JAPANESE MUSIC
AND MUSICAL INSTRUMENTS

1. The dance pantomime "Okame" accompanied by this typical folk ensemble (hayashi) is seen frequently during fall festivals in Japan. See page 49.

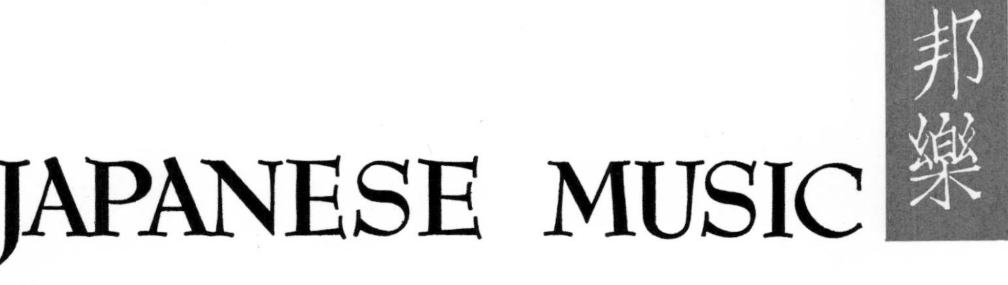

JAPANESE MUSIC

AND MUSICAL INSTRUMENTS

by WILLIAM P. MALM

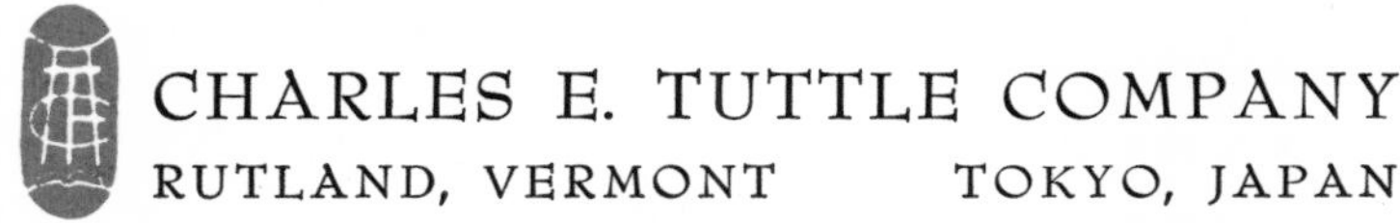

CHARLES E. TUTTLE COMPANY
RUTLAND, VERMONT TOKYO, JAPAN

Representatives

For Continental Europe:
Boxerbooks, Inc., Zurich

For the British Isles:
Prentice-Hall International, Inc., London

For Australasia:
Book Wise (Australia) Pty. Ltd.
104–108 Sussex Street, Sydney 2000

Published by the Charles E. Tuttle
Company, Inc., of Rutland, Vermont & Tokyo
Japan, with editorial offices at
Suido 1-chome, 2-6, Bunkyo-ku, Tokyo

Library of Congress Catalog
Card No. 59–10411

International Standard Book No. 0-8048-0308-0

First edition, 1959
Ninth printing, 1983

Book design and typography
by Kaoru Ogimi
Line drawings and layout of illustrations
by M. Kuwata

Manufactured in Japan

Dedicated to
The traditional musicians of Japan:
May their art flourish
And their creativity be reborn

CONTENTS

LIST OF ILLUSTRATIONS

PLATES

FIGURES

FOREWORD

Basil Hall Chamberlain, in his introduction to Konakamura's *Kabu Ongaku Ryakushi* (A Short History of Song and Dance Music, 1887), ended his remarks by saying: "The result of his labours is a work which will be the despair of future investigators, leaving to them, as it would seem to do, nothing further to discover." Since that time there has actually been quite a bit to discover about Japanese music, not only as it relates to dancing or singing, but also in its instrumental development. Sir Francis Piggott was much wiser when he said that his book on Japanese music, published in 1893,* was only an introduction to the topic.

Since the appearance of Piggott's book there have been no further major attempts in any Western language to deal at all comprehensively with Japanese music, the few papers on the subject being restricted to specialized aspects. The Japanese have produced several worthwhile books, but these have remained buried in the relative obscurity of the Japanese language. The present book, then, has been written in order that the Western world may know the basic facts about the various forms of Japanese music and musical instruments and their place in the over-all history of Japan. Like Piggott's book, this too can be but an introduction to a most complex subject. I am fortunate, however, in having had many more sources to draw upon than did Piggott.

I have tried to include as much general information as possible for the layman and, for the musicologist, have included brief paragraphs and suggestions concerning more technical matters. For those who wish to pursue the matter further, I have also added at the end of the book a bibliography, a list of recommended recordings, an outline of musical notations, and a guide to Tokyo's somewhat hidden world of Japanese music.

In general, the book has three main orientations: the history of Japanese music, the construction of the instruments, and the music itself. The materials for the history section are drawn primarily from the Japanese sources listed in the Bibliography. The musical analyses are for the most part based on my own research. I have tried to make each chapter a self-contained unit. This has necessitated some slight repetition of information. The organization is, however, as chronological as possible, and reading

* For details concerning this and other publications mentioned hereafter, see the Bibliography.

straight through the book should give one a grasp of the over-all evolution of Japanese music. Thus, whether one's interest is in a special form of Japanese music, music in general, theatre, Japanese culture, or simply intellectual curiosity, it is hoped that this book will prove both informative and entertaining.

As to editorial matters, long marks to indicate prolonged vowels in Japanese words have not been used in the body of the book. They have, however, been included in the index, together with Japanese characters and glossary-like explanations of technical terms. At the suggestion of the publishers, italics for Japanese terms have usually been used in the text only when the terms are initially used or defined, and not thereafter. Throughout the text Japanese names are given in the Japanese fashion, surname first.

I am indebted and here express my thanks to many persons and organizations for the illustrations in this book: Engeki Publishing Company: Plates 77, 78. Mr. Francis Haar: Plates 36, 38, 75, from his book *Japanese Theatre in Highlight*. Hogaku Company and Mr. K. Machida: Figs. 38–41. Iwanami Motion Picture Production Company: Plates 6, 7, 11, 20, 34, 35, 39, 42, 72, 79, 83–87. Japan Broadcasting Corporation: Fig. 21, from their publication of folk music, *Nihon Minyo Taikan*, the Kanto volume. Japan Travel Bureau: Plates 19, 33, 40, 51, 53, 81, 182. Kokusai Bunka Shinkokai: Plate 26. Mr. I. Kurosawa: Plates 88, 89. The Mainichi Newspapers: Plate 48. National Theatrical Study Institute: Plates 5, 17, 18. Tokyo National Museum: Plate 2. Tokyo University of Fine Arts: Plates 21–23. *Toyo Ongaku Kenkyu* magazine: Fig. 24. Mr. C. Yoshida: Plate 76. All other photographs were taken by myself. The line drawings of musical instruments are by Mr. M. Kuwata.

In closing I wish to express my sincere thanks to the many individuals who made my task easier. Dr. Kishibe Shigeo deserves special mention as my musical mentor in Japan. Miss Takemoto Kazuyo was an ever-efficient and courteous *arbeiter*. My thanks also to Messrs. Edward Seidensticker, Howard Hibbett, and Richard Lane and to the members of the Japanese Folk Theatrical Institute for services rendered. This book is the result of two years of research done under a grant from the Ford Foundation, for whose help and understanding during my period of field work I must express my sincere gratitude. It should be added, however, that the opinions expressed herein are my own and do not necessarily reflect those of the Foundation or its officers.

Finally, I want to thank the men to whom this book is dedicated: the traditional musicians of Japan. Without their coöperation an effective book on Japanese music would be impossible. I only hope I have been able to do their profession full justice.

W.P.M.

April, 1959

JAPANESE MUSIC
AND MUSICAL INSTRUMENTS

謡うも舞うも
法の聲

Both music and dance
Are voices of the Way.
—Zenji Hakuin

PROLOGUE: THE O-MATSURI

In a tiny restaurant the young lady on the television screen who was dancing to "Indian Love Call" was given sudden competition. A red-faced, golden-eyed lion rushed in, clacking his wooden jaws and shaking his stringy hair in a violent and determined effort to bring good luck to the shop and good fortune to himself. An elderly man in kimono and derby hat stood outside nonchalantly playing a lively accompaniment on his bamboo flute. A more prosperous lion might have had a drummer also, but this was the time of the *o-matsuri* festival and the drummers were all busy. Three of them were only a block away, sitting on a newly built stage next to the neighborhood shrine and busily beating out a highly syncopated accompaniment to the flute strains of *Edo-bayashi*, a music as gay and lively as Dixieland.

The crowd which had gathered at the sound of the deep-toned temple drum was not paying conscious attention to all this joyous music. Nevertheless, caught up in the spirit of the music, they were happily providing linguistic counterpoint to the flute's *tessitura* flights. Children in the gaily colored kimono were primarily concerned with buying little squid and octopuses dipped in soy sauce, netting goldfish from large pans into plastic bags, or hiding their doll-like faces in clouds of cotton candy.

The lion pranced on to the next store, and a new set of musicians arrived to do battle with the hapless young lady on the television set: the entrance curtain was suddenly pushed aside, and in came three girls of rice-fed proportions, who struck up a folk song inviting the patrons to the festivities at the shrine. Even the noise of Japanese-noodle-eating could not drown out their song, which in effect announced the beginning of a Japanese version of a church canvass. It is doubtful that the most friendly, well-dressed vestryman could tear a parishioner from his gastronomical pursuits half as easily as these three plump peasant girls could with their music and dancing. The rhythmic strumming of the three strings of the *shamisen* gave an effect surprisingly similar to American mountain banjo music though the drum and the dance of simple, beckoning gestures added a distinctly Japanese flavor.

Having firmly defeated the ballet of the Indian maiden, the three blue-and-white kimono went out once more into the street. Here was a riot of color and sound to rival the carnival scene in Stravinsky's *Petrouchka.* The young men and boys were all dressed in blue *happi* coats with large, red *matsuri* characters on the back. They had their hair tied back with blue and white towels and their faces painted white with rice powder. They milled around the shrine shed waiting to start the procession which is the center of the festivities. One young boy was doing his best to add to the merry confusion by straddling the huge shrine-drum as it stood in its cart and beating on it in the rather unimaginative rhythm of "pom, pom, pom-pom-pom," quite out of synchronization with the rhythm and meter of the stage musicians not twenty feet away.

In the midst of this whirl of people and sounds, mixed with the ever-present cacophony of car horns and impatient three-wheeled motorcycle trucks, appeared a somber priest with a huge basket-like hat completely covering his head. Apparently oblivious to the fierce competition, he wandered from door to door playing soft, woody melodies on his bamboo recorder, stained by myriad dusty fingers and the neglect endemic in the life of a dying profession. His windy tune ended. A coin dropped into the white box hung around his neck, and he went on to the next store, seemingly indifferent to the anachronism of his profession, his fate, or the function his guild once performed throughout Japan.

Any thoughts of lugubrious sentimentality, however, were soon pushed aside by a great shout that came from the men as they brought the shrine bouncing out of its shed. It was a highly ornamented black-and-gold miniature temple, and on its roof stood a golden phoenix, flashing and flapping its wings in the sun as the shrine was jostled about by the youthful shoulders that supported it on its wooden beams.

A group of boys assigned to pull the drum wagon took up their positions, and the girls fell in behind as the procession began. The older men set the cadence with large poles topped with metal rings which rattled majestically as the poles were pounded against the pavement. A much faster rhythm was set up by the short-breathed chant used by the shrine-carriers as they trotted along – but what a way to carry a shrine!

This was a folk festival, and the dignity Westerners usually associate with shrine processions was very much out of place in the crowded, narrow streets of Yoyogi-Uehara, in Tokyo. The custom has always been that the shrine is carried to everyone's house, bringing more good luck than even the busy lion can provide, and at a dearer price. However, the transportation of the shrine from place to place was not so much a procession as a tug of war. First one side of the shrine and then the other would take the offensive and the poor phoenix flapped wildly as the shrine canted perilously from one side of the road to the other. Needless to say, there were plenty of extra bearers to give the contestants a rest.

The big shrine was followed by smaller ones so that the younger boys could get some early training in shrine-carrying and also, of course, get in on the fun. Off they went, much as their fathers and grandfathers had before them, with the possible addition of a police escort who stopped traffic and considerately blew their whistles in time with the chanting. . . .

This is not an imaginary scene, but an accurate description of September 22, 1955, in Tokyo. Such scenes have been part of every September in Japan for decades, and there seems to be little doubt that they will continue for many decades to come. Though television antennas cover the slate-tiled roofs and jazz echoes across Lake Chuzenji in Nikko, the vitality and popularity of traditional music still seems to be firmly rooted in the daily lives of the Japanese people. In the Meiji Stadium, the afternoon crowd cheers and sings its school songs much as does any American sports crowd, but when evening comes, fires are lit in the adjacent park and people gather to dance *bon-odori* in celebration of the autumnal equinox. The man who repairs your automobile may also sing *yokyoku*, the music of the noh plays dating from the fifteenth century, while the businessman and fellow strap-hanger in the fast-moving subway may be seen poring over the words to a *kouta* song in preparation for a lesson at the end of a day of selling textile machinery. One could go on indefinitely citing examples of such traditional musics existing in modern surroundings. The systematic presentation of these musics, along with the exposition of their historical backgrounds and musical characteristics, is the theme of this book. This is the world of *hogaku*, the traditional music of Japan.

CHAPTER ONE THE PRESENT AND PAST OF JAPANESE MUSIC

I. Japan's Musical Life

Japan is presently attempting to support two musical cultures at one time: Western music and traditional music. Of these the former is easily understood by the Westerner because it is part of his own heritage. If one wishes, one can spend a busy season attending symphony concerts, lieder programs, and piano recitals. There is even a fairly wide choice of opera companies, and such operas as *William Tell* and *Hary Janos* have a better chance of being seen in Tokyo than in the United States. At the same time, those of more modern tastes can join the Society for Contemporary Music or attend concerts given by Japanese composers of *musique concrete*. There are also the new works by Japanese composers that are played at every concert of the Tokyo Symphony. Traveling artists now make Japan a regular part of their itinerary, and one need seldom feel starved for Western music in Japan, though it may not always be of the best quality.

At the same time, there is an equally large part of Japan's musical life that is either completely incomprehensible to the Westerner or greatly oversimplified for him by convenient stereotypes provided by only partially-informed writers. This music is *hogaku,* a word which means music that is uniquely Japanese. This traditional music of Japan should be recognized as a highly evolved art form, a music that has as many facets and approaches to beauty as the music of the West. The scope of hogaku includes orchestral music, chamber music, opera, and a host of vocal forms. The approach may be different from that of Western music, but the aesthetic goals are essentially the same. This very difference is one of the best reasons for studying Japanese music or, for that matter, the music of any non-European country. Such studies provide an opportunity to view an equally logical but different system of musical organization. This, in turn, may give us a new view of our own music. In addition, there is the sheer hedonistic desire to increase our response to unfamiliar artistic media. If one appreciates Schubert songs, kouta enjoyment takes only a little reorientation, and a lover of opera should find Japanese narrative singing tremendously exciting.

There is really a third world in musical Japan, one might call it a limbo, and this is music written by modern Japanese composers using traditional materials in a new orientation. In some cases it is a concerto for *koto*, in others, a string quartet using Japanese folk songs as themes. In either case, the results are often novel and sometimes they are even good music. This fascinating subject, however, is the topic for a different book. We are concerned here primarily with the indigenous music from its beginnings to its present condition.

One of the reasons why the study of hogaku is so interesting is that it conveniently symbolizes the position of the traditional in Japan today. Though Japan is called the most Westernized country in the orient, she is carrying many burdens of the past while attempting to assimilate and create within the new patterns of the West. Some of these traditions will be dropped and others will change their shape in order to fit into their new environment. Still others appear to be important enough that they will be kept intact despite their different surroundings. Within the boundaries of Japanese music all three of these reactions can be found. The reasons for the continued vitality of one form and the decline of another can be ascertained by a more detailed study of each case. In such studies the form must be evaluated both as music and also as a manifestation of the artistic needs of a certain social class. In general, we can say that those forms which survive today have been able to maintain interest musically and fulfill social needs. However, before one can understand clearly hogaku's position in modern society, one must first have some idea of its place in the general history of Japan.

II. Music and Japanese History

The exact ethnological origins of the Japanese are not clearly known. However, from ancient times there have been waves of migrating cultures applying pressure on whatever indigenous culture there may have been. It is characteristic of the Japanese even today that they seem to be able to sustain the most intense cultural invasions and yet maintain enough independence to make use of these foreign cultures in a different way. It is impossible to tell how much of this was true in prehistoric times, but in addition to the Chinese, Korean, Mongolian, and Southeast Asian influences found in archeological remains, there seems to be something that can be explained only as indigenously Japanese. Of course, technically, we cannot speak of the prehistoric Japanese in any national sense, for the inhabitants of the islands were divided into many small clans which showed little signs of merging until around the first century A.D.

Tradition claims that the Yamato people were the first to foster the concept of an imperial clan to which the other groups owed allegiance. The strength of this Yamato clan began in Kyushu, the southernmost of Japan's main islands, and the next few centuries of Japanese history are basically concerned with the gradual extension of imperial Yamato power in a northerly direction.

Musically, this age represents the period of primitive forms, primarily folk music. Where the music appears to have been more complex, it probably came from isolated Chinese or Korean colonies and was not native music as such. In fact, to learn more about ancient Japanese music we must turn to Chinese sources, as Japanese was not as yet a written language.

In the chronicles of the Wei dynasty of third-century China we find an account of a visit to the islands of Japan which includes a mention of music, dancing, and singing as part of a funeral wake. Another sixth-century chronicle tells of a group of Chinese scholars sent to Japan from Paikche, an ancient kingdom in southwestern Korea. Among these men of learning were listed several musicians. From such scraps of information we get the impression that music was an important thread in the general fabric of Japanese life from the earliest times.

The first native literary products, the *Kojiki* (A.D. 714) and the *Nihon Shoki* (720), give us some indication of music's place in early mythology. The most famous tale is that of the Sun Goddess, who was insulted by her brother, the newly-appointed guardian of Hell, and retired into a cave, leaving the world in darkness. It was in order to coax the Sun Goddess to return that Ame no Uzume danced her lewd and humorous dance before the other gods who were assembled at the mouth of the cave. Since the music, dancing, and resultant laughter aroused the Sun Goddess' curiosity enough to bring her out of hiding, the theatrical arts got off to a good functional start even in Japanese mythology. In addition to such myths, the *Kojiki* and *Nihon Shoki* contain some two hundred poems which may very well have been recited to music.

By the time of these writings we have come to the end of what is called the ancient period of Japanese music history. Such music was all of a folk nature and probably rather simple and repetitious in style. There is no evidence of any independent instrumental music or the development of anything that could be called art music. Such instruments as did exist were a cithern called a *wagon* or *Yamato-goto,* a bamboo flute (the *Yamato-bue*), and various simple percussion instruments. Our primary source concerning these instruments are the *haniwa* statues that are found in ancient tombs (Plate 2). The only piece of actual music from this period is a tune called "Kume Uta," which is said to date from the days of the first traditional emperor of Japan, Jimmu. The melody, however, has no doubt gone through many changes since then.

The first major historic period in Japan, the Nara period (553–794), saw the initial struggles to establish a national government and an attempt to impose a Chinese social and intellectual order on the rustic clans of Japan. The period name comes from the city of Nara, which was laid out in 710 in accordance with the plans of a famous Chinese city. One can imagine what a Mecca of miracles China must have seemed to the Japanese, who were without a written language, permanent cities, a centralized government, or any religious concepts beyond a rather indefinite pantheism. In every category of life Chinese models were used, often with little thought given to their suitability. Some of the results were a polysyllabic language being forced into a monosyllabic script, the planning of cities too large to populate, and sweeping reform edicts without the power to execute them. There was also a wholehearted embracing of the doctrines of Buddhism and Confucianism.

When the imperial household was weary of its web of intrigue and insurrection, or when a nobleman sought rest from his struggles with Chinese philosophy, edifying relaxation was provided by the government bureau of music. Much as early American classical musicians had to be from Europe, the Nara court musicians were all from China or Korea. There is even a tale, said to date from the third century, of Korean musicians instructing the Japanese to save the timber from wrecked ships because it was properly seasoned for instrument construction by the salt water and the sun. Thus, foreign music and dance began to move out of the colonies and became part of the life of the new intellectual centers of Japan very early in the Nara period.

The great literary anthology of this time, the *Manyoshu* (eighth century), contains some four thousand poems, many of which are believed to be aristocratic revisions of ancient folk-song texts. The *Shoku Nihongi*, a historical chronicle of the late eighth century, tells of ritual and music performed at the dedication ceremonies of new shrines and temples. The most famous example is the founding of the Todaiji temple, at which hundreds of musicians and dancers are said to have performed. Music thus became an ancillary to the early development of Japanese architecture and the other fine arts.

The music of the Nara period can be classified as belonging to the first international period in Japanese music history. The court music was all of Chinese, Korean, or Indian origin and was played primarily by foreign musicians in its original style. While the poetry anthologies indicate that folk music had continued its steady pace, the historical records and relics show us a music that was primarily instrumental and often connected with the dance. At the same time, the music of the Buddhist service became known throughout Japan and exerted some influence on the native vocal style, though

2. This ancient tomb figurine (*haniwa*) is playing a prototype of the wagon zither. See page 25.

perhaps the influence was mutual as in the case of Gregorian chant and early European folk songs. In sum, the main feature of the music of the Nara period was the importation of foreign musicians and music of both a sacred and secular nature. As yet the native genius seems to have had little influence on this music nor were the native musicians held in particular respect. The parallel of this situation with that of America in the early nineteenth century is quite striking.

During the Heian period (794–1185) there were signs that the Chinese influences were beginning to be assimilated and modified. Great changes occurred in the governmental system, with the position of the emperor becoming weaker while the power of the regent became stronger. This strength was consolidated under the exclusive control of the Fujiwara clan. While the imperial troops did battle with the Ainu tribes in the north, the court turned more and more to the problems of etiquette and ritual. The northern frontiersmen paid little attention to the pious edicts of the distant emperor, while the noblemen, stripped of all political power, found themselves immersed in one of the most ultrarefined societies in history. The favorite courtier was the man who could improvise the best poem in Chinese, while the women made use of a phonetic script to produce Japanese literary works of great acumen and vitality, mixed with a Gothic-like sentimentality. Beneath this surface of silk and delicate lacquer flowed a writhing torrent of intrigue and suppressed desire. Fame and banishment were eternal potentials, and the distance between them was no farther than his lordship's chambers. One might tempt fate by the mere pushing aside of a bamboo curtain or by passing beyond a gilded screen that served as some semblance of privacy in this life within a jade goldfish bowl.

This was also the period of one of the most famous feuds in Japanese history, that of the Minamoto (or Genji) and the Taira (or Heike) clans. It ended with the defeat of the Taira in 1185, but out of the ruin came a legacy of legends that has provided endless inspiration for the fine arts. There also appeared the concept of the samurai, the faithful warrior, whose loyalty was more important to him than his life. Above him loomed the figure of the military dictator, who would soon find the effete court a likely place to garrison his troops and send his orders.

The most famous literary product of this age, the *Genji Monogatari* (*The Tale of Genji*) by Lady Murasaki, is replete with scenes of music.[1] In this wonderful tale of romance, music and poetry seem to form the very matrix into which the characters are set. Every truly "refined" person in the book can play at least one or two instruments, and

[1] See Lady Murasaki, *The Tale of Genji*. Trans. by Arthur Waley (New York, Mifflin Co., 1935).

we find that one of Genji's fondest memories of Lady Murasaki is the music lessons he gave her on the lute. He was led to another of his amours by the sound of a koto, so beautiful that he was filled with passion for the unseen performer. In good romantic tradition she was, of course, equally as lovely.

The music of the Heian period still employed a host of Chinese instruments and forms, but the musicians themselves were more often Japanese. The people of the court took up music with a passion, and it gradually developed distinctly Japanese characteristics. While one often thinks of this music as being instrumental, it must not be forgotten that almost all of it contained a poem at some point. The Japanese fine arts in general seem to have been inseparable from literature and, in fact, seem to take their basic orientation from the written word. A lovely scroll may be the invocation of a Chinese poem, while the *biwa* lute has always served as the supporting vehicle for poetry and sagas. The Heian *gagaku* court music comes closest to a pure instrumental form, but even here a chorus is common. When there is no chorus, there is often a dancer who still links the music to some ancient myth or historical event. This court music is a block of sound. It does not move but allows other things to move through it. In this way, it has managed to survive to the present day, apparently with relatively little distortion. Such a continuous line of patronage has no parallel in the history of Western instrumental music, though in all fairness we must add that the Western emphasis has been more on evolution than on preservation.

In the field of purely vocal music the Heian period produced Buddhist hymns and also many secular songs. Among these songs were those specially composed for use at the many banquets that figured so heavily in the court schedule. One can imagine the long, matted rooms filled with soft faces and clothes of every hue. As the properly attired guests partook of the properly displayed foods in the proper order, these banquet songs added just the right amount of sentimental impropriety to season the evening and the conversation.

The Heian period, then, represents the heyday of court music and the beginnings of native influence on imported music and instruments. Again we must reflect for a moment that beyond the capital there must have been a great body of folk music that floated unnoticed and unrecorded over the muddy rice fields.

The Kamakura period (1185–1333) produced the military dictatorship of Yoritomo and a tradition of the shogun, or the man controlling the shogun, as the true ruler of Japan. The warrior became the dominant figure in the government as well as in battle. However, in order to avoid the insidious softness and intrigues of the court in Kyoto, the military established a separate headquarters in Kamakura. All real authority now stemmed from the empiric and untutored north. The ambitious men of Kyoto were soon found at the side of the military men of Kamakura advising, administrating, and helping form a new feudal system, the effects of which are evident to this day. This system differs from the Western concept of feudalism primarily in the unusual sense of clan unity and the interlocking obligations incumbent on both lord and vassal.

During this period Buddhism increased in popularity, especially among the common people, on whom the effects of evangelism were immense. The ethics of the warrior class had a more philosophical base, and the influence of Zen Buddhism was very strong. The contrast of the military life and the contemplative severity of Zen complemented each other to such an extent that, even as late as World War II, officer candidates were required to study Zen. Perhaps some of Zen's appeal may have been its special type of austerity, for the greatest fear of the military leaders was the loss of a Spartan-like pride they had engendered in their men.

One of the most famous memorials to military virtue is the *Heike Monogatari* (*The Heike Story*)[2], which was written originally for recitation to the accompaniment of the lute (*biwa*). This long saga retells the battles of the Taira and Minamoto clans, which figured so strongly in the previous period. While extolling the deeds of the past and the impermanence of life in general, this tale set the standard by which many a Kamakura warrior vowed to live.

Unfortunately, the disdain of court life did not last in more peaceful times, and the warriors were soon aping the manners of the courtiers they controlled. The Kamakura regency seemed in danger of falling, when the country was distracted by Kublai Khan's attempt to invade Japan. Individual valor and two truly miraculous storms destroyed the Mongolian Armada, but the days of the regency were already numbered. In 1333, Kamakura and the power of the shogun disappeared in a holocaust which was a portent of the bloody days to come.

By the Kamakura period most traces of the international character of Japanese music had disappeared. Court music in general was declining, while there was a steady growth of more theatrical arts for the entertainment of both the court and the military headquarters. The comic dances of *dengaku* were so popular that certain officials were censured for neglecting their duties in order to enjoy the daily performances. Lute-accompanied sagas of military glory had a steady audience, and the form developed greatly in style and technique. Buddhist chanting likewise became more popular and exerted a stronger influence on the secular music of the time. Its style is said to have

[2] A. L. Sadler, *The Heike Monogatari*. Tokyo: Kimiwada Shoten, 1941.

permeated even the drinking songs. Indeed, there was a mixture of sacred and secular elements in Kamakura music that reminds one of a similar condition in the music of Gothic Europe.

In general, the music of the Kamakura period is marked by a new emphasis on vocal and more dramatic music. This tendency will be seen to gather momentum in the periods to follow and represents the beginning of a genuinely native music movement. The days of imperial power were over, and the arts reflected the change to a feudalistic society with a style that was better suited to the new roughshod patrons.

The Muromachi, or Ashikaga, period (1333–1615) is characterized by a degeneration of larger socio-political units into smaller ones. The centralized government of the Ashikaga shoguns was replaced by the rule of powerful independent land barons, and the concept of clan loyalty gave way to the spirit of unity only on a family level. Under the new code, an individual no longer felt any dishonor in changing sides during one of the many feudal wars that plagued this period as long as he remained true to his immediate household.

The period began with rival emperors and a war of succession and ended with a disastrous rivalry for the position of shogun. The warriors committed the fatal error of moving to Kyoto and were soon caught up in a life of luxury based on the theory that the acquisition of art objects and intellectual syncophants represented success. While the local officials were busy acquiring neighboring fiefs, the Kyoto warriors were engaged in tea ceremonies or attending the many new theatrical entertainments that had been devised to amuse them.

War and revolt were rampant, and blood flowed more thickly than the ink of the many painters who found patronage with the military or the church. When the blood had dried, the social system of Japan was found to be completely changed, with the family now as the central unit. When the ink had likewise dried, there remained a legacy of art, permeated with Zen and new Chinese influences, but full of vigor and independence. The brilliance of the famous Golden Pavilion in Kyoto makes us forget the sordid struggles that formed a background for the gentle conversations that went on within its serene walls.

In this period the court was poverty stricken to the extent that one emperor had to sell his autographs to subsist, while the military class luxuriated in a manner often in excess of their treasuries. Due to an increase in foreign trade, the first signs of a strong merchant class appeared. Meanwhile, the history of individual families is replete with tales of rapid expansions and sudden demises. This left many a samurai without a master and hence without a conscience. This uneasy balance of classes needed only a few more drops of insurrectional blood to tip the scale and pour the entire society into a new mold in the following century.

The outstanding feature of the Muromachi period's music is the growth of the theatrical arts. Public and private performances of dance-dramas and acrobatics became increasingly popular and prepared the way for the development of the noh drama. At court, the traditional music suffered greatly, though it is recorded that even during the period of the terrible Onin War (1467–77) the court managed to keep up the annual *kagura* dances at the shrines. Some notices of folk music appear, especially as concern its influence on performances at the shogun's palace in the Muromachi district of Kyoto. Short ditties (*kouta*) are recorded, as also are an ever-increasing number of narrative songs. Itinerant storytellers wove their tales on the street corners, often with only the beating of a fan for accompaniment, little realizing that they were preparing the way for one of Japan's greatest musical forms, the *joruri*.

At the same time, a simple bamboo recorder began to be heard, played by wandering priests who were soft heralds of a greater music to come. In short, the Muromachi period was a time of musical potential; a material and psychological build up for a flood of activities that was soon to burst upon the artistic world in a torrent of color and sound.

The first break in the dam occurred in the latter half of the Muromachi period, which is often called the Momoyama period (1534–1615). This new stream of music came from the noh drama, which was the final refinement of the many entertainments mentioned earlier. While this timeless and subtle art was being gently molded by Kannami and his son Zeami, a broken and blood-soaked Japan was hammered back together by a final set of wars under the leadership of Oda Nobunaga and his associate Toyotomi Hideyoshi. It was Hideyoshi who first sounded a warning to the newly-arrived Christian missionaries that Japan was tolerant of all religions as long as they did not threaten the uneasy security of the state. Disdain for this warning and the foreigner's overconcern with mercantile rather than spiritual advancement brought about the martyrdom of many a simple follower of the Cross.

Hideyoshi also sacrificed many a Buddhist soldier in his unsuccessful attempts to invade Korea. In the meantime, a three-stringed guitar called a *jamisen* was invading, with greater success, the southern part of Japan and adding another potential to the gathering musical forces.

In addition to the development of the noh drama and the introduction of the jamisen, the Momoyama period is important for its improvement in instrumental construction. The early bamboo recorder was changed into the shape of the present-day *shakuhachi*, while the old court cithern was modified into a more sonorous koto. The jamisen was changed greatly into the shape of the shamisen, and the art of drum-making was raised to such a level that a Momoyama drum is prized in Japan much as a Stradivarius violin is in the West.

The Tokugawa, or Edo, period (1615–1868) represents one of the most unique attempts to maintain a *status quo* in all world history. The first Tokugawa shogun, Ieyasu, instigated a system of government that was based on the principle of immobility in every class. The court was subsidized but reduced to a life of ceremonies; the feudal lords were relocated so as to neutralize their power and prevent conspiracy, while the warrior's great perquisites were contingent on obedience to the shogun. The power of religion was broken forever, first by splitting up the dangerous Buddhist sects and secondly by ruthlessly suppressing the Christian movement. The final hymn of the slaughtered Christians of Shimabara was also the swan song of Western influences in Japan for more than two hundred years. A tiny Dutch colony, called Deshima, in the harbor of Nagasaki remained as Japan's only legitimate contact with the West. She deliberately shut out the world and sought peace and stability under a military dictatorship that had no wars to fight but waged a constant, if finally unsuccessful, battle against change.

Beneath the stolid, unchanging letter of the Tokugawa law, however, there was a swift current of new forces that eventually overflowed its confines and revolutionized Japan's entire social structure. The major turbulence resided in the lowest class in the Tokugawa hierarchy, the merchants. When the capital was moved to Edo, now known as Tokyo, a new concept in cities was begun in Japan. Here was the new seat of government and an important new commercial center of Japan. It was filled with the pensioned-warrior class and the hostages which the shogun held to insure the loyalty of the country lords, all restless, repressed, and in need of distraction. This was provided by the greatest flourishing of the entertainment world in Japanese history.

Such a large city had many needs, and the merchants were quick to provide the necessary services, at an almost unnecessarily high profit. The Tokugawa law had effectively immobilized the feudal and warrior class, but the despised merchants found that circumventing the law lost them no prestige (since they had none) while it often made them very rich. The period presents a picture of the gradual decay of the samurai and the covert rule of the moneylender. Beneath the entire society were the rice farmers. They were called upon to provide the basic wealth, but were given no share in it; in fact, at one time they were even forbidden to eat the rice they grew. When these lower classes moved out from underneath the rigid upper layers, the entire structure collapsed. The history of the Tokugawa era presents the fascinating saga of an attempt to change an agricultural society into a commercial society despite government resistance and the lack of one of the vital components of commerce, foreign trade.

Throughout this tale, however, we find a secondary theme, the development of a bourgeois art. As was noticed in the previous period, there was an increasing interest in the theatrical arts in Japan. This reached its zenith in a segment of the Tokugawa period known as the Genroku period (1688–1703), during which the pleasure districts of Tokyo, Osaka, and Kyoto became the very centers of Japanese life. Here the class distinctions had less meaning. The merchant could openly display his new-found wealth, while the samurai could forget his recent poverty in the blandishments of paid companions, wine, and the distractions of a host of kabuki and puppet theatres. This was the famous *ukiyo*, the "floating world," in which Japanese society drifted until the sheer weight of pleasure-seekers burst the entire structure wide open. However, despite the upheaval engendered by the re-entry of Western culture in the late nineteenth century, many of the patterns of thought and action drilled into the people of Edo by the shogunate are still firmly entrenched in the modern population of Tokyo, as of all Japan.

Musically, the Tokugawa period saw the rise of shamisen music, the flourishing of the koto, the shakuhachi, and a vast development of music for the drama, in short, an advance of all that one usually thinks of as the traditional music of Japan. The period can be compared favorably with the early nineteenth century in Europe, when the symphony, the opera, and chamber music were in their prime. While the plays of Chikamatsu were declaimed with an almost hysterical intensity by the joruri singers, the ancient noh plays found refuge in the patronage of a few conservative officials and eventually were able to gain a following among those middle-class persons who wished for a sense of refinement. The kabuki theatre, however, was nurtured on the shouts of approving townsfolk and solicited its patronage with brilliant costumes and dramatic plays. In kabuki, audience participation and a good cry are as essential as they are in Italian opera.

Thus, we have in the Tokugawa period a manifestation of almost every type of music known in Japan. The court musicians provided the necessary leisurely pace for the ceremonies that were the only *raison d'être* of the imperial court. The blind priests continued to recount past glories to the accompaniment of the lute or solicit alms by means of the bamboo recorder. For the secular blind men there was the teaching of koto, which had become popular among the lonesome ladies who served as political hostages in Edo. The tottering aristocracy took solace in the noh drama, while many of the samurai fled to the gay quarters. Meanwhile, the townsfolk luxuriated in a new sense of power, which included the right to an immense variety of dramatic and erotic music. Since the farmer had traditionally been considered an ignorant but all-providing drone, his music flowed on as always. The placid river of folk music showed signs of branching into regional styles, but it remained basically undisturbed, primarily because it was ignored. The tales of Edo, like the romantic novels of Europe, paint scenes of rustic festivals and peasant merrymaking, but as in the case of their European counterparts, their authors often chose to disregard the despairing eyes that belied many a farmer's smile.

The Tokugawa period is a treasure house of Japanese music and represents the zenith of all the traditional arts. However, the basis of the Edo society was unrealistic and, rather than growing, it merely became bloated until it was fatally punctured by the masts of the black ships of Commodore Perry.

The Meiji period (1868–1912) can best be summarized by saying that the floodgates were opened. Western culture inundated the land and the outlines of tradition were only dimly discernible in the torrent of new ideas. The Japanese endemic weakness for being "modern" or "smart" was never more virulent than in the late nineteenth century. From the Heian to the Momoyama periods, familiarity with some element of Chinese culture had always been considered "chic," and in the Tokugawa period, fashions and language were guided by the leading actors and geisha of the day. In the Meiji era, however, it was one's knowledge of steam engines and anatomy or an ability to do second-rate oil paintings that counted.

The samurai class made one last show of strength but was crushed by an army trained along Western lines. The shogunate had been caught in its own propaganda, for the emperor rose to power on the prestige they had provided, plus the backing of those who saw the danger behind the approaching black ships and felt that the country could only be saved from Western dominance by overhauling her outdated social structure and by adopting Western techniques of warfare and administration.

It is significant that the first Western music in the Meiji era was military. Bandmasters were part of the cadre of foreigners solicited by the regime, and the gentle nuances of the koto were drowned out by the brassy heralds of a new age. The most fatal intrusion for traditional music, however, was the cold, opaque moon of harmony that eclipsed hogaku's source of life. The beauty of Japanese music lay in an extremely subtle melodic style, which became leadened and deadened by the addition of factual tonic and dominant chords. Those musicians who resisted the trend were called old fashioned and fell on evil days. Thus, the beginning of the Meiji period presented a picture of the traditional arts on the defensive in what appeared to be a losing battle.

In the Meiji period, Japan began to change from a mercantile nation to an industrial and colonial power. She learned to run her trains on time and taught her children to sing "Annie Laurie," but still she found the Western attitude toward her rather patronizing until she discovered the secret to esteem in the West, war. Her battles with China were considered an inter-Asian affair, but the West took sudden notice of Japan when she thoroughly defeated her nearest Caucasian nation, Russia. Japan learned her lesson well, but the bones of thousands of soldiers that are scattered over the Pacific are symbols of her failure at the final examination. Since then Japan has not proved to be a very apt pupil of democracy, and what course she may take in the future is an unreadable enigma. Part of the answer may be found in a careful reappraisal of her past, but it would be rash of a musician to attempt to play the prophet.

Musically, we can note that the rise of militant nationalism in the twentieth century had certain salubrious effects on traditional music. Shamisen and koto music fitted the jingoism of the times, and court music was opened to the public for the first time as a type of cultural propaganda Whatever the motives, the traditional musics have shown a steady resurgence of strength except for those unhappy years of the great debacle. The impact of the West left its mark, but the exact degree of influence is not yet apparent. Again, past history might give us some clues.

As was mentioned earlier, Japan completely adopted the ways of eighth-century China during the Heian period. Along with Chinese literature, architecture, government, and religion, she coveted Chinese music. As a matter of fact, the only survivals of T'ang Chinese music are found in the *To-gaku* music of the present-day court orchestra of Japan. What Japan had wholeheartedly adopted she gradually began to adapt and in time produced arts which were built on Chinese models yet different and distinctly Japanese.

One is tempted to make a comparison of this seventh-century situation with the Meiji Restoration of 1868. There is perhaps some justification for supposing that Japan may again slowly bend these foreign ways to the inclinations of her native genius, but there is one important factor that must not be overlooked. Japan took on the manners of China at a time when she had little developed a culture of her own. The ways of the West, however, were superimposed on a highly developed culture with hundreds of years of development behind it. The first reaction of this foreign catalyst was the complete subjugation of the native arts, but today both styles seem to be growing in strength and stature. How malleable each will become is one of the most interesting questions in Japan today. For our purpose the important thing to notice is that the traditional arts *do* still flourish and give some indication of preparing to advance again with restored self-confidence and with an audience of enthusiastic listeners.

Now that our rapid survey is finished, what general trends can be found in the growth of Japanese music? First, there is the dominant position of vocal music. Every instrument developed under the aegis of the human voice. The first instrumental solos were created to serve as interludes to the verses of songs. One might even study Japanese music as an ancillary to literature, for so much of the time it serves primarily as a vehicle for words.

This leads to the second main observation, which is that Japanese music history is marked by a steady growth of theatrical music. A seventh-century census lists a special clan dedicated to the telling of stories, while ancient records show the function of Shinto priests as being primarily ceremonial. This early concern with the theatrical side of entertainment and religion grew to ever-increasing importance, until it was completely out of proportion in the Tokugawa period. A sense of balance has returned since then, but a foreigner cannot but be struck by the indigenous theatricality of nearly all the Japanese people.

In our discussion of the development of the clan and family spirit we have neglected to note its effect on the teacher-student relations of Japan, which is also a special characteristic of the Japanese music system. Education on any level is an extension (or contraction if you will) of the obligations between the lord and vassal. Even in the cynical present day a music teacher has a right to expect a loyalty from his pupils, and the student instinctively feels a veneration toward the master. The word *sensei* in Japanese has far greater implications than the word teacher does in English. Sensei is one's mentor, and if his teaching seems inadequate for one's needs, it would be a gross breach of etiquette to look for someone new. Not only would this be very discourteous but one would lose the fellowship of the fraternity of the other students and gain the suspicion of any new group into which he might try to enter. Not to "belong" is one of the greatest tragedies in Japanese life. The intensity of this social pressure in Japan is far greater than in the West. This was the great legacy of the Tokugawa period, and even the humble shamisen teacher and his pupils were and, to a great extent, still are bound by these unwritten laws.

As the center of Japan's political history slowly moved northward from Kyushu to Kyoto, to Kamakura, to Edo, there was an equally steady growth of independent Japanese music forms and instruments. In general, the pattern was that an instrument would be introduced in the south via Korea or the Ryukyu Islands and would then gradually change as it moved to the north. The most complete metamorphosis occurred with the shamisen, but the music of the koto, shakuhachi, biwa, and the court also became more original while traveling the well-worn Tokaido road from Kyoto to Tokyo.

Now, standing on the shore of the present, we are able to view the currents of musical progress as they pass by the major landmarks of Japanese history. If water seems to have been used frequently as an analogy it is because water is such an important factor in Japan's existence. The Japanese live on a strip of land crowded between the mountains and the sea, and they must depend on the ocean for their fish and on the rain and mountain streams for the cultivation of their rice. A Japanese student was once heard to say that he wanted to go to America just so he could see with his own eyes a vista of land in every direction. Before launching into a detailed study of the many forms that make up Japanese music, it is wise to reflect that a feeling of confinement has been inbred into the Japanese character by the very geography of the land. Japanese history is the story of crowded masses of men rushing up and down this narrow strip of preferred land; Japanese arts likewise present an attempt to move within very prescribed boundaries. Given these rather rigid limits, one must be prepared to appreciate the consummate skill with which the Japanese artists were able to refine rather than expand their techniques. If one's personal taste is found to be incompatible with the results, at least one can learn to respect the highly developed organization and moments of genius that are integral parts of the finer products of this kaleidoscope of sound, this hogaku, the traditional music of Japan.

CHAPTER

TWO

RELIGIOUS MUSIC

I. Shinto Music

INTRODUCTION: Shinto, "the way of the gods," is Japan's indigenous form of religious expression. Since the days of its mythical origin, Shinto has experienced a continual fluctuation between heydays and dogdays, but it has never had and probably never will have a total eclipse in the land of the rising sun. Shinto shrines are still a part of every village scene as well as most big-city wards. Though they have no regular weekly services and sometimes not even a full-time priest, there is a daily stream of workmen and housewives who may be seen dropping by to toss a coin in the offering box, rattle the shrine gong, bring the spirits to attention with a clap of the hands, and say a short prayer. Besides the prayers of thanks or supplication, there are often prayers of remembrance. These are usually directed toward some recently departed relative, but such prayers are not so much a form of ancestor worship as they are an overt recognition that there is an indestructible link between the generations past and the generation present. Shinto is based on the concept that this present generation owes the past an eternal cultural and spiritual debt. This debt is paid with remembrance, and the Shinto shrine is constructed of symbols which are meant to help recall the past, whether it be last year or two thousand years ago.

The business of blessing or purifying is one of the main functions of most Shinto ceremonies. In ancient times the Shinto priests seemed to have been entirely concerned with the problem of purification and keeping sacred places free of defilement. Today, one will still see on the site of new buildings a sacred square formed by ropes strung between four small trees. In the center of the square, offerings are placed much in the same manner as was done centuries ago. Even fire engines, airplanes, and new atomic reactors require some form of Shinto benediction.

Shinto became an instrument of nationalism during the 1930's and suffered correspondingly with the end of World War II. However, the thousands of modest shrines that dot the rice fields or occupy a shelf in stores, restaurants, and homes attest to the fact that Shinto has become imbedded in Japanese life not so much by government policy or evangelism but by its very antiquity and perhaps by its convenience. For example, in the country it serves as a form of fertility rite, while in the city it becomes a kind of personal spiritual lobbyist much like the patron saints of Christianity. There have been no religious wars over Shinto because there are really no theological issues to fight about. The Buddhist church was wise enough to recognize its usefulness to the people and harmlessness to the church with the net result that at one time Buddhist priests also served in Shinto ceremonies. Indeed, any study of things religious in Japan is complicated by the fact that Shintoism and Buddhism are tremendously intermingled.

From the musical standpoint the problem is even more acute. The most virile form of religious music in Japan is that used in various folk festivals, but it is not always possible to say which music is Buddhist and which is Shinto. In fact, sometimes the same piece is used for both with only the words changed. The lion dancer who opened the prologue of this book is a very lively example of the continuous influence of Shinto music on everyday Japanese life. This same lion may, however, turn out to be Buddhist on a different day. With a reminder that any categorical discussion of religious music in Japan is a semiartificial organizational device and does not always represent actual musical or historical distinctions, let us look at the main styles of Shinto music.

KAGURA - TRADITIONAL COURT MUSIC: *Kagura*, "good music," is the generic term for Shinto music. It is usually divided into two main subdivisions: 1) *kagura*, the music used for imperial Shinto functions or for the more formal parts of ceremonies at local shrines, and 2) *sato-kagura*, Shinto folk and festival music. The Japanese with their love for categories have made a dozen further distinctions in kagura, but for our purposes these two are sufficient.

The famous dance of Ame no Uzume described earlier is considered to be the origin of Shinto music as well as everything else musical and choreographical in Japan. It should be noted that from the very beginning this music was associated with dancing, for this connection has remained firm to the present day. Thus, any discussion of kagura music automatically is concerned with the dances as well.

The ancient records contain accounts of kagura from very early times, and many of the poems that have survived are texts to kagura songs. Besides the story of kagura's origin, its poems, and lists of compositions and composers, there are also reports of various special performances. For example, in the chronicles of Emperor Chuai (circa A.D. 200) as found in the *Kojiki* the following account is given (see ref. 4, I, 153):

When the emperor was preparing to go to war he went to the Ashibi shrine in Kyushu and performed for the gods on the lute. After he had finished, his minister entered the tabernacle and sought the gods' opinion of the venture.

WAGON

This habit of an imperial performance as a prelude to the pronouncements of an oracle was retained for many generations until professional musicians fell heir to the duty. Even then, music was still considered a necessary attribute for the emperor as well as his court.

The songs of kagura fall into two basic types: 1) *torimono*, songs meant to praise the gods or seek their aid, and 2) *saibari*,[1] songs meant to entertain the gods. In both cases the accompaniment is basically the same. It is analogous to Bach's sacred and secular cantatas in which the musical style is quite similar but the words are different. In the case of kagura there are two poems which will show the difference more clearly.[2]

I. A Torimono Poem

As darkness falls on the perilous slope of the mountain,
I cut a staff of sakaki *wood.*
This wood is from the mountain of god,
And with this sacred staff in my hands
I pray for the safety of this poor mountaineer.

II. A Saibari Poem

Flying away, flying away,
The cranes head for Tamino Island,
As the tide flings the waves
On the beach of Naniwa.

The above saibari poem is typical of a genre of Japanese poetry which was very popular in the Japanese court. However, it should be added that among the saibari poems many pieces can be found which apparently came directly from Japanese folk music.

The most famous religious dance is "Azuma Asobi," which survives (in a less ancient form) in the present-day repertoire of the court. Its exact origin is not clear but there are references to such a dance as far back as 763. From the musical standpoint it is important because the accompanying instruments are also listed in ancient records.

The first of these instruments is the *wagon* (pronounced wa-gon′) or the *Yamato-goto*,

[1] *Saibari* is different from the later *saibara*. See ref. 25, 636–7.
[2] For the Japanese texts see ref. 4, I, 159.

a six-stringed cithern (Plate 33). It is claimed as one of the few completely indigenous instruments of Japan. Support for this theory is found in replicas of the wagon that are found in prehistoric figurines (Plate 2), though the shapes of these instruments resemble certain Korean forms. The remains of a wagon prototype were found recently in the excavations of an ancient house site to further prove its antiquity.

By the end of the Nara period we have fairly definite information as to how the wagon was tuned and played. By this time, however, the influence of Chinese music theory was very strong, and it is difficult to tell how much of the original character of the wagon had survived except for the fact that its musical style seems quite distinct from that of imported Chinese citherns.

The basic tuning of the wagon is shown in Figure 1. The note D has been chosen as the basic pitch, because this is the starting pitch of the Chinese mode in which the piece "Azuma Asobi," mentioned above, is said to have been played. The actual base for the tuning, however, is flexible. In Figure 1 the strings are numbered according to their distance from the player, number 1 representing the nearest one.

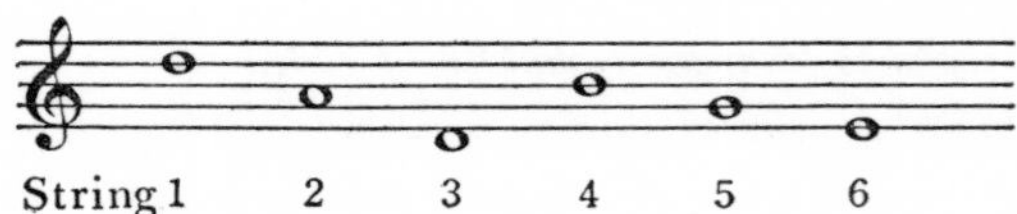

FIGURE 1. The tuning of the wagon

FIGURE 2. The folk pentatonic scale

The tuning of the wagon is done by placing an inverted v-shaped bridge under each string and moving these bridges so as to make the strings the proper length to produce a given pitch. These bridges were originally the forked branches of trees, hence their shape. This branch-fork shape is one of the characteristics that makes the wagon different from similar Chinese citherns.

The most interesting musical features of the wagon are its tuning and its melodic structure. The Western harp, the cithern, the modern Japanese koto, and other such instruments are usually tuned so that a sweep across the strings will produce a scale and thus make the playing of melodies relatively easy. The wagon, however, is tuned more like a guitar, that is, the notes of adjacent strings are some distance apart. The unique feature in the case of the wagon is that the tones do not progress in a regular

KAGURA-BUE

order from low to high but form two separate, broken chords. These notes put in normal order form the pentatonic (five-toned) scale found in folk music all over the world (Figure 2). In Japan this is the basis of the so-called *ritsu* scale (see Figure 5). Thus, the wagon combines features of both the melodic and harmonic types of plucked string instruments. As might be expected its use also reflects this mixture.

Wagon music consists of various arrangements of four basic patterns named *zan*, *ji*,

FIGURE 3. The four wagon melodic patterns

oru, and *tsumu* (Figure 3). The rhythm and tempo may vary, but the music always remains within the framework of these four patterns. Since the melodies of the other instruments vary greatly, it becomes obvious that the wagon part cannot join in the exposition of any central theme. Instead, these patterns are used as signals for phrase endings or the beginning of a new section. In this respect, it serves what is called a colotomic function, i.e., it divides the music up into sections and does not have any particular significance harmonically (in the usual sense of the term) or melodically. More will be said of this when court music is discussed in Chapter III.

The next instrument used in kagura is the *kagura-bue* or *Yamato-bue* (Plate 30). This is a six-holed flute made of bamboo. In appearance it is much like the noh flute except for the number of holes. The notes produced from this flute are the same as the scale shown in Figure 2. Special fingerings will produce other pitches, but these notes remain basic. The actual pitch of the instrument will depend on the length, which varies. This instrument is also claimed as an original Japanese creation though it went under Chinese influence in the Nara and Heian periods.

This flute, along with a nine-holed, double-reed instrument called the *hichiriki* (see Chapter III), are the melodic instruments of the kagura trio. The melodies used today come from a variety of sources, but primarily from the more ancient songs of the court orchestra (gagaku).

SHAKUBYOSHI

SUZU

In addition to these three fundamental instruments others are often added. In ancient times there was usually a chorus of singers who also seem to have played a percussion instrument called a *shakubyoshi*. This is a small wooden clapper that produces a sound somewhat like the single click of castanets, though the tone is thinner. It can still be heard at court concerts, especially if a chorus is used. It acts rather as a time beater for the singers. In addition, other instruments from the court orchestra are found in use together with drums from many sources. Classically speaking, however, the trio mentioned above forms the center of all such Shinto music.

The types of kagura are many and from the historical viewpoint seem almost endless, but a few forms stand out as basic. We have mentioned the "Azuma Asobi." This is typical of the male dances which form the center of most imperial ceremonies. The generic term for such dances is, unfortunately, kagura, an already confused word. For the sake of clarity, I shall call all such dances male kagura in contrast to the other court dances and folk kagura. These male kagura fall basically into the two types mentioned earlier, dances paying homage to the gods (torimono) and dances staged for the entertainment of the gods (saibari). In the first type the main dancer (called the *nincho*) usually presents rice wine or a sacred *sakaki* branch to the shrine. The second type covers a host of styles from sword to mask dances. The greatest fund of these dances remains within the court itself.

In Kyoto, Nara, and at the Ise shrine one may still see *mikomai*, one of the two main styles of female Shinto dancing. There are also folk mikomai (Plate 5). It was pointed out earlier that sacred dancing had its mythological beginning with the performance of a female goddess. This tradition of female dancers and sorceresses continued on for several centuries. The mikomai, originally a boy's dance, is now performed in traditional Shinto female robes, white powdered faces, and a hairdo in the style of the Heian period. The main musical comment to make about mikomai is that the dancers usually carry a small tree of bells called a *suzu* (Plate 5). This instrument is still in great use in folk dances and ceremonies, particularly Shinto ones. The classic mikomai accompaniment remains the wagon, flute, and hichiriki trio, to which may be added a few drums or other instruments borrowed from court music.

The second main type of female Shinto dance is the *shirabyoshi*. This dance was performed by girls who received special training and were also called *shirabyoshi* after the name of their dance. These dancers can boast of a very long and occasionally lurid past. During the Heian period there were regular schools in the court for the training of dancing girls for the shrine (and the palace) as well as other schools for male dancers and musicians. The shirabyoshi, however, seem to have been particularly popular. It is said that the Shokyu War was caused by the shirabyoshi favorite of the emperor. Many classic love affairs in Japanese literature involve these comely and apparently many-talented young ladies. For example, Gio, of *The Heike Story*, and Shizuka, the sweetheart of Japan's military hero, Yoshitsune, were both shirabyoshi.

The music used by these girls was usually a form of song known as *imayo* (see Chapter III). Besides the use of imayo, which in its final form evolved into a form of court "popular" music, the instrumental accompaniment for the shirabyoshi also showed the early secularization of these temple dancers. Instead of the traditional Shinto trio, an hourglass-shaped drum called a *tsuzumi* formed the mainstay of the rhythmic background, while a flute and occasionally other drums were also used. These dancers were at their zenith during the Heian period and suffered a steady decline thereafter. However, they have left behind a legacy of romantic tales and song-poems which help us recapture some of the flavor of the opulent age in which they lived and loved.

At present kagura is restricted primarily to Kyoto, Nara, Ise, and the imperial palace, although various simplified folk versions are also found elsewhere. Before passing on to the folk styles of Shinto music, however, certain characteristics of Japanese music that have already appeared in these early forms should be noted. For example, there are the stereotyped melodic patterns used in the music of the wagon. This principle will be found at work throughout this entire survey of Japanese music. It is interesting to note that it seems to have appeared even before the entrance of Chinese and Indian music influences. Also, it should be noted that pure instrumental music does not appear. Though the Shinto service is often performed in a simple unaccompanied chanting called *norito*, pure instrumental music is unknown. Thus, from the very start Japanese music is seen to be linked with literature, dancing, or some ceremonial action. This is a link that remained intact for centuries and is one of the keystones to the understanding of Japanese music.

SATO-KAGURA - FESTIVAL MUSIC: In any agricultural society the seasons and the main agrarian events are marked by official ceremonies and sacred sanctions. The same is true in Japan. The New Year, the spring plowing, the midsummer growth, the autumn harvest, and the winter snow are all greeted by a festival, or *matsuri*. While these basic patterns are found throughout Japan, the particular form that each local festival takes shows a surprising amount of variety. However, by looking at a few specific cases

O-DAIKO

of this so-called sato-kagura (village kagura) one can learn what to expect from any future encounters with similar folk events.

For foreigners, perhaps the most frequently seen folk festival is the fall festival occurring in late September or early November.[3] This festival is most readily accessible because it is celebrated in the large cities as well as in the country. The prologue of this book is a description of a Tokyo o-matsuri. It gave a picture of the shrine procession and its surrounding festivities, but now it is time to look at its music in greater detail.

The main source of music for such festivals is a small band of musicians called the *hayashi*. This term stands for many different ensembles, but in city festivals the hayashi usually consists of three drummers and a flutist (Plate 1). One drummer is assigned to the *o-daiko* while the other two play on rough-hewn versions of the *taiko*. The taiko heads are lashed together with rope and tightened by a second encircling rope (Plate 1). Its structure is like that of the taiko used in the noh drama, except that the skins are thicker as are the ropes and the wood. The playing method also differs. Instead of a delicate playing stand used for noh drums, the folk taiko is tipped up in front by means of a stick that is shoved into the ropes. Sometimes the drum is merely placed on the edge of a box. The sticks (called *bachi*) used to play this drum are smaller than those used for the noh drum. Modern design has appeared in this folk instrument, and many taiko are now tightened by means of large nuts and bolts. If these drums seem rather un-Japanese in their lack of delicacy it must be remembered that many are homemade and that they are subject to severe weather changes on open-air stages and to the rough handling of folk musicians.

The o-daiko has a convex wooden body and two tacked heads. In performance either one or both heads can be used. It is usually set on a crate (Plate 5) or tipped, with one head toward the player. The music is played on either the skins or the rim by means of two blunt sticks.

[3] Japan changed from a lunar to a solar calendar in the Meiji period. Thus, some festivals are celebrated on dates calculated on the old system and some on the new.

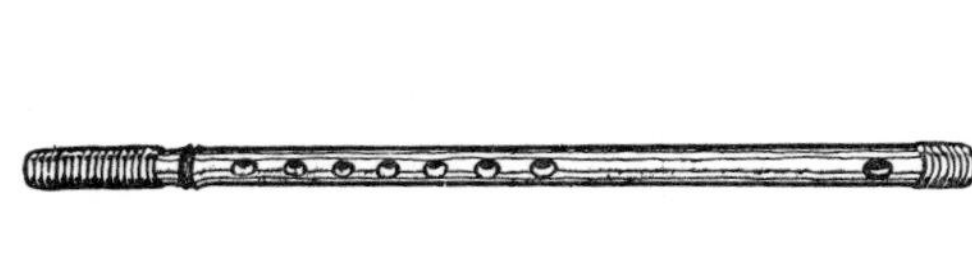

TAKE-BUE

TAIKO

The flute used in these folk hayashi groups is usually a simple bamboo pipe with six or seven holes called a *take-bue* or *shino-bue*. Not only do the length and number of holes vary from group to group but the manner of playing is also different. There are many Japanese folk flutists who play with the flute to the left instead of the normal right-hand position.

The folk hayashi is open to considerable variation. Other styles of drums are used together with singers and special percussion instruments. The most common addition is the *atari-gane*, a small brass gong suspended or held in the hand and played with a bone mallet set on a stick. By hitting at different parts of the gong a pleasant variety of tones can be produced. It is normally struck on the inside as seen in Plate 4. Instruments the size of the one shown here are usually called *suri-gane*.

These ensembles are often named after the name of the particular district from which they come or the particular type of music they play. For example, there is a Kanda-bayashi from the Kanda district of Tokyo and the popular Edo-bayashi, which is the repository for much of the festival music of old Tokyo (Edo). This music is considered as a folk form though it is now usually played by professionals. It has been discussed in the religious chapter, however, because of its close connection with Shinto festivals. For one thing, it is often used to accompany folk kagura dances. During o-matsuri one can see many of the most common sato-kagura dances: the comic female dance (*okame*, Plate 1), the bumpkin dance (*hyottoko*), the dog dance (*nimba*), and the always popular lion dances (*shishi-odori*, Plate 6).

Both the dances and the music are repetitive, and each section is performed many times before any contrast is presented. Frequently, these repeats are in sets of three or nine, as three is a lucky number in Japan. City kagura dances are more like performances for public entertainment than most of those seen in the country, although they still retain the fundamental choreographical concept of the efficacy of magic numbers. Though the spirit may be lost the tradition remains. Such prolonged repetitions become boring if one follows the dance too closely. However, such dances are not meant to be watched continuously except, perhaps, by the gods. For the onlooker, casual observation mixed with conversation is the best approach to the enjoyment of such performances. The same can be said for many oriental theatricals and folk events such as Chinese operas and Javanese shadow plays as well as Japanese kabuki. The idea of mixing attention with subliminal awareness is the key, I believe, to both the organization and appreciation of many such stage productions.

Since the music for an o-matsuri type of festival is not directly related to special ceremonies, its form is different from that of the usual religious music. There are a certain number of set pieces which are played in a given order and then repeated in that order as often as necessary. The exact pieces used varies from one hayashi group to another, but such titles as "Kamakura," "Shoten," "Yatai," and "Shichome" are found frequently. If one views these pieces on a country-wide basis, however, one will find that although the titles may be the same the melodies are often different. These names seem to designate broad divisions in the traditional festivals rather than specific tunes.

The drum parts of these hayashi groups are very lively and interesting. When there are two taiko players, it is common for one to set up a steady rhythmic drone against which the other player creates syncopations. However, at certain vital sections of the music, such as phrase endings or codas, the two play the same rhythmic patterns. In the more simple pieces one often finds the drummers playing many repetitions of a single rhythmic pattern of some three or four measures length. Like an Indian *tala*, this rhythmic phrase is played over and over until the flute melody is finished, at which time a special ending rhythm is added. In more complex pieces, the drum part is much freer, though certain parts of the music have special names which represent specific rhythmic patterns. This use of named rhythm patterns will be seen frequently in the chapters to follow.

The big drum (o-daiko) is used less frequently and usually enters during an introduction or a close. Thus, it can be seen that this music is organized to a great extent around rhythmic cadences in contrast to Western music, which is usually based more on harmonic cadences. The Westerner recognizes the end of a piece by the chords that appear, and the Japanese can tell the coda of a kagura piece by the type of rhythmic ensemble and the specific patterns used. Both reactions are culturally conditioned and both are valid means of holding a musical structure together. The entire series of pieces used by the hayashi is connected by flute interludes so that the music never stops until the series is finished and the rice wine is opened for the thirsty musicians. Festival hayashi music is a casual affair and, while not without its complexity or artistic merit,

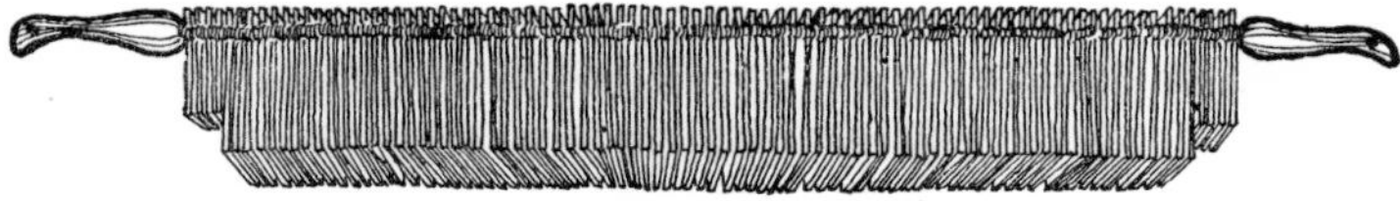

BIN-SASARA

it should be considered primarily in the same light as the tailgate band at a New Orleans funeral. It is meant to entertain both gods and men and seems to do well in both capacities.

If one travels further into the backwoods of Japan one can find some of the most ancient and pure forms of Japanese folk music. A goodly portion of this music is reserved for use in the various seasonal religious festivals. These festivals, while full of entertaining dances, are quite concerned with ritual and magic numbers. Speaking in broad terms, the content of most such events will include a procession, a purification ceremony, sacred dances, a symbolic or real banquet, secular dances, and a climactic event or benediction.

In the mountain fastness of the small village of Niino in Nagano there occurs one of the most famous of these festivals, the Yuki Matsuri, or "snow festival" (see ref. 20). It occurs every year on January fourteenth as an act of supplication that the spring fertility will once again follow the winter barrenness. For several days before, special purification ceremonies and banquets are held, but the festival itself officially begins on the afternoon of the fourteenth with a procession from a temple on one side of the village to the main shrine on the other side. The function of the procession is to carry the masks of the *kamisama*, the spirits, to the main shrine. This shrine, in traditional fashion, is in a forest and on a hill. The music for this procession consists of a short flute melody played over and over with the beating of an o-daiko drum for accompaniment. One should add that the drunken shouts of some of the participants are also part of the music as is a flourish from the local firemen's bugle corps, which forms part of the entourage.

Upon arriving at the shrine, the sacred dances are immediately begun on the special kagura stage, which forms part of most shrine compounds. To the accompaniment of flute and drum, groups of men and boys move through the stately measures of the dances, making sure that everything is repeated three times on every side. The men carry serpentine Japanese rattles (*bin-sasara*), while the boys carry drums. The bin-sasara (Plate 8) is one of a variety of rattles (*sasara*) used in Japanese folk music. Usually they are some form of split bamboo. The bin-sasara, however, is made of plates of wood that are strung together to produce a sharper tone. The men dance to the "jat, jat, jat" of their bin-sasara, always played three times and always left-right-left.

In present-day performances the boys merely carry the drums and do not play them.

These dances take over an hour and, though the crowd drifts off to buy souvenirs or wine, the dances are scrupulously repeated the proper number of times to insure the coöperation of the gods. There is little apparent awe of the spirits, for the dancers talk and even smoke and drink during the performance, but the superstition of the magic numbers still has a great hold on this rural population.

The next set of sacred dances takes place within the shrine itself. They are interesting because they are dedicated to Kannon, the Buddhist goddess of mercy. This is an excellent illustration of the mixture of the Buddhist and Shinto religions mentioned earlier.

The symbolic banquet at this festival consists of the opening of the sanctuary and the placing of proper offerings within it. All the participants in the festival are then blessed with a special wand brought from the inner sanctum. The music of the prayers that follow is of interest. It consists of chanting done to the accompaniment of the large drum and the rattling of bell trees (suzu). This music, called *semmyo* (Plate 10), is closely related to a style of Buddhist hymn singing (*wasan*) to be studied later (compare Plate 10 with Plate 12).

The climactic event of the festival occurs around 1:00 A.M. when a huge pine-tree bonfire is lit. The pyre is ignited by means of a sacred boat which is sent up nine times before it finally touches the trees. The pine burns with a pitchy intensity. Suddenly, through the shower of sparks the first god appears. Standing in the orange glare of the fire and surrounded by shouting men and waving lanterns the dancer truly gives the impression of something supernatural. From their position under the eaves of the shrine roof, the flutist and drummer strike up the tune of "Saiho," and the gods themselves begin to dance. This dance consists of a series of movements each done three times. The entire dance is repeated nine times, with only the ending changed. This is altered in order that the dancer may bless different parts of the shrine at the end of each repeat. The last repetition includes an interlude performed by the drum and the rattle dancers who appeared earlier.

The next dance, "Modoki" (Plate 9), is exactly the same choreographically as "Saiho." Only the mask is different. This is one of the most interesting characteristics of Shinto festivals. There has been no really adequate explanation for this rather curious habit. The only reason given by the peasants is that they want to make sure that the gods have seen and fully appreciated their dances.

As the night progresses toward dawn, a further series of dancers plunge through the smoke to do their bit to entertain the gods. More secular entertainments appear, in-

3. These colorful devil (oni) dancers from the Yasurai festival of the Imamiya Shrine in Kyoto are among the many devil dancers that lend accent to Shinto ceremonies throughout Japan.

4. The devil dancers of the Yasurai festival use gongs called atari-gane. Their drums are folk taiko. For other devil dancers see Plates 82, 83.

5. The dancer-priestess (miko) in this folk Shinto ceremony on the island of Miyakejima, uses a typical ceremonial instrument, the bell tree (suzu). See page 46.

6. The ever-popular lion dances are found in many forms throughout Japan from long creatures like this one to the more common one- and two-man lions. See page 49.

7. Masked dances such as this one from Matsue, Shimane Prefecture, are common in folk Shinto dances (kagura). Note the o-daiko drum to the right. See page 46.

8. This dancer at the Yuki Matsuri, the "snow festival," in the mountain village of Niino in Nagano, uses a rattle (bin-sasara) of ancient origin. See pages 51–52.

9. The "Modoki" dance is one of a series of secular dances performed before the sanctuary in the all-night celebration of the Yuki Matsuri.

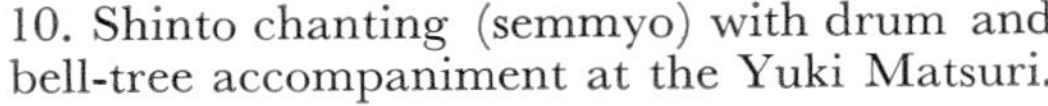

10. Shinto chanting (semmyo) with drum and bell-tree accompaniment at the Yuki Matsuri.

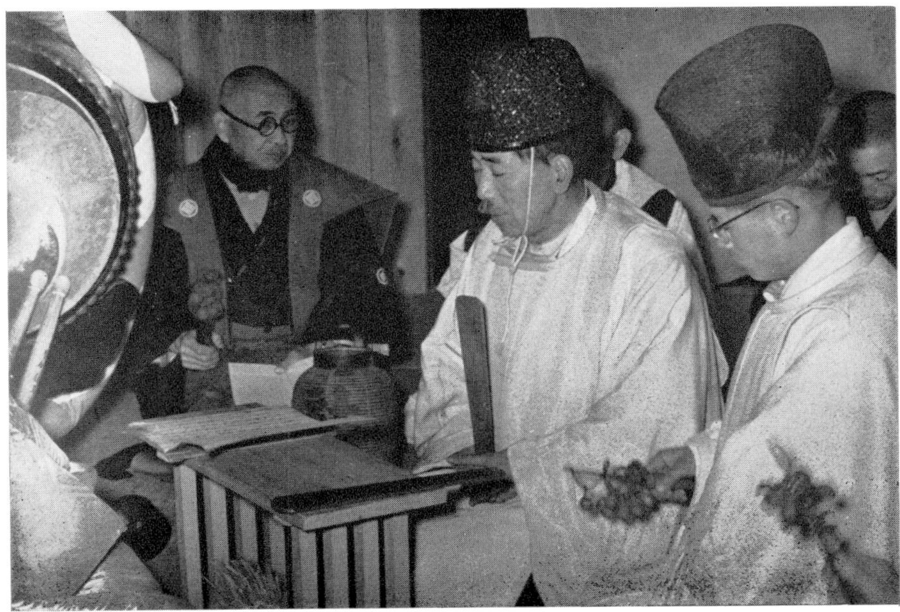

11. A large, wooden fish-mouthed slit gong (mokugyo) sits ready for use as Buddhist priests chant their service while circling before the altar. See pages 69–70.

12. Buddhist wasan singing is often accompanied by the o-daiko drum. See page 69.

13. An old print showing various street musicians of Edo. Ogibyoshi, top left, saimon, top right, and nembutsu priests, below. See pages 72, 73.

14. An itinerant shaman on Enoshima sells sacred texts and chants prayers to the accompaniment of the uchiwa-daiko drum. See page 70.

15. Members of a Buddhist congregation of the Jodo sect practicing goeika music and dancing. See pages 72–73.

16. Bon-odori, such as this example from Miyakejima, are the most common Buddhist-inspired folk dances in Japan. The lack of instrumental accompaniment indicates the antiquity of its origin. See page 73.

17. In this Buddhist folk festival from Nagano the saints seem to literally come marching in. See page 74.

18. The Iwate deer dance is one of the most spectacular folk dances in Japan. See page 74.

19. Street musicians are still popular in Japan, though the instrumentation and the things they advertise may have changed. Their most frequent use today is in front of pin-ball parlors. See Plate 13.

FIGURE 4. The Yuki Matsuri devil-dance music

cluding short, masked comedy skits. There is an extremely interesting dance by two men wearing model horses, which may be an imitation of the ancient imperial custom of having horse races and archery contests on festival days. Another dance, more directly related to the fertility overtones of the festival, is an amorous pantomime between an old lady and old man, both played by masked children. Finally, at dawn three devils, or *oni*, appear who perform a slow stylized fight. One curious element of this dance is that the dancers cannot see out of their masks, and hence each man is moved about by an assistant much in the manner of Japanese puppets.

There is a comic horse dance, which is then repeated as a lion dance, another comic skit, and the festival draws to a close with the singing of a final chant by a group of men gathered around an upturned drum upon which offerings have been placed. The masks are put away, the souvenir sellers fold up their booths, the remaining wine is finished, and the population wanders home for a good sleep, content in the knowledge that the gods are on their side for another season.

The music for the Yuki Matsuri is played by a flute and a drum with the occasional addition of the bin-sasara or the suzu. Figure 4 is the music used for the devil dance (*oni-no-mai*) mentioned above. It is typical of Japanese folk flute music and illustrates one of the common folk scales. This scale, known as the *yo* scale, and its companion *in* scale are said to have developed out of the *ritsu* scale (Figure 5). The musical characteristics of this melody are discussed in Chapter X. It is included here to help capture the ponderous, primitive spirit of the choreography of this folk devil dance.

The Yuki Matsuri displays all the characteristics of a Shinto festival as listed earlier. If one travels about the country, one will see a host of festivals using a variety of masks, dances, and ceremonies. The basic outline, however, will remain about the same. It is the pleasant task of future anthropologists and ethnomusicologists to ferret out the many fascinating details that remain undiscovered in the world of Japanese Shinto folk festivals. For the more casual observer they provide a colorful spectacle and a pleasant memory of Japan.

Before closing the topic of Shinto music one should mention the music of Tenrikyo, a modern religion founded around 1830 and now separate from Shinto. The foundress, Nakayama Miki, used a kind of kagura in the services accompanied by a variety of instruments. Today court music is used in some of the temples for certain religious, memorial, or marriage services. The dancing used by Tenrikyo consists primarily of hand gestures like Buddhist mudras. There is a newer Japanese religion, however, which is called the "dancing religion" because its followers express their faith in real dance movements. While the many new religions of Japan that made their appearance since the end of World War II offer interesting studies in syncretism and spiritual activity, musically one must still look to the classic Shinto and Buddhist traditions for the significant religious musical heritage of Japan.

II. Buddhist Music

THEORY AND PRACTICE: Western music is based on two great traditions, the music theories of ancient Greece and the extension of these theories by the Catholic church. Our scales, modes, notations, and concepts of consonance and dissonance are all deeply rooted in this background, though the present-day products may seem to be very distant indeed. By the same token, Japanese music is based on two equally great theoretical foundations, the music of ancient China and the music of Buddhism.

Buddhism entered Japan in the Nara period and continued to grow in influence and power during the subsequent Heian and Kamakura periods. Coming primarily through Chinese sources, Buddhism became an important purveyor of Chinese culture and ideas. Among the intellectual accoutrements of this Chinese Buddhism was the theory of singing and composing chants based on sacred texts (sutras) and hymns. This art became known in Japan as *shomyo.*

Yearly, Japanese monks would set out on the perilous journey to China to sit at the feet of the great singing masters of the Chinese monastery of Yü-shan (or Gyosan in Japanese) in order that they might be able to instruct their brethren in the proper manner of praising the Lord Buddha in song. Yü-shan must have been the musical Mecca of the orient, the Rome of ninth-century Buddhism, where Japanese, Chinese, Tibetan, and Indian knelt together to read commentaries on the Diamond and Lotus sutras or to raise their voices in praise of the Buddha, whose serene smile could be seen dimly through the clouds of burning incense.

Buddhism began in India, and the art of shomyo is also said to have originated in the singing of the ancient Hindu Vedic hymns. Perhaps the Japanese monks met Indian teachers of this style during their stay at Yü-shan. It is said that some Indian priests actually came to Japan to teach. In any event, there is some basis for believing that part of this Hindu tradition was also absorbed into the music of the Japanese Buddhist church. However, the organized theory of music as learned by the Japanese is based on Chinese texts and Chinese teachers. This theory was not the exclusive property of the church, for the music of the court also originated from Chinese models. There, the theory was kept fairly intact, while the Buddhist monks, perhaps because they had more time and inclination for commentaries, extended some of the basic ideas. However, for our purposes one can say that the music theory of shomyo and that of court music (gagaku) are basically the same and that they have a common origin in Chinese music theory. Some of the ideas of this theory will be presented here and some in the following chapter, but it must be remembered that they are all basically of one piece.

Buddhism, like Christianity, is fraught with sectarianism. These theological schisms are reflected in turn by various music styles, each responding to the beliefs and ceremonial requirements of a particular sect. For example, in speaking of Christian music one must differentiate between Catholic, Orthodox, Anglican, American Protestant, and many other styles. Likewise, in Japanese Buddhism differences exist in the music of the Shingon, Tendai, Nichiren, and a host of other sects. However, if our discussion is organized around musical types rather than sectarian styles, a better idea can be grasped of the general scope of Buddhist music.

Since shomyo began as the chanting of Buddhist texts in India and went to China before it came to Japan, it is now sung in three different languages. Those songs sung in the ancient Indian dialect are called *bonsan*, those in Chinese are called *kansan*, and the songs in Japanese are *wasan*. Because the Japanese adopted Chinese ideographs for their written language, giving them Japanese pronunciations, it is possible for them to sing Chinese songs with Japanese pronunciations. This form of shomyo developed into a distinct style called *koshiki*.

When we want to know about the background and origins of Western music, we turn to the ancient collections of Gregorian chant or refer to the theories of Odo of Cluny, Guido d'Arezzo (the inventor of *do, re, mi*), and a legion of other monkish scholars. If we seek a similar heritage in Japanese music, we must look to such works as the *Shomyo Yojinshu* by Tanchi (1163–1237) of the Tendai sect or the main codex of the Shingon sect, the *Gyozan Taikaishu* (1496), with its important theoretical appendices by Chokei. By distilling certain major facts from these important works a basis can be formed upon which to build a study of all subsequent Japanese music.

First in any music theory, East or West, is the problem of scales and modes. In shomyo there are two basic scales and a third one over which there are sectarian differences. Ignoring some historical variations in nomenclature, the two basic scales can be called *ryo* and *ritsu* (Figure 5). Each has five basic notes called *kyu, sho, kaku, chi,* and *u.*

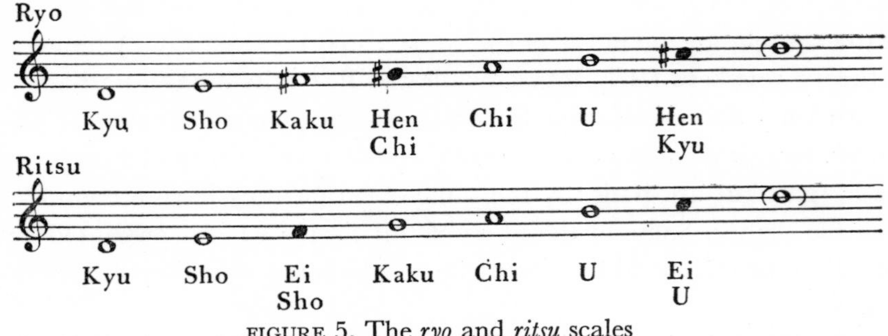

FIGURE 5. The *ryo* and *ritsu* scales

Notice that each scale has two auxiliary tones. The prefix *ei*, like the Western sharp, raises a tone one-half step, while the word *hen*, like the Western flat, indicates that a note should be lowered one-half step. These auxiliary tones are known collectively as *hennon*, literally "changing tones," and are used primarily for modulation.

The third scale is meant to be a combination of the above two, thus its usual name is *han-ryo-han-ritsu*, "half *ryo* and half *ritsu*." Which half goes where is the bone of contention between the various theorists.

In Western music the space of one octave contains twelve possible pitches. Played in succession they are called a chromatic scale. These notes also exist in Japanese (or Chinese) music theory. In Western music seven of these twelve notes are chosen to form a normal scale. The Japanese scales also consist of seven notes, but only five of them are considered vital. In Western music one can take a given scale structure (for example, a major scale) and start it on any one of the twelve notes. In this way C major, E flat major, F sharp major, etc. are constructed. In Chinese music theory such a process is also possible, but one standard Japanese theory (unfortunately there is more than one due to sectarianism) allows only five notes out of the twelve to be used for scale construction. *Ryo*-type scales can be started only on the note D or G, *ritsu* scales should begin on E and B, and the mixed scale should start only on A. Notice that these starting notes are the five basic pitches of the *ritsu* scale as shown in Figure 5. Also note that this *ritsu* scale is the classic pentatonic scale mentioned earlier (see Figure 2). As for the problems of modes within each scale, modulations, and other transpositions, all that need be said here is that these topics are also covered in the theory books. These Buddhist tomes are replete with charts, diagrams, and tables; the symbols of authority for music theorists all over the world. As in the case of many such theoretical works, the charts and diagrams do not always coincide with actual performance practice.

Before leaving scales one more thing should be noticed. The essential difference between the *ryo* and *ritsu* scales is the placement of the *kaku* note. It is one-half step lower in the *ryo* scale. This is somewhat analogous to the situation in Western music in which the important difference between major and minor is the lowered third note in minor. One might call the *ritsu* a major-type scale and *ryo* a minor-type, though it is not safe to carry the analogy too far.

Into these scale molds Buddhist music is poured. As the chanting developed certain standard musical phrases and ornamentations appeared. These were given special names, the exact meaning of which often varies with the particular scale being used. Thus, certain patterns were reserved for use only in the *ritsu* or only in the *ryo* scale though they had the same name. The most common type of ornamentation is called *yuri*, or "swinging." There are many kinds of yuri but their basic technique is the use of a waver or slight change in pitch which colors the line and provides a small sense of rhythm to the melody.

The problem of rhythm is one of the weakest links in the rather rigid chain of Buddhist music theory. There are discussions of the problem, observations on the seven-five-syllable construction of some of the poetry, and the names of certain rhythmic units. In present-day practice and notation (see Appendix II), however, there is really very little one can hold on to except for traditional performance practice.

In the light of all this music theory it is now time to look at actual performance practice. Because of considerable sectarian variation it is not possible to provide an all-

DENSHO

KEI

encompassing example, but by citing one specific case the general style of other sects can be inferred.

The main Tendai temple in the Asakusa amusement area of Tokyo is well known for its hidden image of the goddess Kannon. The following is an account of a morning mass at that temple.

Like the Christian tradition, the faithful and the priests are called to the ceremony by means of a large bell. The Buddhist bell (a *densho* or *hansho*), however, does not have a clapper but is struck on the outside with a hammer in a rapid and loud manner that is associated in the West with country fire alarms. The processional accompaniment is rendered on a large hidden drum of the o-daiko type. The ponderous beats echo through the main hall and create an atmosphere of solemnity to equal that created by the chanting entrance of Christian monks.

The head priest kneels on a dais immediately before the image. Various offerings and sacred vessels are arranged before him, and to his right there is a small, hanging, fish-mouthed chime made of bronze called a *kei*. This is used rather like the small bells of the Catholic mass, i.e., it signals certain special moments in the ceremonial movements of the head priest. For this purpose, two more bells are provided. One is a small hand bell with a clapper which is found throughout the orient and in Japanese is called a *rei*. The other is a bowl-shaped bell called an *uchinarashi* or *kin* which is set on a brightly colored cushion and struck on the edge with a mallet. This latter instrument is found commonly in home shrines and is capable of a very lovely, sustaining tone. It comes in a variety of sizes from monsters of several feet in diameter to very small ones.

The major sections of the ceremony are marked off by strokes on a common, knobbed oriental gong. On other occasions a chime is used.

When the priests are all in their places, a gong is sounded and the first shomyo begins. As in most religious traditions, the opening phrase is sung by a solo cantor, sometimes with the other priests humming softly behind him. The tempo is very slow, and rhythm seems almost nonexistent. Gradually the entire ensemble joins in as the main priest begins the ablutions and blessings requisite to the presentation of the offering to Buddha. Musically, the point of greatest interest is the fact that each priest sings at his own pitch level. Some feel that this is not the intention of the original style, but, be that

KIN

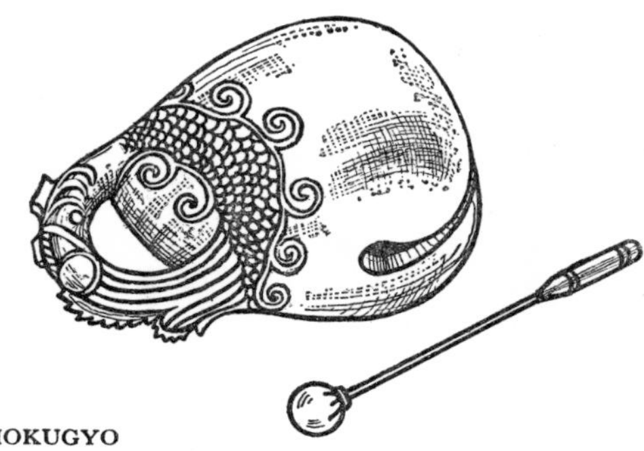

MOKUGYO

as it may, the effect of some twenty men chanting as many pitches is quite striking.

One of the important parts of the normal Buddhist mass is the *gyodo* during which the priests sing shomyo while dropping symbolic lotus petals. Sometimes this is done while parading around the central dais. The fascination of this music lies in the fact that the cantor often sings a completely different piece in Sanscrit, while the other priests chant in ancient Chinese. The Sanscrit piece (called *bai*) gives the same effect as that of a *cantus firmus* in the early polyphony of the Catholic church. The similarity in effect (though not necessarily in sound and form) is really quite intriguing. Perhaps certain ideas concerning psychological and acoustical effects are universal in the field of religious music.

Bells and chimes continue to mark off the progress of the service. The prayers and holy scriptures are read in a simple chanting style like that used for similar sections in many Christian services. Responsive singing between the cantor and the priests occurs during the section in which the priests rise and make obeisance to their god. It is interesting to note that this ceremony, like the Shinto dances mentioned earlier, is often repeated in multiples of three. The mass ends with the singing of wasan, a chant in Japanese. This, unlike the preceding shomyo, is sung in a very steady rhythm which is set by means of an o-daiko type of drum (Plate 12). The poems of these wasan are usually in the seven-five-syllable scheme but are sung in phrases of eight beats. This, as will be seen later, is a fundamental rhythmic orientation in Japanese music. When the wasan is over and the final prayers are said, the wasan drum is given one sharp rap which signals the beginning of beats on the larger hidden drum. These mark the stately measures of the recessional. The Buddhist mass is over.

This, of course, is only one mass of a particular type for a particular sect. Some of the musical variations that should be mentioned occur in the popular Jodo and Nichiren sects. Both have a love of the percussive, and greater use is made of drums and gongs during their ceremonies. Among the endless battery of Buddhist percussive instruments two are especially popular. One is the *mokugyo*, a wooden, fish-mouthed slit gong known in the West as a Chinese temple block. In dance bands it is the "clippidy clop" of many a Western ballad, and in the Buddhist home it is the ostinato over which one chants the name of Buddha as a means of salvation. This persistent wooden

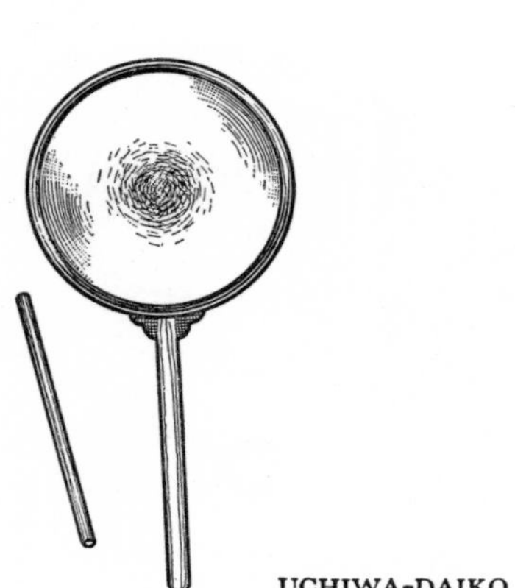
UCHIWA-DAIKO

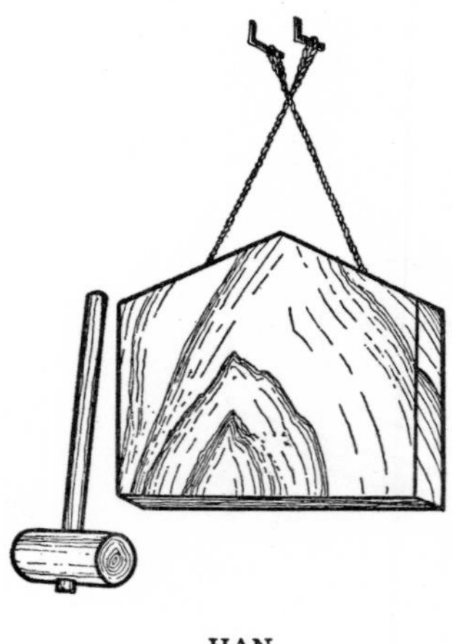
HAN

"tat, tat, tat" has been heard by many a tourist who has wandered through a Japanese village in the early morning or at sunset. One of the most striking uses of the mokugyo can be heard during a high mass of the Jodo sect. At the end of the service the priests begin their steady chanting of wasan. From the side of the sanctuary another priest begins a slower rhythm on a very large, deep-toned mokugyo. This rhythm is picked up by a chorus of women who are kneeling behind him, each with a smaller instrument. They also chant, and the rhythm of their song rises slowly until the temple is filled with an overpowering chaos of rhythm and uncoördinated chanting. It is an excellent and exciting example of psychological considerations overcoming music theory in the shaping of religious music.

The other main percussion instrument of Buddhist music is practically the trademark of the Nichiren sect. It is the *uchiwa-daiko,* the fan drum (Plate 14). A single head is stretched over an iron ring and then attached to a wooden handle. The drum is beaten with a wooden stick, and religious slogans are often written on the head. The Nichiren sect is quite evangelistic, and one can often see one of its followers tramping down the street, pounding an uchiwa-daiko as a means of calling on sinners to repent. These drums are also used in the Nichiren services, the congregation beating out the prayers, while an acolyte provides syncopation on an o-daiko. Under such conditions it is not difficult to see that vocal technique suffers. In any event, there is little chance of drowsing during a Nichiren service. In the more important services of many different sects court instruments are added, but the battery mentioned above is the center of most branches of the Buddhist instrumental tradition.

The monastic life of the Buddhist church, like that of the Catholic, is filled with many office hours and has a concomitant number of special gongs and bells to assist in the marking of these hours. In the cloisters of the famous Zen sect of meditative Buddhism one can find some twenty-odd instruments used to regulate the monk's daily life. Of them, only two will be mentioned here. One is the *han,* a large wooden board which is beaten with a mallet to call the monks to the central hall for periods of meditation. This board (found in other sects too) is often inscribed with a religious poem. Another

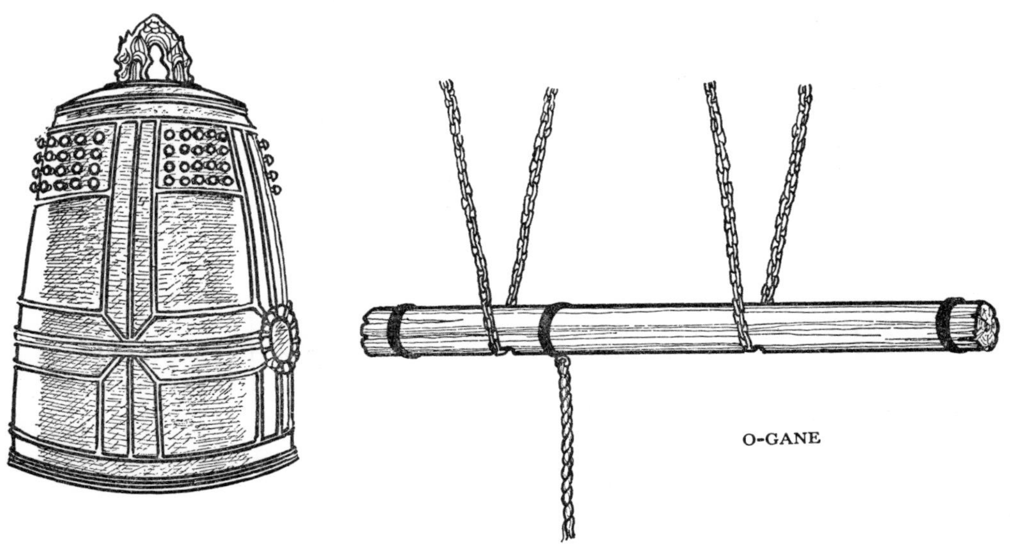

O-GANE

instrument must be mentioned because it is the very symbol of the Buddhist temple as pictured in poetry and remembered by the foreign visitor. This is the *o-gane,* a large bell which hangs in a separate bell tower within the temple compound. It is struck by means of a long, horizontally suspended pole. Its deep, rich tone marks off the hours of the day, and on New Year's Eve o-gane from every part of the city slowly mark the passing year. The great Japanese classic, *The Heike Story,* begins and ends with the solemn tolling of such a bell, for it amply symbolizes the Buddhist concept of the impermanence of this world and the inextricable unity of life, death, and time. One might say that shomyo destroys time in the sense that any deep religious meditation seems to escape temporality, but the o-gane symbolically restores a sequential regularity to life. The Buddhist tradition is rich with such ritualistic and artistic abstractions of its various religious precepts. For the music lover, the ancient art of Buddhist music certainly provides ample testimony to the grandeur of the Japanese Buddhist heritage. The study of this music not only provides a basis for the understanding of many subsequent styles but also gives one an indirect glimpse of what might have been the musical traditions of ancient India and China.

BUDDHIST FOLK MUSIC AND FESTIVALS: Buddhism has a long and distinguished history of evangelism. Its priests traversed vast deserts, mountains, and oceans to bring the message of Sakyamuni to the oriental world. Like all evangelists, they found music very helpful in the process of conversion. Also, like the Catholic missionaries, they realized that the words of their standard ceremonial music were in too foreign a tongue to be of much help in reaching the common people. Therefore, vernacular pieces were composed, sometimes based on existing folk music and often creating a new genre of folk song. In Japan this process began with wasan, the Buddhist chants that already existed in Japanese.

Both the melodic style and the texts of wasan were changed in order to capture the attention of new, less sophisticated congregations. One group of priests created sets of simple wasan which were taught to the large prostitute population of the capital. This form of music became one of the main contributing factors to the imayo music of the Shinto dancing girls mentioned earlier. Other hymns that were written for more rural populations were absorbed quickly into the local folk-music tradition. Hence, many of the older folk songs existent today have a Buddhist overtone to their texts and sometimes a distinct shomyo quality in their melodies. One example, heard on a small island called Miyakejima, comes to mind. During a recording session held on the island, one of the old ladies dragged out of her memory a song in which each syllable was separated by a long melisma in almost a classic Buddhist chanting style. Some of these religious folk songs are still called wasan by the folk singers though frequently they are designated as *bushi*, a generic term used as a suffix with a wide variety of folk songs. One characteristic of the older Buddhist folk songs, besides the chant influence, is the fact that accompaniment is seldom used. Hand clapping or an occasional drum may be added, but music of this category which uses the shamisen is usually of much later origin.

One of the more violent transfers of music from the sacred to the secular occurred with a type of hymn known as *saimon*. These hymns were used in Buddhist, Shinto, and Confucian rites and were later incorporated into the structure of the various theatrical predecessors of the noh drama. In the late Muromachi period, they became popular once more, but by then the secular influence of the above theatricals had become too strong. Instead of praising Buddha, the songs were used to satirize current events and people rather like Carribean Calypso music. These lampoonings were invented primarily by traveling priests called *yamabushi* (Plate 13). Like some of the early European friars, these men had only a very loose connection with the church or its morals. They soon took to recounting dramatized versions of the latest love affairs around town, especially those ending in double suicides. Such music might be called a fifteenth-century musical tabloid. This type of saimon was eventually coupled with the shamisen and became known as *uta-zaimon*, an important predecessor of a genre of narrative music to be studied later (see joruri, Chapter VIII). The only remains of the old saimon are found in certain dirty ditties used in folk theatricals and dances. The religious forms of this music have disappeared. Its real significance, however, lies in its relation to uta-zaimon and the shamisen musics that followed.

Another form of Buddhist folk music is *goeika*. These hymns also originated in wasan and grew to their greatest popularity in the Muromachi period. They were particularly popular as pilgrims' songs and are still used during sacred processions to various shrines. A hand bell and a small gong set on three legs (a *hitotsu-gane*) or an atari-gane are often used as accompanying instruments. Plate 15 shows a practice session of goeika for use in an important ceremony of the Jodo sect. Notice that, as in some of the ceremonies of the newer Japanese religions, a form of religious dancing has been added.

The goeika songs also were contributing factors to the creation of a type of folk song known as *ondo* (see Figure 20). The word *ondo* has become a generic term for various types of folk songs. Usually these songs are antiphonal, with a soloist being answered by a chorus. Like the word *bushi,* ondo is used as a suffix. For example, there is Akita-ondo from the Akita district and Fukuchiyama-ondo from the Fukuchiyama area.

One of the most common types of ondo are those used to accompany the dances of the *o-bon* festival. This is perhaps the best known of all Buddhist festivals. It is a type of All-Souls' Day and occurs in late August or early September, depending on the locality. The dances of this festival, the bon-odori, are the most widespread in Japan and offer a great variety of styles. Like the folk songs mentioned earlier, the older dances use no instrumental accompaniment. Instead there is a chorus of singers, the dancers themselves sometimes entering into the song (Plate 16). Those pieces dating from the Edo period, however, often use flute, drum, and shamisen (see Figure 21). Bon-odori is usually done in a circle with the musicians in the center. The most common style of these dances is rather easygoing, perhaps in keeping with the languid mood of the summer evenings on which they are performed. Plate 16 shows a characteristic movement of both the feet and the rest of the body. Fans are used often along with simple hand gestures. Both men and women dance bon-odori, and there is usually no difference in choreography between them. In fact, one can say in general that bon-odori, like other styles of Japanese dance, is quite hermaphroditic. Like many a Buddhist statue, it seems sexless, although this does not mean that it is not sensual. Such eroticism as may arise from the mass movement of a circle of Japanese girls in summer kimono, however, is more cumulative than direct. Though there are some very lively bon-odori, most of them are rather restrained. Actually, bon-odori is a form of community dancing and hence the steps are simple enough that anyone can join in.

Among the more specialized Buddhist folk dances the best known are the *nembutsu-odori.* They are said to have originated from the *nembutsu* section (literally, the calling of the name of Buddha) of the Buddhist mass. In old paintings one can see groups of priests prancing and beating gongs while performing nembutsu. Nembutsu priests also wandered the streets (Plate 13). A popularization of a nembutsu-odori is said to have been the first dance of the founder of kabuki. As this form evolved among the folk it took on several interesting characteristics. Unlike bon-odori, these dances are not done by mixed groups but always men or women separately. The men often carry drums while the women frequently have their sleeves tied back and wear straw hats. These dances are not done in a circle but usually are in the form of a processional. The accompaniment was originally wasan or nembutsu music. Later various percussion instruments and a flute were added. Today the shamisen is used sometimes. The nembutsu-odori itself has become quite mixed into the general field of folk theatricals so that it is not possible always to say that a certain dance is a pure nembutsu-odori.

In addition to the Buddhist folk music and dances there are many festivals built on Buddhist themes. One of the most colorful is the birthday of Nichiren (November 12th). On this day the followers of that sect form great processions. Everyone dresses in white, and large floats and umbrellas festooned with paper flowers are carried through the streets. The striking musical element is a massed band of flutes and fan drums (uchiwa-daiko). Both the sight and sound of this group reminds one greatly of processions pictured on the reliefs of the ancient civilizations of the Middle East.

For those who are able to explore the countryside there is an extremely interesting festival in Nagano Prefecture, the *Nijugo Bosatsu Raigoe,* during which the saints literally come marching in (Plate 17). For me, however, the most spectacular Buddhist dance is the *shika-odori*, the deer dance, from Iwate Prefecture (see Plate 18). There are many kinds of lion and deer dances in which the dancers also beat drums, but few can match this one in dramatic movement. With two plumes towering out of their backs, a large drum in front, and a fearsome mask covering their faces, the dancers stride about in awesome grandeur. Suddenly, one will bend forward and the two plumes will smash against the ground with a whirl of dust. The thin melody of a bamboo flute seems hardly adequate to keep these ponderous creatures under control. One almost expects them to begin fighting each other, they look so belligerent. This shika-odori is an excellent example of the more virile type of Japanese dancing which is often unknown to the cosmopolitan student of Japanese culture.

The above survey has only scratched the surface of the immense field of Japanese religious folk music. However, even in such a cursory study one can see how thoroughly the religious traditions have impregnated the Japanese folk field. Buddhist folk music equals Buddhist classical music theory as one of the most fruitful areas of study in Japanese music.

III. Christian Music

Christianity first came to Japan in the sixteenth century and went underground with the closing of the country during the Tokugawa period. Its music was the same as Christian music elsewhere and had little effect on indigenous music. The latter in turn did not have much effect on this imported religious music. There are a few folk songs which can be traced to old Christian hymns and there are hymns based on Japanese folk songs. In the latter case the debilitating effect of harmony has rather destroyed any charm the tunes may have had originally. In general, the relatively late arrival of Christian music, its suppression, and its second revival in the wake of Japan's modernization kept it outside the world of traditional Japanese music. Actually, in some cases it acted as a depressive. As late as 1921 one missionary proudly wrote that Japan was turning to civilized Western music and away from those "old fashioned strumming oddities."[4] There is plenty of reputable Christian music in Japan, but there is nothing particularly Japanese about it.

Christian music, however, has had a curious effect on contemporary Buddhist music. Fighting fire with fire, some branches of the Buddhist church have begun to issue hymn books, especially ones for children. They have also installed organs in some of the major temples. It is rather a surprise to hear a kimono-clad cherub serenely singing, "Buddha loves me, yes I know. For the sutras tell me so." Apparently all's fair in love, war, and religion.

IV. Summary

Looking back over our entire discussion of religious music, it can be seen that Japanese religious folk music is all basically the same musically. The choreography, location, costume, and *raison d'être* of each event may be different, but the accompaniment is still built around singing, the flute, and some percussion. The later entrance of the shamisen has also been noted. From this study the tremendous intermingling of Buddhist and Shinto elements in all regions of art and life can be seen. The point was made that many times the same pieces are used for Buddhist and Shinto ceremonies with only the words changed.

On the classical music level, the establishment of the standard Shinto music trio, the wagon, hichiriki, and Yamato-bue was mentioned. The close connection of the various Shinto dance forms with court ceremonies and with the secular theatrical entertainments of the nobility should be remembered.

Finally, the importance of early Buddhist music theory and practice must be emphasized once more. Shomyo, wasan, and their Chinese inspired explanations form a base from which one can watch the world of Japanese music blossom into the host of more familiar forms by which it is known today.

[4] McCausland, Isabelle. "Music in Japan Today," *Musician*, XXVI (Nov., 1921), p. 4.

CHAPTER THREE GAGAKU, THE COURT MUSIC OF JAPAN

I. The History of Court Music

In the summer of 749 the great image of Buddha at the Todaiji in Nara was finally completed. To celebrate this august event the emperor and all his court traveled to the great hall and presented their felicitations to the Buddha with all the dignity and grandeur at their command. Eloquent speeches were read by state ministers, hymns of praise were sung by large choruses of priests, and the full company of court musicians and dancers numbering in the hundreds provided regal spectacles suitable for both the rulers of heaven and of earth. The music for this performance was *gagaku*, the court music of Japan (see Plate 20).

The word *gagaku* means elegant, correct, or refined music. *Bugaku* is the term used when this music is used to accompany dances. Under the continual patronage of the court since the sixth century, this music is perhaps the oldest extant orchestral art music in the world. Through all the vicissitudes of Japanese imperial history a hard core of gagaku music tradition has managed to survive. The net result is that one can hear today music that is over a thousand years old played in a style which is apparently close to the original. Because of gagaku's direct influence from the musics of the Asian continent, inferences can be made as to the type of music found in the ancient courts of India and China. In short, gagaku is one of the most unique musics in the world; a living museum for the music or cultural historian and a rare and exotic delight for the general music lover. Before discussing the variety of instruments used in gagaku and the structure of its music, however, it is necessary to review its distinguished genealogy so that we can fully appreciate its right to the title of "elegant music."

There are three great continental traditions that form the beginnings of gagaku, the ancient music of India, China, and Korea. The Korean music seems to have been the earliest importation. There are references to it as early as the third century, and further indications of its importation in the fifth century. The important influx of Korean music did not occur, however, until the seventh and eighth centuries, when Japan opened her mind to the cultural influences of the entire continent.

The various waves of Korean music that entered Japan went under the names of the particular kingdoms in Korea from which they came (*Shiragi-gaku* in 453, *Kudara-*

gaku in 554, later *Kama-gaku*, etc.). However, the music was not necessarily pure Korean music, since the Korean courts were themselves under constant Chinese influence. In fact, the Chinese form known as *gigaku* (the remains of which are found in certain Japanese folk lion dances) is said to have been introduced into Japan in 612 by Mimashi of the kingdom of Kudara in southern Korea. There is even a hint of Manchurian music coming to Japan via Korea.

All this complex of music was first classified under the general term Sankan-gaku (Sankan were three kingdoms in Korea). Later, it was called Koma-gaku as the music derived from that of the kingdom of Koma came to predominate.

Another foreign style of music that entered Japan came from a land very far from Korea, India. In Chapter II Indian priests were mentioned as having done missionary work in Japan. According to traditionally accepted accounts, an Indian and an Indo-Chinese priest came to Japan in 736 and introduced the musics and dances of their respective homelands. This music was named Rinyu-gaku after a kingdom in Indo-China (Plate 21). Eight of these pieces survive in the modern court repertoire. Their dances are particularly distinctive in their use of grotesque masks which seem very un-Japanese. The choreography of the "Genjoraku" dance in which a masked dancer exorcises a snake has even been traced back to an ancient Vedic legend of India (Plate 22). The accoutrements and choreography of the Rinyu-gaku dances seem quite unique, and one can only wonder what traces of the original music might remain in an orchestra so thoroughly Sino-Japanese.

The paramount foreign influence in gagaku, as in all things Japanese, came from China. The Japanese Imperial Music Bureau (Gagaku-ryo), established in 701, was filled with T'ang musicians and a good number of Koreans. If compared with nineteenth-century America, these men were like the Germans and Italians who controlled American musical activities. During the Nara and early Heian periods Chinese music poured into Japan via the musicians and the returning students who had taken on a "continental" air. This Chinese music found in gagaku, the so-called To-gaku, seems to have been originally developed as banquet music rather than for ceremonial purposes. The greatest source of Chinese ceremonial music was found in the Korean court, where ancient texts and contemporary practice reveal a rich tradition of Confucian ceremonies and dances quite lacking in Japan and now rare in China itself (see ref. 6, II, 206 and ref. 37, 349–81). Of course, some such music did come to Japan either directly or via Korea. However, it makes sense that returning students, albeit scholars, might be more familiar with the banquet music of their Chinese university towns than with the formalities of the Chinese court.

20. Music, dancing, and ceremony mark the completion of a new hall for the great Buddha at the Todaiji in Nara in the eighteenth century just as they did a thousand years earlier. The scene is from a screen painting of the Genroku period. Note the bugaku musicians and dancers spread about the courtyard. See page 77.

21. Rinyu-gaku, an ancient form of court music as shown in the fourteenth-century scroll, the *Shinzei-kogakuzu*. See page 78.

22. The ancient court dance "Genjoraku" as pictured in the *Shinzei-kogakuzu* scroll. See page 78.

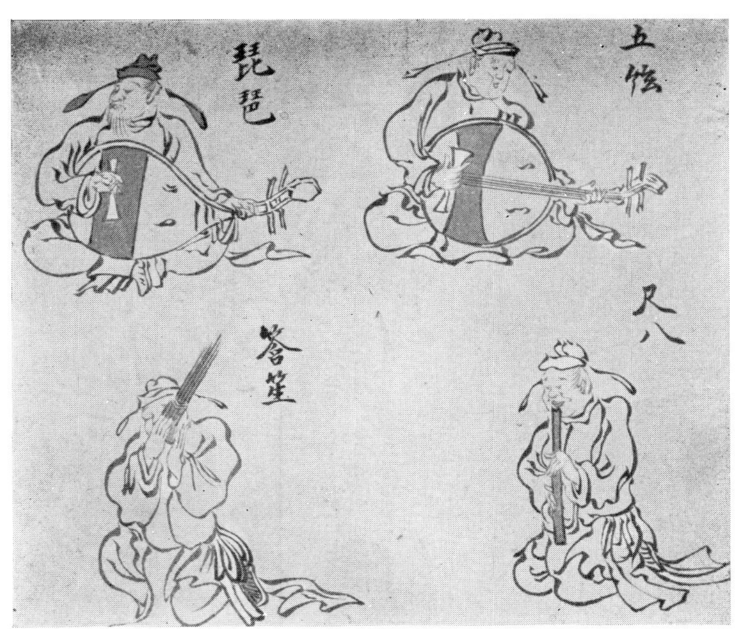

23. The gaku-biwa, gogen, sho, and shakuhachi as shown in the *Shinzeikogakuzu* scroll. See pages 94, 98, 151.

24. A modern artist's conception of ancient party music (enkyoku) in action. See page 90.

25. Bugaku dancers today still wear the same magnificent costumes and fierce masks of the early court dances.

26. The colorful da-daiko drum adorns the imperial music hall during a bugaku performance.

27. Outdoor bugaku performances dedicated to the imperial ancestors are held every year at the Ise Shrine.

28. The imperial gagaku orchestra in the palace music hall. They represent one of the oldest orchestral traditions in the world.

29. A bugaku ensemble accompanying dances at the Gion Shrine in Kyoto. Note the lack of stringed instruments. See page 100.

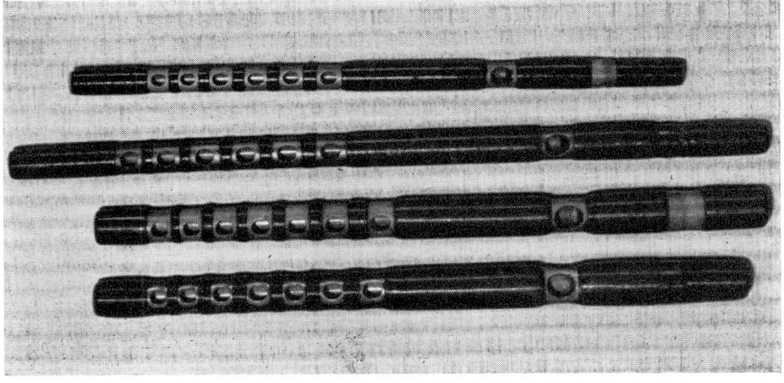

30. Four kinds of Japanese flutes: (from the top) the Koma-bue, kagura-bue, ryuteki, and noh-flute.

31. The da-daiko is Japan's largest drum. See pages 91–92.

32. A shoko gong with an ornate stand used during a Kyoto dance festival in honor of the cherry blossoms. See page 92.

33. A rare outdoor performance on the wagon zither. Note the high bridges. See pages 93–94.

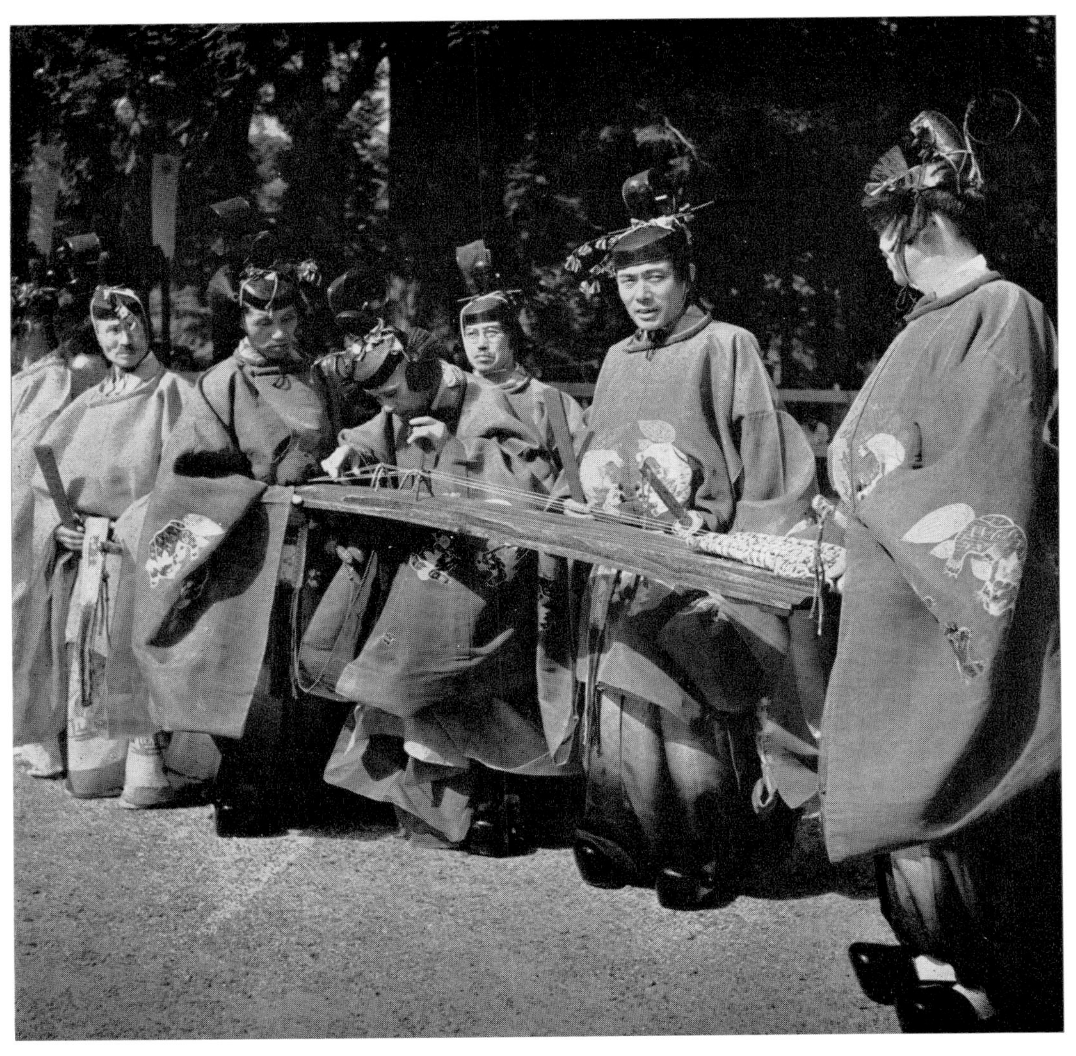

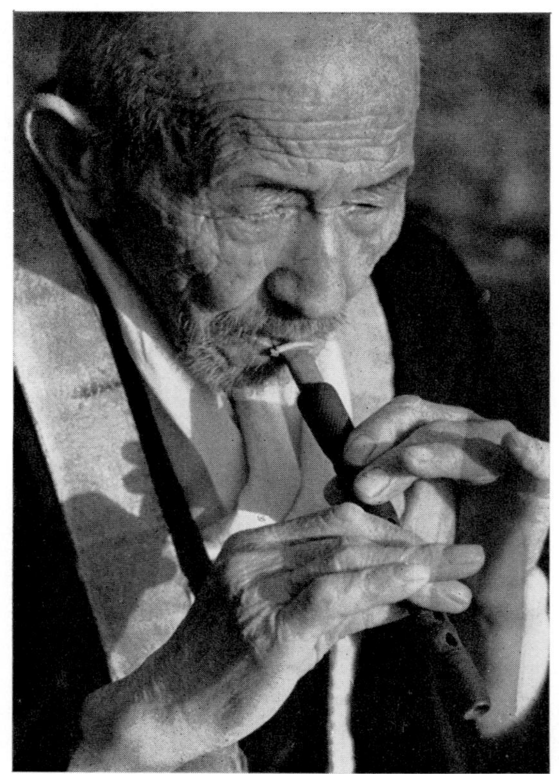

34. The hichiriki is played with a loose embouchure, and great skill is required to control both the pitch and the tone quality. See page 95.

35. Three monks from the Mo-otsuji in Hiraizumi play court-orchestra instruments (from the left: the sho, hichiriki, and ryuteki). This temple is one of the few places outside the palace where one can still hear traditional court music. See page 91.

By the ninth century gagaku had incorporated a confusion of different musics, each with its special instrumentation and style. Music by Japanese composers, known as *wagaku,* was not deemed worthy of performance at the Imperial Music Bureau. Such "home grown" music was relegated to a separate, less-exalted area of the palace, the "big-song hall" (O-uta-dokoro).

Such a wide variety of music was probably a considerable strain on the imperial coffers and was not designed to produce polished music specialists. The need for reform was evident, and the retired emperor Saga with the aid of a group of noblemen spent the better part of the years from 833 to 850 trying to bring order to this chaotic situation. In eighteenth-century Europe it was the so-called Mannheim school of composers who standardized the Western orchestral instrumentation. In ninth-century Japan it was Soga and his followers who created the standard gagaku orchestra. In addition to limiting the number of instruments, they also organized the repertoire into two main categories. Indian and Chinese music were combined under the classification of To-gaku (also known as "music of the left"), while the many styles of Korean music and Manchurian music were classified as Koma-gaku (or as "music of the right"). In addition, many of the old dance pieces were rearranged and new Japanese pieces were commissioned. It is said that these new Japanese compositions had a particularly strong effect on Koma-gaku so that most of the latter's Korean flavor was lost. The origin of the distinction between "left" and "right" music is open to debate, but it smacks very much of Confucian ideals. Such an origin would be a plausible one in view of the Confucian training of a Japanese gentleman of that period.

By the middle of the Heian period gagaku had become extremely popular at court. Not only was it a necessary element in all court ceremonies, but it also was practiced by the noblemen themselves. In a political system in which cloistered emperors often controlled retired emperors who in turn directed ministers who controlled the ruling emperor, there was a surfeit of smaller courts whose problem was more one of ennui than of affluency. Amateur groups known as *miasobi* or *gyoyu* flourished among the courts of these shadow emperors. In addition to selected Chinese pieces, new vocal forms were popular; *roei,* chanted Chinese poems, and *saibara,* gagaku-patterned folk songs. The latter stand in about the same relation to folk music as do the more "folksy" Haydn symphonies. Descriptions of these amateur musicals are preserved in *The Tale of Genji* and other literary works of the period. They remind one slightly of scenes from the court of Frederick the Great or from the mansion of the Esterhazys though they seem to have been somewhat more stiff and formal.

Not all the court music was so sedate. For every ceremony rigid with prescribed behavior there was a banquet with noblemen stiff with rice wine (Plate 24). *Enkyoku*, banquet or party music, was another important part of the music of the Heian court. It was not without reason that another name for this music was *enzui*, "drunken pools." Old anthologies of enkyoku poems reveal rather edifying texts, but one need only compare contemporary college songbooks with the music of a fraternity party to infer that all enkyoku were not concerned with plum blossoms and the snow on mount Fuji. Party music is functional music and as such has a notoriously short life span. Enkyoku melodies no longer exist, but from the various text collections we can gather that this music must have been a mixture of the many religious and secular vocal styles of the period. The melodies were probably watered down shomyo and were not very important musically. However, the study of enkyoku injects a very human spirit into the rather unreal picture most of us have of life in the Heian court of Japan.

In speaking of the shirabyoshi dancers in Chapter II mention was made of another very important form of court vocal music, *imayo*, or "contemporary songs." This music had a double origin. One beginning, mentioned earlier, is found in the simple hymns (wasan) created by evangelistic Buddhist priests for missionary work among the city prostitutes. These imayo might be compared in function to the Bowery hymns of the Salvation Army. The second type of imayo originated when someone became tired of learning the court orchestral music by solfège and decided to put poems to the melodies. This is the reverse of the instance found in Western music history in which syllables were taken out of a poem to form our solfège (*do*, *re*, *mi*). In the court form of imayo many different poems were imposed on one melody much in the way Americans use the tune "John Brown's Body Lies a-Moulding in His Grave" ("The Battle Hymn of the Republic," etc.). This music was, in effect, the "popular" music of the court and the "hit" tune was the melody of "Etenraku" (Figure 7). These so-called etenraku-imayo were often used by female entertainers with words suited to the occasion or to the mood of their patrons.

The Heian period represents the zenith of aristocratic power and affluence. During the subsequent Kamakura period the warriors predominated and gagaku suffered accordingly with the other pastimes of the courtier. Unfortunately, part of the gagaku tradition has always been the secret passing down of the music for one instrument through one clan. Therefore, when the big orchestras were broken up or scattered by the destruction of war, there were few musicians who had an over-all view of the music. At one time the court was hard put to find enough musicians to play for a single ceremony. Eventually, the military themselves found gagaku of use, and in the sixteenth century, by order of Ieyasu, the remaining musicians were split into two main

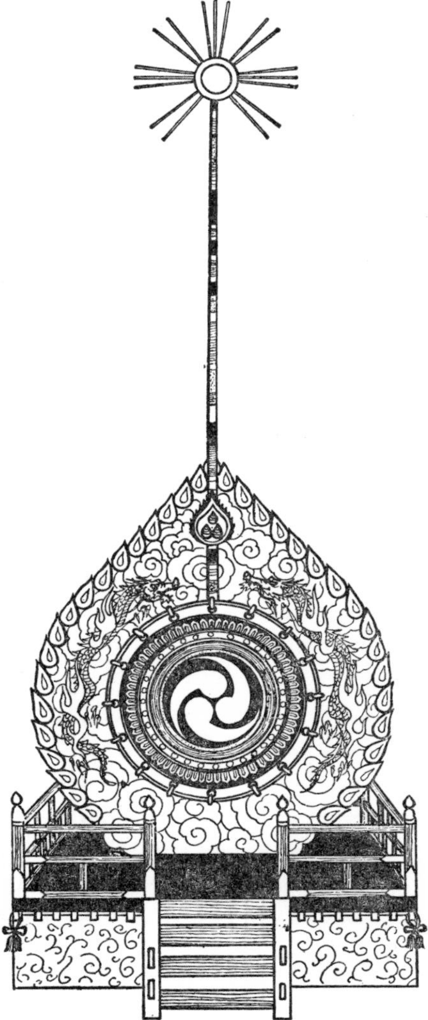

DA-DAIKO

groups, one in Kyoto with the emperor and the other in Edo. This system remained throughout the Tokugawa period. With the coming of Western culture after the Meiji Restoration, the music bureau, now known as the Gagaku-bu, was further reduced to a group of men at the palace in Tokyo plus various musicians at the important shrines. The art that was the responsibility of those hundreds of musicians and dancers at Todaiji in the eighth century now resides in the hands of some twenty men at the imperial palace and smaller ensembles at scattered temples and shrines. The group is small, its position anachronistic, but there is hope for its continued survival as Japan becomes more aware of the many unique features to be found in gagaku.

II. The Instruments

Gagaku is the earliest significant instrumental form in Japanese music. It shares with kabuki music the distinction of having instruments in each of the three basic orchestral units, percussion, strings, and winds. While it does not take as much advantage of the orchestrational possibilities of its ensemble as does kabuki music, it is considered by some to be the only "true" orchestral music of Japan. This opinion is due primarily to the grandeur and solidity of its sound. I think it is more accurate to say, however, that it is one of the main orchestral forms of Japanese music. Because of this, it is necessary to discuss the various instruments which are characteristic of this ancient and serene music.

PERCUSSION: Perhaps the most impressive feature of one's entrance into the imperial gagaku room is the sight of the two monstrous *da-daiko* drums (Plate 28). These huge drums are used to add ponderosity to the choreography of certain dances.

TSURI-DAIKO

NINAI-DAIKO

It is quite an effect when the dancer shifts his weight from his heel to his entire foot in coördination with the roof-shaking thud of the da-daiko. This tone is produced by means of two heavy, lacquered beaters (Plate 31), which are always struck in a left-right sequence. The skin is not as immense as it appears from a distance. The area of skin beyond the rim of the body of the drum is actually a separate piece from the central playing section. The use of separate skins is necessary because a single hide could not cover such an area and still be capable of enough tension to produce a sound. Twisting the ropes that secure the two heads and stanchioning these ropes with large wooden pegs effects the pitch of the drums even though each skin is not one continuous piece. The musical tone of this drum is nil, but its psychological effect is tremendous. Therefore, it is used only in bugaku dance pieces.

The next drum in size is the taiko. It comes in different forms, depending on whether it is to be used in a performance hall, played standing, or used in a parade. The standard gagaku taiko is called a *tsuri-daiko*. This drum has two tacked heads and is suspended on a stand in front of the player (see the center of Plate 28). Only one side is struck. This is done by means of two sticks with leather heads. In keeping with the mythical symbolism of gagaku, the left-hand beat is female and the right-hand beat male. It serves to mark off the larger phrase units by means of rhythm; in musicological jargon, it is known as a colotomic instrument.

The bronze gong that can be seen suspended on a small stand to the left of the taiko in Plate 28 serves another colotomic function. This gong, called a *shoko*, also comes in three sizes, depending on where it is used. As one can see in Plate 32, it is played on the inside by means of two hard-tipped sticks. Its function is to further subdivide the musical phrase by means of single beats. In practice, it is usually heard on the first beat of every measure with a special added anterior stroke every four bars. Its metallic sound supplements nicely the tone of the drums.

Whenever a group of instruments are concerted, it is the custom all over the world to appoint one man as the leader. In the West it is usually the first violinist or a special-

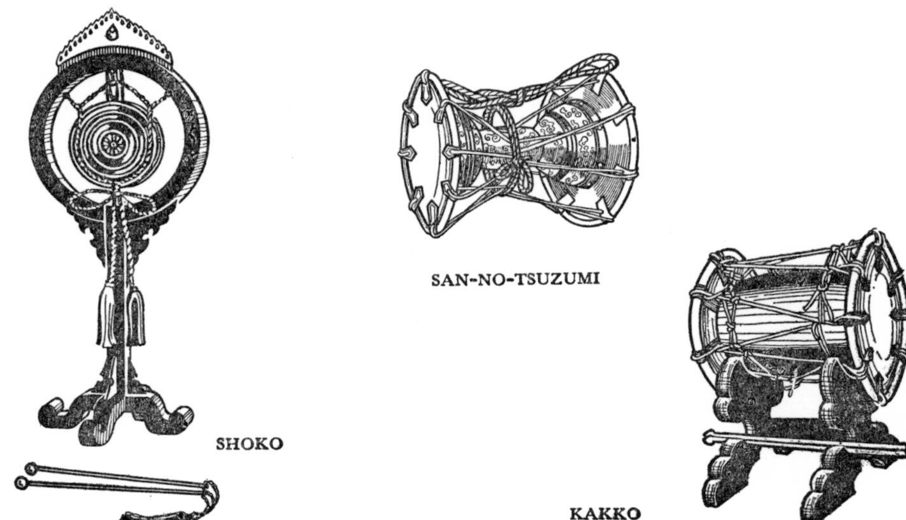

ist, the conductor. In the orient this duty is usually given to a drummer. In gagaku it is the player of the *kakko*, a small, horizontal drum with two lashed heads made of deerskin (Plate 29). Unlike the other drums mentioned, both heads are used. The two drum sticks employed are built more lightly because two of the three basic patterns used on the kakko are types of rolls. One is a slow roll done with both sticks, and the other is a gradually quickening roll done on the left skin. The other pattern consists of a single tap with the right stick. This drum regulates the tempo of the piece by means of these various patterns and, unlike the more colotomic instruments mentioned above, is found prominently in free rhythmic sections as well as being used to mark off the passage of a certain number of beats or phrases. This drum is used in To-gaku.

When Koma-gaku music is performed the leader does not play the kakko but uses the *san-no-tsuzumi*. This is a larger hourglass-shaped drum of Korean origin. It is also laid on its side and has two lashed heads although only one is struck. Ancient scrolls show interesting pictures of this drum which indicate that it originally may have been played with the bare hands (see Plate 21). Actually, it is the only one remaining of a series of four different hourglass-shaped drums which were used in ancient times.

These are the basic percussion instruments of gagaku. Their notation is discussed in Appendix II. Simply stated, the systems involve a series of dots to represent the basic beats and special Japanese characters to indicate the type of strokes to be used. Finally, I should mention again the *shakubyoshi*, two simple sticks that are beaten together by the chorus leader during gagaku vocal pieces. A more ancient form of clapper may be seen in the hands of the first musician on the left end of the group in Plate 21. This instrument is related to the folk bin-sasara mentioned in Chapter II (Plate 8).

STRINGS: There are only three stringed instruments used in contemporary gagaku. The first is the wagon already discussed in the previous chapter. A comment should be added on Plate 33, which shows an example of *tachigaku*, "standing music." For such outdoor performances extra men, called *toneri*, are added to the ensemble to

GAKU-SO

hold the wagon for the player. Their less-exalted task does not prevent them from wearing splendid costumes.

The second gagaku string instrument is the *gaku-so* or simply *so*, a thirteen-stringed predecessor of the popular Japanese koto (Plate 53). Though it is built with all the potentialities of its successor, its use is very restricted in gagaku. Both finger picks (*tsume*) and bare fingers are used to play the gaku-so, but unlike the regular koto, the strings are never pushed down behind the bridges to produce additional tones. Like the koto (and unlike the wagon) the strings, with the exception of the bottom one, are tuned in an ascending scale. There are different tunings for each gagaku mode. The use of the gaku-so is like that of the wagon in that it uses only a few stereotyped patterns plus occasional short melodies or graces. The two basic patterns for the gaku-so are *shizugaki* and *hayagaki* shown in Figure 6. Since the instrument is tuned according to the

FIGURE 6. The two gaku-so music patterns

particular mode of the piece being played, the actual pitches of these two patterns may vary. This may account for the differences between the transcriptions of these patterns by various scholars. This difference could also be due to the variation in performance, resulting from the varying speeds of the compositions. These patterns function colotomically, marking off sections of the music without being genuinely melodic.

The remaining string instrument in gagaku is the *biwa* or *gaku-biwa* (Plate 23),[1] the latter term being used to differentiate it from later models. This pear-shaped lute has four strings and four frets and is played with a small plectrum (*bachi*). The present-day plectrum is different from that seen in Plate 23 as is the hand position. The gaku-

[1] In Plate 23 there is shown also a *gogen*. This is an ancient Chinese "moon guitar" which appeared in early Japanese court music and is similar to a type that was used when performing Ming Chinese music (Minshin-gaku), but it is no longer used.

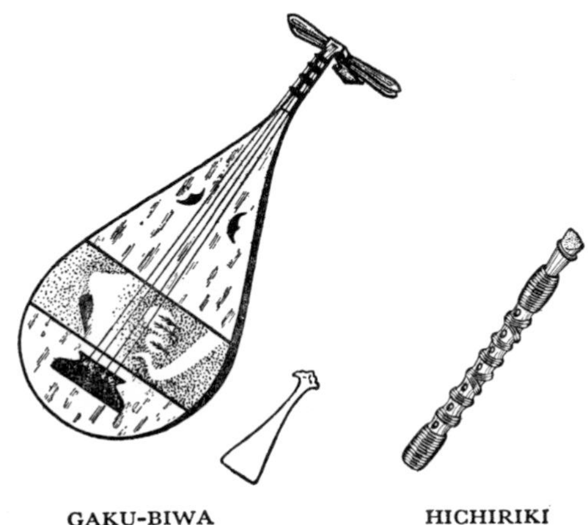

GAKU-BIWA HICHIRIKI

biwa is also used to mark off the passage of time. This is accomplished by means of arpeggios, which sometimes have a two- or three-note melodic fragment at the end. Set in the matrix of the full gagaku ensemble sound, however, the effect of the gaku-biwa is primarily rhythmic. Its notation is mentioned in Appendix II. In closing, it should be noted that unlike later biwa techniques, the strings of the gaku-biwa are pressed down only on the frets, not in-between them.

WINDS: We now come to the heart of the gagaku orchestra. The wind section of gagaku plays an analogous role to that of the strings in a Western symphony orchestra. It is the winds that carry the main melodic line and add the distinctive harmonic milieu so characteristic of gagaku music. Because they are the mainstay of this music they also are heir to many interesting legends and historical commentaries.

The *hichiriki* (Plate 34), a short, double-reed woodwind, is perhaps the most controversial instrument in Japanese music. The sharp-tongued Sei Shonagon in her eleventh-century diary (*The Pillow Book*) has the following remarks to make about the hichiriki (ref. 4, II, 993):

"The horrible sound of the hichiriki is like the noisy crickets of autumn. I can't stand to be in the same room with that sound. One festival day, when I was in the waiting room attending upon her Majesty, I was entertained by the lovely sound of someone playing the flute. Then suddenly another person joined in on the hichiriki. It made my hair stand on end!"

From historical readings it would seem that one seldom took a moderate view of the hichiriki. It either was an abomination or an instrument of great moral and musical power. However, even the stories of its prowess can be interpreted in two ways. For example, there is a famous story in the thirteenth-century *Kokin Chomonshu* (ref. 4, II, 990) about the robber who came to the house of Hiromasa. While Hiromasa hid quaking under the house the robber proceeded to strip the rooms of everything in sight. When he had left, Hiromasa came out to survey the damage. The house was bare except for one item, Hiromasa's hichiriki. The story makes no comment as to why the robber chose not to take the hichiriki but goes on to relate that the forlorn Hiromasa picked up his only remaining worldly possession and began to play. Not long after the robber reappeared and returned all the stolen goods. He said that he had heard the sound of Hiromasa's hichiriki, and it moved him so that he was constrained to give back all he had taken. The story ends with a comment that robbers in the good old days were more sensitive creatures. We can only wonder what the hichiriki players must have been like.

One final tale credits the hichiriki with supernatural powers. In the same chronicle there is a story about Enri, a skilled hichiriki player, who accompanied his father on a trip to a distant province, where he had been assigned as governor. The people in that country were in dire straits due to a prolonged drought. All their prayers for help had been to no avail so they pressed the new governor to see what he could do. Upon hearing this his son immediately went to the main temple and performed for the gods on his hichiriki. Very soon thereafter, the sky clouded and rain began to fall. However, the hichiriki engendered so much rain that there was a severe flood. This heavenly reaction seems open to various interpretations.

By now the reader must have gathered that the tone of the hichiriki is rather distinctive. It has the nasality of an oboe but is much broader in sound. This is due to the thicker reed and the embouchure with which it is played (see Plate 34). This embouchure is necessary in order to produce the many microtonal variations upon the fundamental melody which are characteristic of its music.

The hichiriki was of Chinese origin and came in various sizes. The contemporary gagaku instrument is one of the smallest variety, measuring some eighteen centimeters in length and having nine holes, two on the underside and seven on top. The tube is made of specially prepared bamboo and is wrapped with bands of cherry or wisteria bark. The fingering is directly related to the notation (see Appendix II). Through use of the embouchure and special fingerings a chromatic scale can be produced though it is never used as such. Divisions of smaller than a half step are, as was said, the characteristic technique of the hichiriki. A transcription of a favorite hichiriki melody is seen in Figure 7.

One of the more curious aspects of the hichiriki has to do with the classic method of learning the instrument. Under this system the student learns the entire repertoire by a solfège before he ever picks up the instrument. It was noted earlier how this method eventually led to the creation of a new genre of vocal music which substituted poems for the solfège (see imayo).

The hichiriki, with its strong tone, is the center of the gagaku orchestra and is found

FIGURE 7. A hichiriki version of "Etenraku"

in all types of gagaku music. Over the centuries its strident tone has preserved the "Gothic" quality of Japanese imperial music and has provided a topic of conversation for delicate-eared court commentators of every period.

The other main melodic instrument of gagaku is the flute. Three different types are used. The first is the kagura-bue, already described in Chapter II. This is used when gagaku music is performed with kagura or other Shinto ceremonies. The second type of flute is the *ryuteki* or *yoko-bue* (Plate 30). This seven-holed flute is of Chinese origin and is used for To-gaku music. It is the largest of the gagaku flutes and resembles greatly the noh flute, which will be discussed later. The third flute is the *Koma-bue*

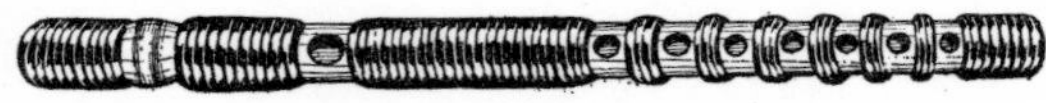

RYUTEKI

KOMA-BUE

(Plate 30), a six-holed flute of Korean origin used in Koma-gaku. It is the smallest of the gagaku flutes. One interesting distinction between these flutes is the color of the piece of brocade that covers the closed end. It is green for the Koma-bue and red for the ryuteki and the kagura-bue as these are the proper colors for their respective dances. It is interesting to note that even in the West today red is still associated with things Chinese.

The notation and technique of the flutes are based on the same principle as that of the hichiriki. Their musical function is to play the same basic melody as the hichiriki but to vary it slightly as it is played. This simultaneous variation of the same melody by several instruments is known as heterophony.

The last of the wind instruments is the most exotic. It is the *sho*, a lovely set of seventeen reed pipes that are placed in a cup-shaped wind chest (Plate 23). By blowing into this wind chest through a mouthpiece and closing certain holes in the pipes, a series of ethereal chords can be produced. The Chinese predecessor of the sho, the *sheng*, is said to be the oldest known pipe organ. Tradition claims that it is meant to imitate the cry of the phoenix. The shape of the sho also is said to be modeled after that lovely mythical bird.

Figure 8 shows the arrangement of the seventeen pipes of the sho in the wind chest and also gives the name of each pipe. Notice that two of the pipes are silent. Recent research[2] has indicated that they were used in ancient times but are now retained merely to keep the aesthetic balance of the instrument. The sho is an interesting compromise of beauty and practicality. Because of the peculiarity of the fingering problem, the pipes could not be arranged in a scalewise order. At the same time, if the pipes assigned to each finger were of the proper length to produce the correct pitch, the shape of the instrument would be very uneven. The compromise consists of two sets of pipes, symmetrically arranged in opposing pairs. On the inner side of the pipes, however, a slit is cut so that the actual acoustical length of the pipes can be varied.

The lower end of each pipe contains a thin metal rectangle in which a reed has been

[2] See ref. 22. This article actually concerns *four* silent pipes because research has shown that two different pipes could be used in the position of each one of the now silent tubes. Which two of these four pipes the player chose to insert depended on the mode of the composition. The contemporary Chinese *sheng*, by the way, has seventeen pipes of which four are silent. It has no substitute pipes.

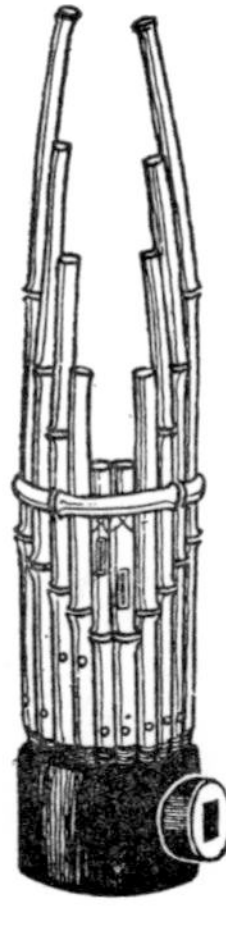

SHO

Otsu
Mo
Shichi
Kyu
Jo
Bo
Hi
Gon
Ya
Sen
Hachi
Ju
Bi
Ku
Otsu
Ichi
Ge

FIGURE 8. The pipes of the sho

cut much in the manner of a harmonica reed. It is a so-called free reed. Each of these reeds is tuned by means of a small drop of wax. They are also coated with a special mixture to prevent the collection of moisture. This is the major problem of the sho player, as a pipe will not sound if the reed becomes too wet. In order to dissipate any dampness resulting from playing, it is necessary to heat the sho over a small charcoal fire. This fire is kept in a white pottery bowl (*hibachi*) which can be seen at every gagaku performance. Whenever there is a free moment the sho players will be seen busily rotating the wind chests of their instruments over the fire.

Although the sho does play melodies in certain vocal forms and in Koma-gaku, its primary function is harmonic. The eleven chords available on the sho can be seen in Figure 29 of Appendix II. The change from one chord to another is accomplished in the middle of the bar. Each chord is begun quietly and brought to a crescendo just before it is time to change to the next chord. To keep the sound continuous, both inhaled and exhaled air are used. In learning these chord changes the student sings a simplified version of the hichiriki melody, using the names of the chords (derived from the name of the lowest note) as text.

Which chords are used is determined by the mode of the composition. Usually they are founded on the basic notes of the melody. However, the use of these chords is somewhat different than the Western concept of harmony. In the West chords tend to color a melody and drive it on by setting it in situations of tension which require release, in music terms, by setting up chord progressions. The chords of the sho, however, do not serve this function. Rather they "freeze" the melody. They are like a vein of amber in which a butterfly has been preserved. We see the beauty of the creature within but at the same time are aware of a transparent solid between us and the object, a solid of such a texture that it shows that object off in a very special way. It is the solidifying effect of the sho which to a great extent gives gagaku its rather transcendental quality. The voice of the phoenix continues to intrigue the ear of man.

Now that the instruments have been explained singly it is time to see how they are combined. There are three basic instrumental combinations; that for To-gaku, Koma-gaku, and bugaku. Plate 28 shows a standard To-gaku orchestra with three sho, three hichiriki, three ryuteki, two biwa, two gaku-so, and one each of the kakko, shoko, and taiko. The Koma-gaku ensemble differs in the fact that the koma-bue is used instead of the ryuteki and the san-no-tsuzumi replaces the kakko. Nowadays the strings are also deleted from most Koma-gaku pieces, though there are indications that they were used in ancient times. The music for bugaku is drawn from both the To-gaku and Koma-gaku repertoires and hence uses the special instruments of the style of music to which its accompaniment belongs. However, string instruments are not used to accompany these dances, whereas, as stated above, the da-daiko is so used sometimes. The reasoning behind this arrangement is that the function of concert music (gagaku) is to display the subtleties of the melody, while the function of dance music (bugaku) is to accompany. Therefore, a simpler, more rhythmic music is required for the latter. Not only do the instruments change but the style of playing the same piece is different when it is used as bugaku. Basically, the difference lies in a more restricted use of the microtonal variations of the melody by the hichiriki.

The vocal forms such as saibara, roei, and imayo use smaller ensembles without drums. Rhythm is kept by means of a shakubyoshi clapper in the hands of the lead singer. In such forms the sho occasionally plays the melodic line.

More facts concerning the use of the instruments in the various forms will be discussed in the section on the music itself. Suffice to say that the instrumentation of each music is rigidly prescribed and based upon a tradition that is centuries old. While such a tradition has stultified any further developments in gagaku orchestration techniques, it has also given us a very rare and beautiful example of music from out of the ancient past.

III. Theory and Practice

As was mentioned in the discussion of Buddhist music, the theoretical basis of Japanese music is Chinese in origin. Figure 5 shows the two main scales of early Japanese music theory, *ryo* and *ritsu.* The Chinese theory provided the same twelve-note, untempered, chromatic scale that is the theoretical, basic tonal material of Western music. With this material the Chinese, like the Western theorists, constructed scales of seven notes each. These scales were permutated in turn into eighty-four modes. By the time all this theory had been Japanized there remained only the chromatic twelve basic tones, two basic scale structures (*ryo* and *ritsu*),[3] and six modes. The Japanese

[3] For details concerning their construction by the process of going up eight half-steps and back six see reference 8.

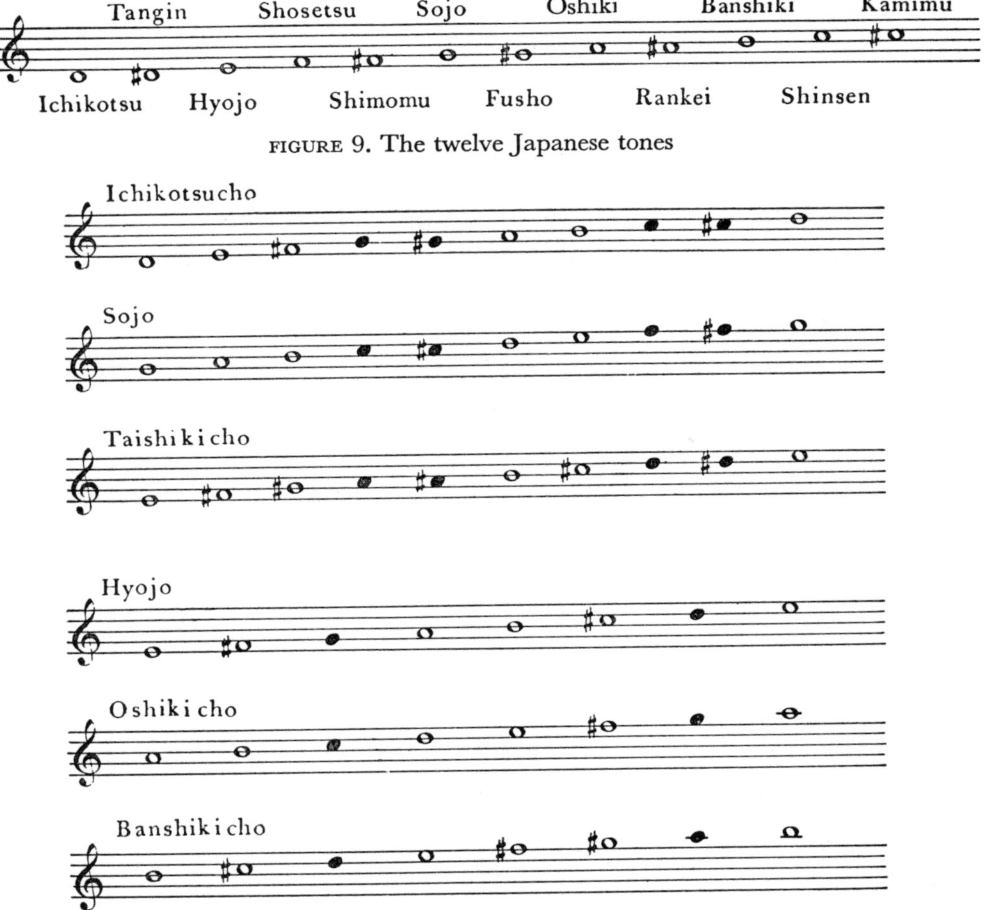

FIGURE 9. The twelve Japanese tones

FIGURE 10. The six gagaku modes

names for the twelve chromatic tones are shown in Figure 9, starting with the note D, as this is the basic pitch of the Japanese tonal system. Antiquarians still love to use these terms when writing about music, and they also are found in the nomenclature of koto music.

The six modes are divided into three *ritsu* and three *ryo* modes. These are shown in Figure 10. Notice that the *ryo* mode beginning on E has a special name in order not to confuse it with the *ritsu* scale that begins on E.

The basic function of these six modes in gagaku is to provide means of transposing compositions, or of playing pieces at different pitch levels. In Western music, when we find that we cannot sing a tune at a certain pitch, we start on a different note and sing exactly the same tune at that new level. This is the usual Western concept of transposition, but the meaning of the term in gagaku is different. When a gagaku melody is rewritten at a different pitch level, the melody itself is changed. Gagaku theory calls these pieces *watashimono*, pieces that have "crossed over." Thus, when a piece is played in a new mode it becomes actually a new composition, a paraphrase of its parent melody. A piece is never moved from a *ritsu* mode to a *ryo* mode but only within the three modes of each system. Pieces originally in the *taishikicho* (the *ryo* E mode) are never transposed. The explanation for all these restrictions is that the instruments of gagaku cannot easily play the necessary chromatic tones to make any further transpositions. This is slightly analogous to the limitation of keys in early Western instrumental music caused by untempered tuning.

The rhythmic theory of gagaku allows for three basic rhythmic structures; units of eight, four, or two beats. The eight-beat structure (*nobe-byoshi*) is used primarily for slow pieces, the four-beat unit (*haya-byoshi*) for medium tempo, and the two beats (*oze-byoshi*) for faster pieces. If a composition mixes units of two and four it is called *tada-byoshi*. When a fast tada-byoshi piece is used for dance it is sometimes changed into alternate measures of two and three beats. This beat is called *yatara-byoshi*.

So much for the basic theory. The next question is how are pieces actually constructed and held together? The basic aesthetic theory of gagaku and of much of the music thereafter is contained in the words *jo-ha-kyu*. Jo means the introduction, ha is the breaking apart or exposition, and kyu is the rushing to the finish or the denouement. The theory, as it penetrated the various fields of Japanese music, came to be applied to entire compositions or to individual phrases. It has the tenacity of the theory of question and answer, arsis and thesis, in Western music. In the chapters that follow we shall see more specifically how jo-ha-kyu is applied to other Japanese musics.

The pieces of the gagaku repertoire are classified as small, medium, and large pieces. The distinction may have originated from the number of men required to perform the accompanying dances. Whatever the origin, it is worth noting that there seem to be differences in the scales and in the forms of pieces used with these three classifications. The large and medium pieces usually follow the tripartite jo-ha-kyu form though there are indications that some pieces (for example, "Goshoraku") interpolated a fourth section, *ei*, between the ha and the kyu. The smaller pieces tend to have only a ha and kyu section. At the present time it is common to combine various pieces in order to create a jo-ha-kyu form.

This formal structure can best be understood by looking at a full-blown gagaku piece and seeing what occurs during the three sections mentioned above.[4] In a dance piece the jo section occurs during the time when the dancer moves from backstage to the central stage. In orchestral pieces, this is often the time for a *netori*, a short phrase that is meant to set the mood of the mode in which the piece is written. First the sho enters with its particularly lovely phrase. It is followed, in turn, by the hichiriki, the flute, and finally the kakko. Then the biwa and the koto play their rather short melodies. The netori is actually a highly refined abstraction of the age-old custom of tuning up. A similar process can be seen in the evolution of the early instrumental music which created the overture in Western music. The gagaku netori is serene and subtle but has an archaic flavor that reminds one of similar seventeenth-century opera overtures in the style of Monteverdi. At the end of the introductions to certain Koma-gaku pieces the melodic line is taken up by the various winds in what amounts to a short stretto, each beginning at a slightly different time. It is one of the rare instances of such near-contrapuntal action in Japanese music.

After this introduction the main body of the composition begins.[5] A solo flute starts the main melody with the three percussion instruments (taiko, shoko, and kakko) usually in attendance. After the second main accent of the taiko (which usually occurs on the first beat of the seventh bar) the rest of the winds enter, the flutes and hichiriki playing the same basic melody, while the sho provides a tone cluster as a harmonic matrix. Usually on the last beat of the eighth bar the first biwa arpeggio is played, its accent always coming on the first beat of the measure. On measure thirteen, the gaku-so enters with its first standard phrase. From there on until the last eight bars or so of the composition, the ensemble plays tutti; there is no further attempt to change the sound.[6] The color of the ensemble's tone is very rich but during the ha and kyu parts it remains essentially a monochromatic richness.

Though the dynamics and tone color of the orchestra do not change there is usually a gradual increase in speed as the piece progresses. Finally, a special coda, called a *tomede*, occurs in which only the first-chair men perform. The tempo becomes very free, the pace slackens, the chord of the sho thins out to two or three notes until finally only the biwa and gaku-so are left. They play two or three very slow notes, the biwa

[4] The transcriptions in ref. 23, I, are all small or medium pieces and do not contain first (jo) sections.

[5] From here one can refer to any piece in ref. 23, I, or to the melody in Figure 7.

[6] There is one form called *nokorigaku* in which the cadences of various repeats of the music are played by different groups, the final cadence being given to the strings. This, however, does not alter the fact that once the basic instrumental sound was conceived, no attempt was made to orchestrate it in the Western sense of the term.

ending with the dominant or tonic note of the mode and the gaku-so ending the composition with a single plucking of the tonic.

This is standard procedure for gagaku pieces, though the lengths of compositions vary and specific instrumental entrances do not always occur exactly as stated above. Notice that such a melody as shown in Figure 7 is in an A-B-A form. Under the process discussed above the netori would be an introduction to such an A-B-A form and the tomede acts as a coda. When one of the vocal forms is performed, like saibara,[7] the process is somewhat different. The voice takes the first-phrase solo, marking time with a shakubyoshi. The chorus and instruments enter on the second phrase and proceed in the same tutti fashion until the poem is completed. In such cases there is no final coda. If roei is sung the first phrase of each stanza is sung by the soloist. During the rest of the time the chorus and instruments (if any) are used.

Much of the pleasure of gagaku is in its rare archaic flavor. To those who are accustomed to the dynamic drive of Western symphonic music the static beauty of gagaku may seem very strange. In the West, music has been defined in terms of aural form in motion, but in gagaku both the formal and progressive elements have been minimized, leaving only the beauty of sound, the exotic creature in a slightly clouded drop of amber. One can find a similar musical phenomenon only in the court *gamelan* music of Java. Perhaps if gagaku took fuller advantage of the tonal possibilities at its command or moved with a less predictable tonal and formal structure, it would gain flexibility only to lose its really outstanding value in world music culture.

Listening to gagaku is a history lesson in sound and a transmigration back into the soul of the Heian courtier. As it stands it is a shadow of its former self and yet it is still one of the clearest adumbrations left of the grandeur and artistic taste of the court of ancient Japan.

[7] See ref. 23, II for a transcription.

CHAPTER FOUR
NOHGAKU, THE MUSIC OF THE NOH DRAMA

I. Introduction

The chorus place their fans before them and the flute rings out with the ancient melody of "Shidai." The tune floats across the fine-grained expanse of wood that is the stage, passes briefly the surrounding moat of pebbles, and informs the audience on the other side that soon the five-colored curtain over the stage entrance will sweep inward and up to allow the first character to begin his voyage along the covered passageway that is said to divide the spirit world from the real. A noh play has begun.

Such a scene is available to anyone in Japan who can forget the curse of the clock and pass with the actor over this bridge into another world. Beyond the aesthetic and literary enjoyment so often extolled by devotees of the noh, perhaps there has been added in modern times the really rare pleasure of a chance to escape from temporality. Certainly such joy is never known by that group of people at concerts in the West who always rush out during the last movement of a symphony in order to catch the 5:53 train or be first in line at the check room. Unfortunately, Japan has become quite Westernized in this respect, but there are still a number of Japanese who can savor these rare moments of timelessness. Noh is a study in literature, theatre, aesthetics, and a type of *gesamtkunstwerk*, but for the moment let it be examined simply as music. It must be understood that noh, more than Western opera, is a *gestalt* of equally contributing arts, none of which can honestly be said to be more important than the others. Thus, when the bonds that hold them together are severed temporarily for the sake of discussion, the individual art forms may seem to be something less valuable than the whole. Perhaps no other music has been so delicately refined, and if on hearing it one finds it dull or a trifle undernourished, it may be because such delicacy can easily be destroyed when taken out of its original context. With this in mind let us turn first to the historical background of noh and noh music.

II. The History of Noh Music

The prototypes of noh were a good deal more raucous than it is in its present form. Its ancestors are not to be found among the stately court dances as might be expected, but rather in the popular entertainments which formed a contrast to the pomp of Heian ceremonies.

Three types of entertainment are said to form the historical basis of noh: *sarugaku, sangaku,* and *dengaku. Sarugaku,* "monkey music," is believed to have originated as a shrine pantomine ritual-play which was later turned into a comic, popular theatrical. As the theatrical aspect of sarugaku grew Chinese acrobats were included in the program. This genre was called sangaku. The sangaku acrobats were a part of Heian city life in much the same way that the jugglers were an integral part of the market-square scene in medieval Europe. The third influence, *dengaku,* "field music," originated in rice-planting dances performed by the peasants. These were later brought into the court as a relief from the formality of ceremonial choreography.

As sarugaku and dengaku developed they became more organized and also more difficult to distinguish. By the Kamakura period the words "sarugaku-no-noh" and "dengaku-no-noh," used to denote the two prototype noh forms, had become almost synonymous. For our purposes the only differentiation that need be made between these early forms is that sarugaku originated as a temple ritual, dengaku as a folk-dance form, and sangaku as acrobatics.

The popularity of sarugaku or dengaku was immense among both common people and noblemen. Indeed, there were a host of various theatricals which vied for the public interest, both inside the temple and shrine compounds and without. Like the medieval morality plays of Europe, various theatricals appeared in conjunction with religious ceremonies for the enjoyment of the populace and the priests. The most famous remnant of this old tradition is *Mibu-kyogen* (Plate 37).[1] These pantomime plays are performed in the compound of the Mibu Temple in Kyoto. Their mixture of comic, religious, and historical plays is a very good example of the spirit that probably existed in the early days of noh.

Among the many theatricals of ancient times one of the best known was *jushi,* a type of light entertainment performed after the Buddhist New Year's ceremonies. This became so popular that it was performed all year around, and performers were even invited to the various aristocratic estates to give *hiru-jushi,* "afternoon jushi." There was also a form called *ennen,* a type of priestly entertainment which eventually became public. In the late Heian period it seems that temples were as busy perfecting their ennen repertoire as they were working on their religious chanting. Finally, the word

[1] Plate 37 shows the finale of the comic play, "Horokuwari," which opens every performance. The plates which are being knocked off the edge of the stage are covered with names. By breaking these plates all sin and bad luck is destroyed. Any plates that survive the fall are smashed by the hordes of little boys who are always waiting below.

furyu should be mentioned, a very ambiguous term which meant a variety of things from Heian foppery to religious processions similar to the Mardi gras. At one time the government issued prohibitions against furyu, by which they meant not only street dances and entertainments but also the habit of dressing up in one's very brightest clothes on official holidays for visiting the shrines in order to compete for moments of sartorial glory. The Easter parade, it seems, is not unique to the West. Furyu is noted in the history of noh because one often finds the words "ennen-no-furyu" or "sarugaku-no-furyu" in the study of noh music. The lively dances and music of furyu, however, should be treated separately as components of a form of folk theatre.

Jushi, ennen, furyu, and other such early entertainments all had their influence on the most important precursors of noh, sarugaku, and dengaku. The popularity of dengaku with the common man is noted in a tale from the *Taiheiki*, dated 1349. At that time a competition was held between two leading troupes of dengaku players. Stands were set up on a river bank and a huge crowd assembled to view the show. Partisan feeling apparently equalled that of a Western hockey game, for at one point the enthusiasm of the spectators ran so high that the bleachers collapsed. Panic ensued, robbers and soldiers moved in, and the day ended in bloodshed. This did not seem to dampen the popularity of dengaku or sarugaku. In fact, these two forms continued in the public favor even after the founding of noh and did not completely decline until the advent of kabuki in the sixteenth century.

Another chapter of the *Taiheiki* tells of the popularity of dengaku among the nobility (ref. 4, I, 704). It relates that in the Genko era (1331–33) dengaku was very popular and the shogun, Hojo Takatoki, invited the two main actor clans, the Shinza and the Honza, to his palace that he might see it himself. He became so captivated that he neglected his official duties and spent his days enjoying dengaku. When these troupes performed the nobles threw jewels at the actors' feet until there was a regular mound of precious gems on the stage. One night, the court was having a drinking party, and Takatoki in a drunken state got up to dance dengaku in his old and clumsy style. However, he soon stopped for there appeared at the door a group of about fifteen players whom no one recognized. They danced beautifully and the sound of their lovely voices attracted a maid-in-waiting outside the room. She slid open the door to peek at the actors and to her surprise saw that they were all in the shape of grotesque animals. She quickly sent for the warrior, Tokiaki, who came rushing to the banquet hall with his sword unsheathed. The players heard him approaching, however, and disappeared. When Tokiaki entered the room he found the shogun drunk and asleep, while the light of his lamp revealed the footprints of animals all around the room.

When the shogun awoke he remembered nothing of the occasion and feigned to be unafraid of this ghostly occurrence. Nevertheless, the records report that he soon thereafter gave up dengaku and took to staging dog chases.

As sarugaku and dengaku prospered, sangaku lost favor, and the acrobats were eventually replaced by comic plays called *kyogen*, "mad words." The greatest change in these forms, however, occurred in the Muromachi period when Kannami Kiyotsugu (1333–84) and his son Zeami Motokiyo (1363–1444) attempted to instill a more serious manner into sarugaku-no-noh. Originally minor functionaries at a shrine in Nara, these men were brought by the shogun, Yoshimitsu, to Kyoto, where they developed their special form of sarugaku-no-noh, later known simply as noh. In seeking a proper musical medium for their new form they borrowed quite heavily from Buddhist chanting (shomyo). This was natural not only because of shomyo's great dignity and solemnity, but also because the stories of the noh dramas were very Buddhist in spirit. The original sarugaku used an orchestra of three drums and a flute. These were retained in the newly developed noh.

Thus, a one-time Shinto priest under the patronage of a secular leader (who apparently admired him as much for his looks as for his acting) combined sacred chanting with popular theatrical conventions and sections from well-known verses to produce one of Japan's most unique art forms, the noh drama. One might call it the greatest pastiche in the theatrical arts, for though none of the individual elements were particularly original with either Kannami or his son Zeami, yet their combination of these elements into a dramatic mold was an act of true genius.

Though the texts for the noh were based on popular Buddhist ideas, the originators of the noh were primarily under the influence of the spirit of the esoteric Zen sect. Hence one finds in Zeami's major writings a repeated emphasis on the Zen-derived concepts of restraint and allusion as basic to noh. These tenets were followed by the first school of noh, the Kanze, and, as far as can be told, they have been retained in the present-day Kanze theatre as well as in the later offshoots of Hosho, Komparu, Kita, and Kongo.

III. The Structure of a Noh Play

From behind the curtained stage entrance come the hoarse, wooden tones of the flute playing "O-shirabe," the traditional warming-up exercise of every noh performance (Plate 39). As the last notes drift away, the curtain swoops upward and the musicians enter in slow, stately procession. Their order is always the same; first the flute, then the shoulder drum, next the side drum, and last the floor drum. Two drummers carry *shogi*, simple, black camp chairs, which they set up in front of the pine-and-bamboo painting that forms the traditional backdrop of every noh stage. As these musicians approach from the left, the chorus (*ji*) enters through a small door at the far right-hand corner of the stage. The drummers and the flutist, collectively called the *hayashi*, sit in a row facing the front of the stage with the shoulder and side drums in the middle, the floor drum to the left, and the flute to the right as shown in Plate 39. The latter two are seated on the beautiful but hard cypress-wood floor which has been specially polished to reflect the gorgeous costumes of the performers that are soon to appear. The chorus arranges itself on the right-hand side of the stage. Thus, with great serenity and dignity the musicians and singers take their place for the beginning of the noh drama.

Thick books have been written about the noh plays, their structure, and their philosophy. For our purposes, however, it is necessary only to understand the basic outline of the plays and how the music fits into this outline.

A day of noh usually consists of five noh plays and three kyogen comedies. There are, in addition, separate performances of sections from noh plays and "arrangements" of text excerpts. These are found most often in student recitals and derive their musical structures from the basic principles of noh itself as will be explained presently.

Kyogen comedies do not, as a rule, use music. They are performed in a special type of heightened speech often set within poetic rhythmic units. However, certain plays do contain singing. This is usually in the style of noh singing or a parody of it and need not be discussed separately. Since kyogen is comic, many party songs are found in its repertoire as well as boisterous versions of famous noh pieces. It is believed that certain Muromachi folk songs have survived also as kyogen "small songs" (*kokyoku*). During certain kyogen dances the drums and flute of the noh are used for accompaniment, but again the music is derived from that of noh. There are, of course, special differences to be found in the music of kyogen, but for the purposes of our survey it can be considered as essentially the same as noh music.

Classically speaking, a program of noh should include one number from each of the five kinds of noh; plays each respectively featuring a god, a warrior, a woman, a mad woman or certain miscellaneous subjects, and a devil. The music structure of each play varies depending on the character portrayed in much the same way that Western opera structures vary with their plots. However, by discussing a typical play one can understand these particular variations.

Noh plays are centered around one actor, the *shite*. The second main actor, the *waki*, serves primarily as a foil for the exposition of the shite's character. Thus, the formal elements of the play are closely linked to the actions of the shite and to his particular personality.

The aesthetic basis of noh form is the introduction-exposition-denouement concept (jo-ha-kyu) mentioned in the discussion of gagaku music. In noh, it is classically organized into five main units, or *dan*. These are usually placed in a two-act framework, four sections being in the first act and one in the second. These dan are further subdivided into more specific dramatic or musical units. There are differences of opinion as to exactly how these smaller units fit within the five dan, primarily because there is a great variety in their use within the noh repertoire itself. It is analogous to the problem one faces when analyzing Bach fugues on the basis of textbook fugue form or trying to fit all of Beethoven's sonatas into one formula. In noh there is also some confusion of terms between those which represent formal units of the play and those which apply to types of music that can appear in several different formal units. In the discussion that follows I shall try to make a distinction between these two types of nomenclature. In essence, a noh play is organized as follows:

1) Jo, the introduction. This unit is the first dan. It contains the introductory music, the appearance of the secondary actor (waki), and the general setting of the scene and preparation for the appearance of the principal actor.

Musically, the most important unit is the *shidai*. This music is meant to represent the character of the supporting actor. Originally several types of shidai existed, but today most plays begin with the *so-shidai*, the priest entrance music. There has been a theory put forward that the shidai always ends around the pitch A and that the actor begins his speech a fourth lower on E and gradually rises to A. Though pitch varies with the type of play being performed, it has been noted that A tends to be a basic pitch for many noh plays. Though the actor may move away from it, the chorus leader, if he is good, brings the pitch back to this standard A during the chorus sections.

2) Ha, the exposition. This unit theoretically has three dan. The first contains the entrance of the principal actor and his first song. It has two important musical units, the *issei* and the *michiyuki*. It may also contain its own introductory music (shidai). The word *issei* means the first song. Its musical structure is strictly regulated as, in fact, is the melodic movement of all noh music. The issei in general concentrates on the upper and middle range of the noh singing register. The rhythm, unlike the melodic movement, is quite flexible and open to variation by the individual actor. Issei sections are found sometimes in the introductory section of the play, sung by the supporting actor.

The michiyuki section occurs when the principal actor travels from the greenroom on the left to the stage via a covered walk that connects them (*hashigakari*). The music is dependent on the personality of the character. Often there is no music at all when the actor first appears. This heightens greatly the effect produced by the slow-moving mass of ancient costumes and the evocative mask, the famous accoutrements of noh. When the michiyuki is sung, one of two types of *uta*, or "song," is used. These are the *sageuta*, which is relatively short and low in range, and the *ageuta*, which is longer and higher. These names are also applied to various songs throughout the play as well as to those used in the michiyuki.

Another musical unit that appears in different sections but especially during this second dan of the play is *sashi*. This is a type of heightened speech. It is like an opera recitative in that it serves as a bridge between more lyrical sections.

In the third dan of the piece (the second dan of the exposition section) the plot is furthered by means of questions and answers between the two actors. This section is known as the *mondo* or sometimes as the *mondai*. Much of this is carried on in a recitative style. The drums often provide a rhythmic background for this conversation. The chorus commonly completes this section with a commentary on the dialogue. This is done in a more melodic style.

There are several special sections that may appear at this time, depending on the plot. One of the most common is called the *kudoki*, a section appearing during tender, feminine scenes. This word in a similar connotation will appear again in our study of shamisen music.

The fourth dan of the play (the final dan of the exposition section) brings the first act to its climax. It contains two basic sections, the *kuri* and the *kuse*. The kuri is significant musically because it has the highest note in the composition. The pitch itself is also called kuri. During this section the basic emotional tension of the plot is revealed. It is one of the most difficult sections to sing.

The kuse is a dance and is considered to be the center of the play. It is meant to be a full exposition of the spirit of the principal character. It is thought to be one of the important elements Zeami borrowed from other theatricals in his creation of the noh. As the highlight of the play, its music is subject to detailed melodic rules. These govern where the melody should start, what notes should be emphasized, and where it should end. There are three main sets of rules which are applied as required by the length and spirit of the text. The drums add an important rhythmic base for the dance.

The fourth dan of the play is closed by means of a section called *rongi*, which is again a period of exchanges between the two actors either in heightened speech or in song.

The chorus frequently ends the act with a song known as *nakairi*. This term is also used to designate the interlude between the acts.

Other units may be used between the acts. For example, a short kyogen, performed by a special kyogen actor, may be adopted. This may or may not be related to the central plot of the noh play. It is usually recited without accompaniment. During this time the main actor is busy backstage changing into the costume of the new role he will play in the second act. Instead of a kyogen, one may hear a hayashi interlude in which the drums play in an attenuated temporality that gives one that feeling of timelessness mentioned earlier. Long moments of silence are broken by the soulful cries of the drummers and by the sparse, resonant drum tones. Sometimes the flute joins in, its lone melody likewise seemingly devoid of rhythm or tempo. The over-all effect is literally out of this world.

3) Kyu, the denouement. A transition into the final dan is formed by a song called the *machiutai*, the "waiting song." Soon thereafter the main actor reappears in his new role, usually that of some supernatural being. A first song (issei) and dialogue (mondo), similar to those found in the first act, are used, but the highlight of the second act, like the first, is a dance. This is called the *mai*. Its music is dependent on the character of the dancer. The accompaniment may be hayashi alone, the chorus alone, or more often both, especially at the end. These dances and those of the first act are often performed separately. Such performances are called *shimai* and are popular among amateurs and professionals alike.

After the dance there is usually a recital of a short poem called *waka*, the name of a Japanese poetic genre. The play ends with a final commentary by the chorus called the *kiri*.

Putting the information given above into an outline, the classic form of a noh play is as follows:

Jo—Introduction
- First dan: shidai

Ha—Exposition
- Second dan: issei and michiyuki
- Third dan: mondo
- Fourth dan: kuri, kuse, and rongi

(*Nakairi—Interlude*)
- Kyogen or machiutai

Kyu—Denouement
- Fifth dan: (issei, mondo,) mai, waka, and kiri

36. The austere noh stage is built out into the audience area and has a ramp (the hashigakari) leading to the greenroom. The noh instrumental ensemble consists of the o-tsuzumi, ko-tsuzumi, and flute, shown here left to right, plus the taiko drum. See Plate 43.

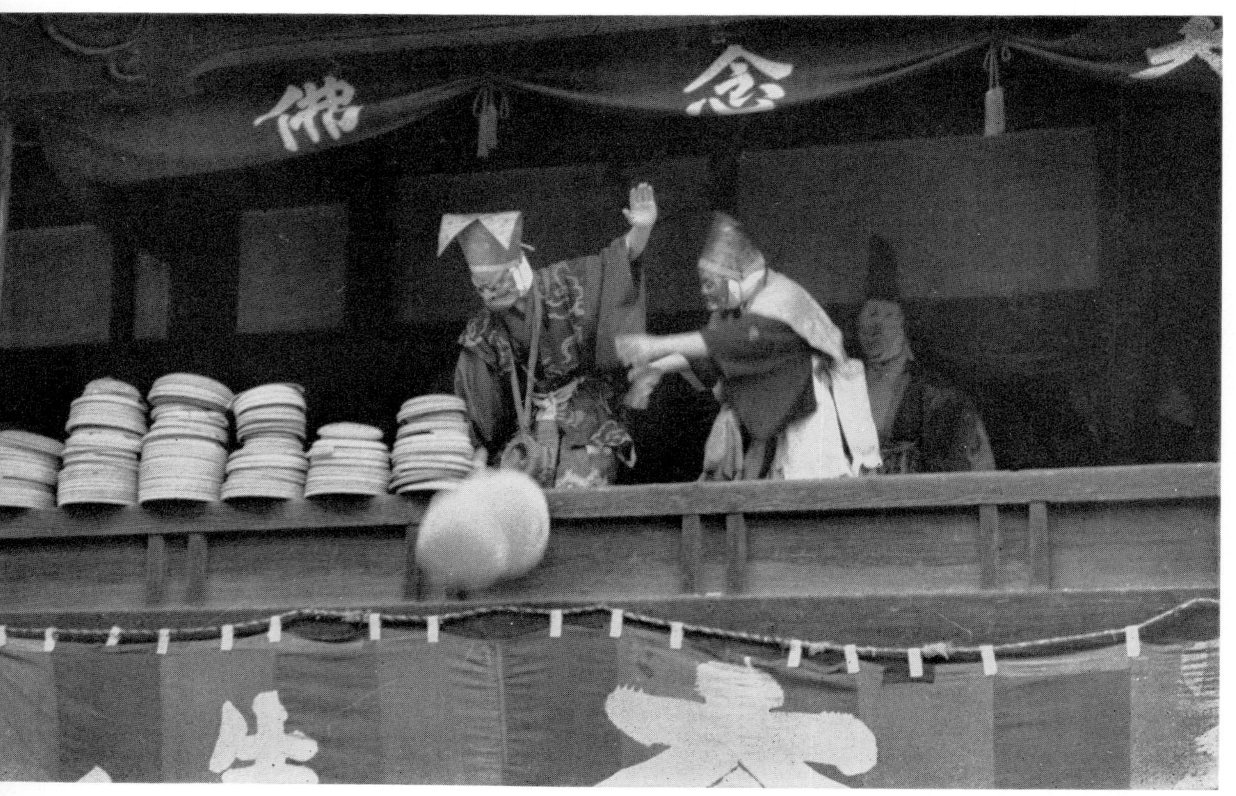

37. The Mibu-kyogen pantomime plays of Kyoto resemble ancient European morality plays and retain the style of the early folk theatricals that inspired the creators of noh. See page 106.

38. The noh flute is the only melodic instrument in the noh ensemble. As in the case of the gagaku flute the holes are covered by the middle joint of the fingers, producing the half-holed effects idiomatic of its music. See page 121.

39. Before every noh performance the musicians play the warm-up piece "O-shirabe." The lead actor adjusts his constume in the background. See pages 108–9.

40. Traditional Japanese music is taught piece by piece through rote methods. The drum instructor beats out the rhythm of all the parts with two fans on a special box called the hyoshiban. See page 124, also pages 170–72, 177.

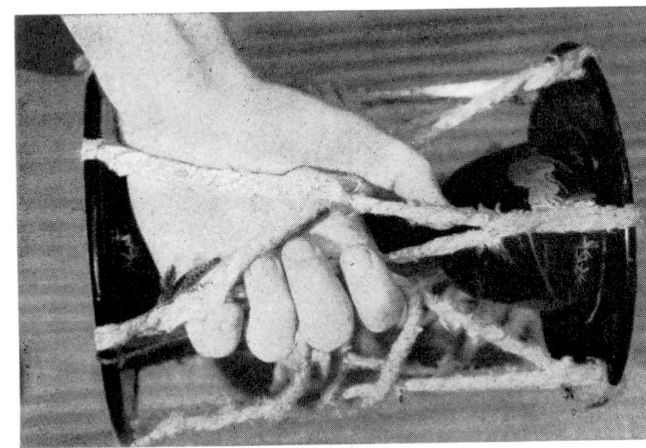

41. The ko-tsuzumi hand position allows the player to squeeze the ropes and hence change the tone.

42. The ko-tsuzumi must be reassembled at every performance so that the rope tensions will be correct for weather and stage conditions.

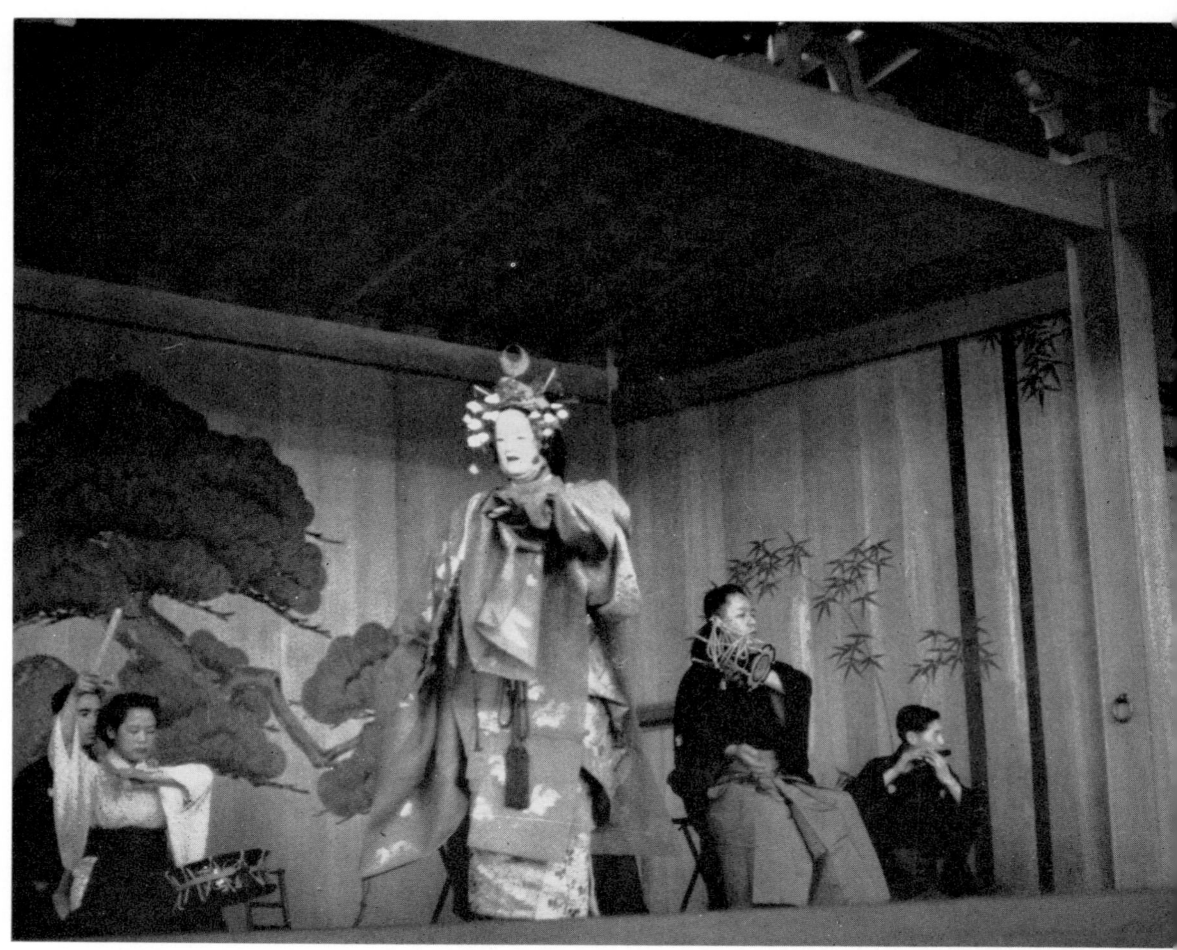

43. The taiko drummer is shown executing the kashira stroke during the play *Hagoromo*. See page 125.

NOHKAN

In the long history of noh there have been many rearrangements and distortions of this order, but it has remained the basic point of departure. There is much satisfaction to be derived from noh as good theatre, but if one compares it with Western drama, it often seems to be lacking any real plot line. Nothing seems to have happened by the end of the play, and the two acts frequently have little connection. This could be explained by comparing the plays with the tea ceremony, which developed concurrently with noh. The purpose of both the play and the ceremony lies not in the form but in the objects presented and the atmosphere created. In either case, one should not seek only an intellectual understanding but rather savor the highly specialized aesthetic experience. It must be remembered that the influence of Zen Buddhism, with its love of allusions and emphasis of non-logical procedures, was strong when noh was developed.

In noh everything is restrained in an attempt to produce as pure an aesthetic atmosphere as possible. If one approaches a noh play looking for the Western concepts of extensive plot development or strong character delineations and interrelations, many plays will seem very poor indeed. This does not mean that noh cannot be appreciated on its theatrical merits alone. However, if one is willing to accept for the moment the artistic tenets purported by the creators of noh, one may find a very pleasing and different form of enjoyment in the theatre arts.

IV. The Ensemble

THE NOH FLUTE: The noh flute, called the *nohkan*, is a relative of the ryuteki studied earlier (Plate 30). Both are made of well-dried bamboo that has been split lengthwise into eight or fourteen strips and turned inside out so that the bark is on the inside. This reversed tube is then bound together with very thin bark, usually cherry. Only the holes are left unbound. The inside is lacquered red, and the outside is black. A gold relief is often inserted in one end, just to emphasize the flute's beauty and value. Though the length is around thirty-four centimeters, the internal pipe is only twenty-nine centimeters, as the flute is solid from the mouth hole to the closed end.

The nohkan has no definite pitch as it is the only melodic instrument, but the seven holes produce notes in the vicinity of C sharp, B, A sharp, a, g, e, and d. In actual playing there are a tremendous number of other tonal gradations used.

Besides this difference in scales, the most important and unique feature of the noh flute as against the gagaku flute or, for that matter, any other flute, has to do with the tonal variation of overblown notes. When one blows strongly on a normal flute it will produce a pitch an octave higher. The noh flute, however, overblows a little flat. As one progresses up the scale the notes become flatter until the seventh tone (C sharp) produces not an octave but a minor seventh (B). The reason for this phenomenon is that a thin tube has been inserted into the flute between the lip hole and the first finger hole. This tube upsets the normal acoustical arrangements expected from a flute and is one of the most unusual features of Japanese instrumental construction. The reason for this device is not clearly known, but one hint might be found in the tonal system of noh singing which is founded on a basic range of a minor seventh (see page 128).

The music of the noh flute consists of the arrangement of a large number of stereotyped patterns. Each section of the play as listed above has special melodic patterns which are not used in the other sections. These patterns themselves are internally constructed of still shorter standard patterns which may be found in the other sections but arranged in a different order. Because of the great importance of the kuse and kuri, however, there are certain phrases that are used there exclusively. This helps to point up the uniqueness of these sections. This use of special phrases for emphasis is a device often found in Japanese music as a formal aid. It is somewhat like the use of the six-four chord just before the cadenza in a classic concerto. Once the listener has been trained (Pavlov style), he reacts immediately to the sound and knows that the cadenza will follow. In a similar way, the enlightened noh devotee recognizes these exclusive signals (of course, not always consciously) and is mentally prepared for the denouement that follows.

The flute serves five main functions: 1) it signals parts of the play (as in the shidai), 2) it accompanies the dance and sets the tempo (as in the kuse and the mai), 3) it adds another timbre and creates atmosphere in the hayashi interludes, 4) it sets the pitch for the chorus (particularly in the michiyuki and kuse), and 5) it heightens the lyricism of certain poetic passages.

At present there are three schools of noh flute, the Isso, Morita, and Fujita. The main points of distinction between them are notation, embellishments, and the use of microtones. For example, one of the Morita school's main characteristics is that few pitches are played clearly, but rather they are preceded and followed by a sliding of the tone. This "blurring" of the pitch may have developed in order not to compete with the melody of the singers, which is never the same as that of the flute.

Most of the tones used in noh-flute playing are produced by very strong air pressure. This forceful attack produces a great deal of wind noise which requires a bit of acclimatization on the part of the listener. The sound is quite piercing and definitely not recommended for small rooms. On the open stage, however, it is quite effective. It must be remembered that originally these dramas were given on an outdoor stage in a palace or temple compound.

The noh flute, like the gagaku flutes, is fingered in an interesting manner (see Plate 38). The holes are covered by the middle joint of the fingers and not the tips as in most Western flutes. This helps to produce the indistinct, half-holed effects so idiomatic in noh-flute music. In addition, there are times when the pitch does not change but the tone quality is altered by raising one of the fingers.

Noh-flute notation is discussed in Appendix II. Simply stated, it is based on a solfège and written within the characteristic eight-beat phrase of noh. The most extensive flute parts occur during dance accompaniments (*mai*) or in hayashi interludes (*gaku*). Their difference is primarily in length, the gaku pieces being longer. Formally, they are organized into an introduction, several related units (dan), and a coda. These flute units use a typical Japanese variation technique. After a short introduction, a basic melodic line, called the *ji*, is presented and repeated several times. The various dan that follow take this basic melody and continue to repeat it, adding subtle melismas and pitch variations to it. They also interpolate entirely new material between some of the repeats of the ji. This material in turn may be varied in the following dan along with the original melody. The original ji returns at the end, and the piece closes with a short coda, often the first line of the ji. This concept of variation by means of extending the length of the sections with new material is found often in other Japanese music, particularly koto music.

When the noh flute is used within the normal progress of the play it plays shorter melodies. The most important of these are the *ashirai*, a group of short phrases which set the pitch for the chorus. They are found particularly in the michiyuki and kuse sections. Though the noh flute's pitch is not always the same, the player can produce a desired pitch by half-holing or "lipping" the tone up or down as Western woodwind players do. Since the same melody may occur in many different plays and in different places it is up to the performer to fit his part in with the specific music or text of each situation. Perhaps this is one reason why there is no detailed rhythmic indication in flute notation. One must simply learn by experience. When the flute is used in combination with the taiko drum, its rhythm is determined by that of the drum part. The close connection of these two instruments is extremely interesting and may be based

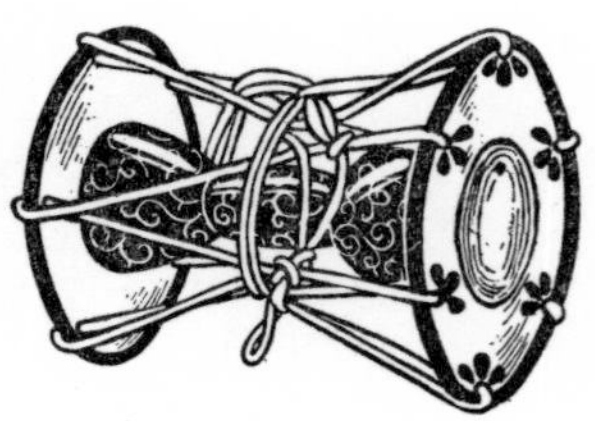

KO-TSUZUMI

on some ancient folk precedent. Its origin has not as yet been traced, but its continued use is noticeable in kabuki music as well as in the noh.

As the only melodic instrument in the noh instrumental ensemble, the noh flute is particularly effective. It amply illustrates one of the main operative principles of Japanese art, that of deriving the maximum effect from the minimum material. The indefinite quality of its tone and its music are eminently suitable for supporting the drama without interfering with the declamation of the poetry. The nohkan and its music are an excellent solution to the problem of the use of music within a drama.

THE DRUMS: There are three types of drums used in noh; the *ko-tsuzumi*, *o-tsuzumi*, and the *taiko*. The ko-tsuzumi, though the smallest of the group, is the most important drum in noh and is one of the unique Japanese contributions to the world of music. It is related to the san-no-tsuzumi in the court orchestra, which in turn has Korean relations. Its final form and manner of playing, however, seem to be something unknown in either court music or the music of Korea and China.

All the noh drums consist of five basic parts; a wooden body (*do*), two skins (*kawa*), and two sets of ropes (*shirabe*) which hold the skins to the body (Plate 42). The body of the ko-tsuzumi is made of zelkova wood. Like a good violin, this wood must come from just the right tree growing in just the right place. The inside of a good drum is hand carved with special patterns called *kanname*, which are deemed very important for the tone of the drum. The lacquer outside may make a drum an *objet d'art*, but it is the carving inside that makes it a good or poor musical instrument. The skins of the ko-tsuzumi are made of horsehide. They are stretched over iron rings and then stitched at the rear with hemp thread. These stitches are covered by the inner black lacquer circle one sees on the face of the drum (Plate 40). The back of the skins is built up with clay so that the body will fit snugly onto the center of the skins. The only major difference between the back skin and the playing skin is that a small patch of deerskin is placed in the inside center of the back skin. This controls the reverberation of the skin and hence the tone. Another control is exerted by small patches of paper which are applied to the outside of the rear skin immediately opposite this inner patch. This paper, called *choshigami*, is newly applied at each performance and has an amazingly significant

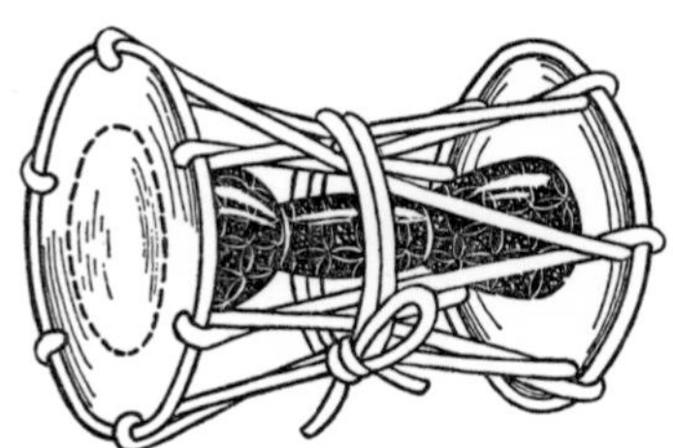

O-TSUZUMI

effect on the tone of the drum. The number of papers applied depends on the weather, the tension of the ropes, and perhaps the whim of the player. The application and wetting of this paper is a puzzle to many a newcomer to a noh or kabuki performance. It has the look of a private conversation between the musician and his drum.

One set of the ko-tsuzumi ropes holds the two heads against the body while the other is looped loosely around the drum. By squeezing this encircling rope, tension is created on the skins, which raises the pitch of the drum. The manner of holding these ropes varies with the school of drumming as does the exact manner of tying the ropes. Plate 41 shows one of the common styles. Notice that the little finger is anchored by means of an extra loop of string, called a *kojime.*

The five basic sounds of the ko-tsuzumi are onomatopoetically named *pon, pu, ta, chi,* and *tsu. Pon* is produced by striking the center of the head. Two to four fingers of the right hand are used depending on the school of drumming followed. The ropes are held loosely until the moment of impact when they are squeezed quickly to produce a lovely liquid waver to the tone. The coördination and perfection of this technique is the *pièce de résistance* of Japanese drumming. *Pu* is similar to *pon* but lighter and played with only one finger. *Ta* has a wonderful crack to it and is produced by hitting at the edge of the head with two fingers while exerting maximum tension on the ropes. *Chi* is a lighter version of *ta* played with the ring finger. *Tsu* is executed by leaving the hand on the front head and allowing the rear one to produce the tone.

When the drum is not in use it is often tied up by a separate rope known as a *shimeo.* The tying and untying of this rope is ideally done with careful ceremony, and it takes simply one or two lessons to perfect the correct technique. Stage manners are equally as important as playing technique in the study of noh drumming.

The o-tsuzumi is similar to the ko-tsuzumi except for its larger size and the addition of rings carved on the outside of the drum. Cherry or Chinese quince is considered the best wood, and the inner carving is simpler. The skins are usually cowhide and are constructed like those above except that they are bigger and unlacquered. There is no need to build up the back of the heads with clay as the thickness of the doubled-over hide suffices to hold the heads on the body. The front head is slightly thicker than the rear and no control patches or control papers are used.

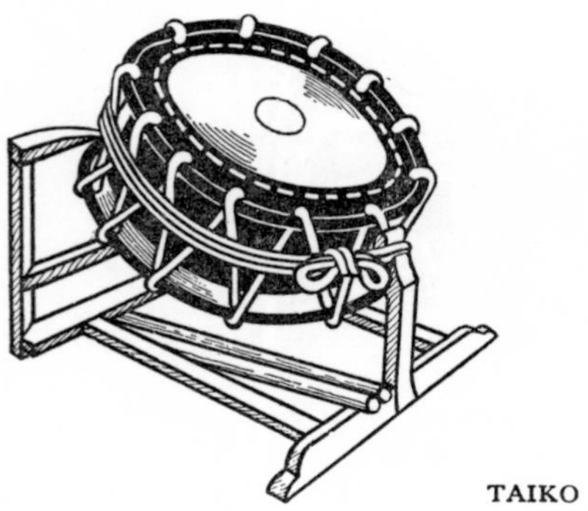

TAIKO

One reason why the o-tsuzumi heads are not lacquered is that they must be heated for at least an hour before a performance. This shortens the life of the skins, and in professional circles a set of skins is not used after ten performances. During noh performances a freshly heated drum is often brought on stage halfway through the play.

Held on the left hip (Plate 36), the o-tsuzumi is struck with one to three fingers of the right hand. Sometimes these fingers are covered with hard papier-mâché thimbles known as *yubikawa*. These enhance the sharp dryness of the drum's characteristic tone. Sometimes deerskin thimbles are used to produce a softer tone. The palm of the hand can be protected by another deerskin covering (an *ategawa*), which is tied to the hand with thin threads. The traditional fan carried by all musicians serves as an emergency device for the o-tsuzumi player. If the head should split during a performance, he can beat out the rhythm with his fan instead. The fan is also said to be used when a lighter accompaniment is desired, though this is seldom seen in performance.[2]

The rope system of the o-tsuzumi begins with one set which holds the heads very tightly against the body. The second rope (in this case, the *kojime*) is looped through five strands of this binding rope and pulled together in order to make the body even tighter against the skins. There is an extra rope (the *donawa*) which serves only a decorative function, draped from the drum onto the floor in front and behind the player. Since the functional ropes are quite tight they do not offer any margin for further control on the tone.

Tone control for the o-tsuzumi comes from the proper movements of the entire arm. The basic sounds are *chon*, which is the strongest, *tsu*, the weakest, and *don*. The latter is produced by leaving the hand on the drum after the impact and letting the rear head produce the sound as in the *tsu* beat of the ko-tsuzumi.

The last member of the noh-drum family is the taiko. Instead of the tsuzumi hourglass shape, it is of a barrel form. The body averages twenty-six centimeters in diameter and fifteen centimeters in height. Zelkova wood is considered the best for the body, and the skins are made of either horse or cow. Carving inside the body is not so

[2] In drum lessons the teacher sits opposite the pupil and beats out the rhythm of all the parts with two fans on a special box called a *hyoshiban*. It is quite a feat of coördination, as various kinds of beats are indicated by different strokes with the fans. All the time the teacher is singing the words and correcting the student (see Plate 40).

important. The construction of the skins is basically the same as that of the tsuzumi skins except that they are larger. The top skin is thicker than the lower, and a patch of deerskin is attached in the center to which all the blows are directed. There is a thinner patch immediately below this one for the purposes of tone. The rear head has no additional patches.

The taiko rope system is similar to that of the o-tsuzumi in that it is very tight and requires a great deal of strength to secure properly. One set of ropes holds the skins to the body, and the other set encircles the drum. The drum is set on a special stand which grips the encircling ropes and holds the drum off the floor so that it can resonate freely. The taiko is played with two thick sticks (*bachi*) with beveled ends. Their length averages thirty centimeters.

The basic sounds of the taiko are divided into three groups; small, medium, and large (*sho*, *chu*, and *dai*). The tones may be stopped by leaving the stick on the skin. This stopped sound (*osaeru*) is characteristic of the taiko. Another very typical taiko technique is the so-called *kashira*, which is heard so often at cadences. This movement consists of the left arm carrying the stick over the right shoulder while the right stick is lifted high (Plate 43). It is a striking effect when the left stick suddenly shoots forward instead of the expected right. The drum calls (*kakegoe*) which accompany this movement add to its excitement. More detail concerning the various strokes of the taiko will be found in the discussion of taiko notation in Appendix II.

One final note should be made concerning the playing technique of the taiko. Unlike the loose wrist common in Western drumming, the taiko calls for a straight arm from the elbow to the fingers. The sticks are held loosely but there is no drum rolling in the Western sense of the term. The technique abets the special restrained tone of this rather large drum as does the deer patch which slightly muffles the tone. Much more sound could be made on the taiko, but the Japanese musician has chosen to limit his technique and concentrate on the chosen tone spectrum and the grace of movement involved in producing a tone. This preoccupation with the style of tone production as well as the tone itself adds greatly to the finesse of a good noh performance.

The original function of the noh hayashi was probably dance accompaniment only. Later, it began to provide a rhythmic matrix for many of the songs and choruses until it gained certain sections for itself. The music of the flute parts has already been discussed. The music of the drums consists also of a series of stereotyped patterns arranged in a certain prescribed order.[3] The patterns of the o-tsuzumi and ko-tsuzumi are most

[3] For a detailed study of how this music is organized see: Malm, "The Rhythmic Orientation of Two Drums in the Japanese No Drama," *Ethnomusicology*, Vol. II, No. 3 (September, 1958), pp. 89–95.

intimately connected though they do not always play the same pattern at the same time. The same names for various rhythmic patterns appear in the music of all three drums, but it does not mean necessarily that they all use the same pattern at the same time. The notation for the drums shown in Appendix II is primarily a teaching device, and in a professional's music book one will usually see only the names of the patterns written along the text of the play. Since there are some two hundred such patterns, it takes several years before one can read easily such a score. There is also the problem of the exact relation of these patterns to each specific situation. This can be learned only by experience. It is the guarded secret of teachers who inculcate this esoteric knowledge by a slow rote method. An added problem is that each guild interprets these patterns in a slightly different way. This makes it difficult and sometimes impossible for certain drummers to perform together. If a student learns a certain school of ko-tsuzumi, then he is automatically committed to learning other special schools of o-tsuzumi, taiko, and flute in order to coördinate his knowledge. When musicians of various clans perform together, they must meet before the performance and decide whose version of each play they are going to use. Occasionally this is not done and there are some unfortunate discrepancies between the parts.

Perhaps the greatest surprise to anyone hearing noh for the first time are the shouts of the drummers, the *kakegoe*. It was said that noh is set in a very flexible rhythm. These calls between the drummers serve to mark the time between these flexible beats and may have originated as practice devices which were later taken into the performance itself. As they were further abstracted, they became an integral part of the over-all tonal picture of noh. Serving both a practical and aesthetic function, they evoke one of the many special qualities associated with the noh drama.

The hayashi was mentioned as consisting of the three drums and the flute. However, the full combination is not always used. Commonly only the flute, o-tsuzumi, and ko-tsuzumi are found. Even when the taiko is added, it is usually used only during dance sections. One of each instrument is used in noh with the exception of the dance "Okina" in which the hayashi consists of one flute, one o-tsuzumi, and three ko-tsuzumi. In special performances of noh selections one may hear an *itcho*. This is a section of a noh drama performed by one or more singers and one drummer. If the music comes from the *issei* section of the play it is called *issei-itcho*. In such music the drummer must synthesize the complete hayashi part on his one instrument. For this reason livelier sections are usually chosen. The problem is rather like the one faced when reducing a symphony at the piano. Sometimes such drum parts become improvisatory, though only within definite limits. There is another form called *itcho-ikkan* which uses one drum and one flute with or without singers. On rare occasions one may hear an itcho for solo drum, usually the ko-tsuzumi. Such a performance offers an excellent opportunity to appreciate fully the tonal variations possible on that drum.

All the music of the hayashi is set within a frame of eight-beat phrases. Though many patterns are shorter than this, they are always learned in relation to the noh eight-beat system, the so-called *yatsu-byoshi*. However, the most interesting element of this construction is that most patterns begin on the second beat. The first beat is often completely silent, leaving the music to be performed in seven beats. This orientation of the accent away from the first beat has an interesting parallel in the rhythmic concept of Javanese orchestral music. The practical use of seven of the eight available beats is another example of the number seven in the structural concept of noh music.

The hayashi of the noh is one of Japan's unique contributions to music. As used in noh and further developed in kabuki, it is perhaps the most original concept in all Japanese music. Its sound, musical structure, and relation to the drama are all quite rare. This idea may be understood more clearly after a discussion of the vocal music of noh, though the best way to understand it is to hear for oneself the power and uniqueness of the hayashi.

THE SINGING: *Yokyoku*, the singing of noh, derives its style from Buddhist chanting. Along with the vocal style of the temple, it has retained through the ages the solemnity and introspection that is associated with religious music. Its sparse melodic style has carried the masterpieces of medieval Japanese playwrights over the centuries into the present time. It evolved under the aegis of aristocratic patrons and now seeks its greatest support among the common citizenry with whom it has become fashionable as an edifying and recreative amateur accomplishment. One of the most pleasant incidental memories of Japan was an impromptu concert of yokyoku performed by a carpenter during his "tea break." The sensitive Japanese male is fortunate in that there are several such artistic yet "manly" arts in which he may find an outlet. For example, yokyoku (along with party songs) has become popular with many businessmen. Thus, noh singing has found a place in modern society as a social grace as well as being an integral part of the theatre.

On the stage, yokyoku (also called *utai*) is sung by both the actors and the chorus. The chorus leader (*jigashira*) is said to control the tempo of the chant by prolonging the sounds. In fact, there is a complex process of adjustment constantly going on between the chorus, hayashi, and the actors. This continual elasticity is a prime factor in the movement that lies barely visible beneath the placid surface of the noh play.

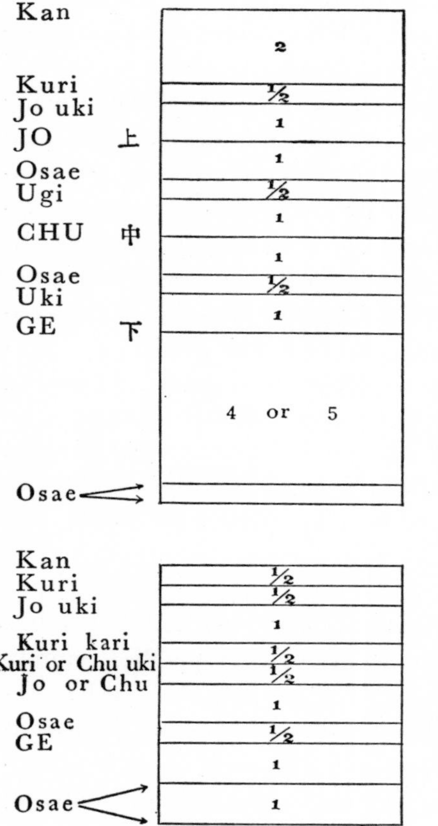

FIGURE 11. The yokyoku tone system

The special voice quality of noh singing originates in the abdomen. Graces and vibratos are added to the tone to give it variety. The pronunciation of the words is an abstraction of ancient styles and further removes the plays from the everyday world. To appreciate noh as sound or as literature, it is necessary to steep oneself in a different language much in the way one approaches Chaucer in the original. In both cases, what is lost in the immediacy of comprehension is gained in the transcendental euphony of words as sound.

Noh plays are set in two basic styles. One is called *kotoba*, or "words." It is the heightened speech style mentioned earlier and is used as recitative. As such it has little in the way of definite pitch or melody. The other style is called *fushi*, "melody." This style is analogous to the aria sections of an opera. In noh there are two basic ways in which these more melodic sections can be performed. The first is called *yowagin*, the "soft" style. It is used in lyric scenes and seems to be the earlier style. During the Tokugawa period, however, there was added a *tsuyogin*, "strong" style, which was used in masculine and warlike scenes. These words are also used as general terms denoting the strength or weakness of delivery desired within a single phrase rather like the Western crescendo and decrescendo.

In the light of our earlier discussion of the flute, which overblows a minor seventh, it is interesting to note that the yokyoku tone system is also based on the interval of the minor seventh. Figure 11 shows this system in its classic form. The tone *jo* (A) is the pitch center, *chu* (E) is the next in importance, and *ge* (B) is an alternate final tone. The distance between each tone is a perfect fourth, which adds up in musical parlance to a seventh (B to A). Around each of these main notes is clustered a group of nearly related pitches which are tonally attracted to one of the main tones. In Western music it is analogous to the tendency of the seventh note of the major scale (*si*) to resolve up (to *do*).

Each chant in the yowagin style is constructed in such a way that these three main sounds carry the greatest burden of the melody, while the other notes function as means of traveling back and forth between the main tones. It already has been noted in the discussion of noh form that the particular type of melodic movement used in each section is strictly regulated. Nothing is left to chance. The words of the text and the over-all form of the play both exert a control over the melodic line.

One idiomatic restriction on the melodic movement of noh music is that one cannot move directly from *jo* to *chu* or from *chu* to *ge*. Instead, one must first go up to a nearby tone and then drop to the lower pitch. This cliché is heard again and again in noh music. Entire formal units have their melodic conventions as well. For example, the climactic kuse sections begin on *chu* (E), work up to *jo* (A), and end on *ge* (B). The higher pitches in general are withheld until moments of greater tension.

In the more militant tsuyogin pieces the pitches *jo* and *chu* are the same note (E) and *ge* is a minor third lower (C sharp). The basic movement is between these two pitches though, as can be seen in Figure 11, the outer limits of the range are much wider. Looking at the entire repertoire of noh singing, one can find about eight basic melodic units, each with a yowagin and tsuyogin form. By combining these in a variety of ways, a highly expressive but restricted melodic style has been developed. Such a style is in keeping with the aesthetic and dramatic demands of the noh play itself.

The rhythmic structure of noh singing is also based on the eight-beat phrase system though it may be treated very freely. The regulations determining the number of syllables sung within these beats are known as *nori*, literally, the way the poem "rides" the rhythm. Nori can apply to the general style of an entire composition or to the execution of a single phrase. There are three basic nori, but the most idiomatic of them is the *hira-nori* which is used for the five-seven syllabic lines. As these rules are applied to each phrase they are slightly modified to fit the particular situation. The rules and detailed explanations of these situations come under the title of *ji-byoshi* (see ref. 29). The study of ji-byoshi is one of the most interesting and also the most detailed of the various techniques requisite for a good noh singer.

Given a music of such elastic rhythm, indefinite pitch, and restricted melodic movement, it is not surprising to find that noh notation is not very detailed. In essence, it is a simple set of neumes. In practice, there is much that must be known beforehand in order to sing these neumes correctly. This notation is discussed in Appendix II.

V. Summary

The noh drama has been presented in bits and pieces. It is now time to view it as an artistic entirety. Growing out of a host of early theatricals, noh found a means of uniting the arts of music, dance, drama, and décor in such a way as to retain the best elements of its predecessors while deleting their mutual inconsistencies when combined in the noh theatre. This was done by building each play on a central evocative theme, creating poetry in keeping with this mood, and maintaining and developing this idea by means of all the other dramatic arts. Each art was held in check so that the reality of the theme would not be destroyed by the intrusion of the reality of the component arts. In noh, the balance between highly refined abstraction and the dramatic necessity of human emotions is one of the most delicate and perhaps most successful attempts in world drama.

Musically, the singing and the rhythm of the hayashi have been shown as subject to intense systematization. The singing is centered on the poetry, and the hayashi remains alert to the rhythmic and emotional changes of the poetry and the movement of the actors. The flute, as the only melodic instrument, provides a necessary contrast to the mauve tone colors of the singing and the percussion of the drums. The calls of the drummers have been cultivated until they have become not only rhythmic signals but also important elements in the general emotional mood of the plays.

The structure of a noh play has often been likened to a mosaic. Each dramatic or musical unit is a microcosmos, answering the logical requirements of its own little universe. These pieces of various emotional tints are put together in such a way that each reinforces the over-all mood of the frame in which they are set. This frame is not necessarily a plot in the Western sense but rather the quality inherent in the "idea" behind the implied plot.

For the musician, the main interest may be in the "horizontal" conception of music. Western music can usually be analyzed "horizontally" or "vertically," that is, one can follow the composer's ideas as they progress in time or take one particular instant and discover what the relation of the various lines is to each other. In simplest terms, it is like studying both melody and harmony. In noh music a vertical cross section of the music will often reveal apparent chaos. The chorus and the flute are involved in two completely separate melodic lines while the drums may be playing rhythmic patterns of dissimilar lengths and names. If one views each passage in a horizontal manner, however, one can see each part working in concord with the basic requirements of the text. The text is the clue to the understanding of much of the music. It is the *raison d'être* for most of the rules that have grown up around the music. This intimate connection is one of the best examples of the literary orientation inherent in most Japanese music.

The music of noh is not the product of one mind. After the poem has been written it is passed on to the various hayashi players and main actors who compose their own parts. Such a system can only be successful with a music that is highly systematized. Noh theorists have seemed sometimes a bit precious in their aesthetic and dramatic writings, but when plays have been entrusted to the care of sensitive actors and musicians, the results have been something quite lovely and unique. A good noh play has a composite beauty, a beauty derived from many different minds and from all the theatre arts.

Noh presents a fascinating paradox. As a dramatic form one would expect it to relate to time and place, yet it often evokes timelessness. There is much truth in the usual translation of the word noh as "an accomplishment," for in the field of the theatre that is indeed what it is.

CHAPTER FIVE
BIWA MUSIC

I. Introduction

Beneath the ancient gates of Kyoto there has passed a multicolored pageant of disorderly events known as history. The slaty eyes of the gargoyles and dragons that festoon their eaves have viewed imperial grandeur, religious pomp, and periodic holocausts resulting from ceaseless struggles for power. If those fabulous creatures have a memory, perhaps they can recall also the regular temple fairs. The strident chaos of buying and selling still assaults their stony ears, but from the depths of their memories they may be able to conjure up the twang of a biwa and the tense voice of a blind storyteller who sat within the shadow of the gate. Though these men were as sightless as the gargoyles, they re-created with their music much of the same color and pathos of the events to which those creatures bore witness. For a few pennies the shopper could rest from his haggling and relive via the blind priest-musician the famous legends of mighty warriors and lovely ladies in their moments of glory and of death.

The blind biwa priests are no longer seen at temple fairs, but the spirit of their songs remains in the theatre music of Edo and in the modern biwa-concert schools. The glowering audience of temple-tile creatures has been replaced by pseudo-Baroque cherubs that cling to the prosceniums of modern theatres. However, the human listeners are basically the same. They still love a good story, and as long as there are biwa musicians with enough talent to re-create the old tales there will be someone to hear them. What the gargoyles may remember, mankind can still imagine with the help of the biwa and its music.

II. The History of Biwa Music

The biwa, like the Western lute, has come in many sizes and shapes and from many cultures. The biwa as used in Japan today has two main sources, India and China.[1] There is a legend that Buddha had a blind disciple to whom he taught the art of singing sutras to the accompaniment of the biwa. Another legend claims that the son

1 Historically speaking, there are three different-shaped lutes that are known to have entered Japan. Only two of them, however, are in use today. For a detailed study of their origin see ref. 38.

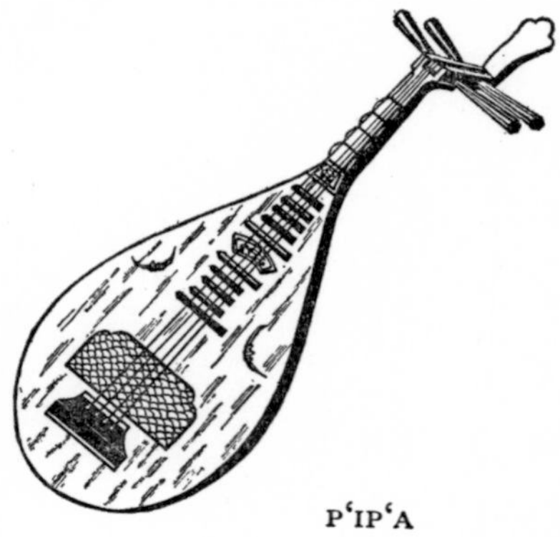

P'IP'A

of the famous Buddhist king, Asoka of India, became such a blind biwa player. There is much disagreement concerning the real origins of this music, but it is fairly certain that it was transferred to China around the third century. There, this instrument, known as the *p'ip'a*, was further evolved, apparently under central Asian influences. It is this Chinese-style lute that seems to have come to Japan sometime in the Nara period.

In Chapter III one of these early instruments mentioned was the gaku-biwa used in the imperial gagaku music. In addition to its use in the orchestral ensemble, it seems to have had an extensive solo literature as well. Playing the biwa was an important social grace for the courtier of the late-Nara and Heian periods. The great literary monument to that age, *The Tale of Genji*, is replete with scenes in which the biwa plays an important role. Likewise, the biwa appears in genre paintings as often as the lute is found in pictures of the European Renaissance. Unfortunately, the solo music for the biwa was mostly secret pieces, and only a few as yet unstudied remnants of its notation exist. If the performance style was at all similar to that of the orchestral biwa, it must have been very simple and meant to be primarily a vocal accompaniment.

While the nobility were busy with their music and their amours, a very different kind of biwa music developed in the south of Kyushu. Here blind priests using a smaller biwa, more like the Indian models, appeared singing sutras to appease the local earth gods. There are many legends concerning the entrance of this music into Japan. Some place it as early as the seventh century, but it was not until after the tenth century that such priests really appeared in great numbers. The best known story of the founding of this *moso-biwa*, or "blind-priest biwa," concerns the Enryaku temple in Kyoto. The story relates that when the temple was built the grounds were found to be infested with poisonous snakes. In order to drive them away, eight blind biwa-playing priests were brought from Kyushu to perform their sutras. Apparently they were successful, for four biwa priests were retained permanently in Kyoto. One of the priests who returned to Kyushu was particularly famous for his talent and was recalled to the capital whenever any plague or other natural calamity made it incumbent to exorcise the spirits. This man was Jojuin, the traditional founder of the Chikuzen school of

MOSO-BIWA

blind biwa players. The other main school, the Satsuma, was said to have been founded by one of the priests who stayed behind in Kyoto. This priest was called Manshoin. The supposed relation between these two men varies considerably with the school allegiance of the authors of the various histories of blind-priest biwa. The important thing to notice is that the difference between Chikuzen and Satsuma styles existed even in the early blind-priest traditions. The term "blind priest" is used here in order to differentiate between these early Satsuma and Chikuzen styles and the musics using the same names that appeared later.

These singing priests led a wandering life. Traveling from village to village, they sang their magic sutras wherever a local god had shown signs of being obstreperous or displeased. Their clientele came more and more from the peasants and less from the big temples and noblemen. Eventually their music became known as *Kojin-biwa*, named after Kojin, a household kitchen god. By the Kamakura period many of these men were reduced to beggars. They ceased to travel and spent their days lying about temple gates and seeking alms with a few stanzas of their once magic sutras. It is possible that some of these men may have begun to improvise stories in order to attract more attention and hence more alms. In any event, these itinerant sutra singers laid a foundation for much of the great theatre music that was to follow.

In the decline of the blind-priest biwa, the Chikuzen school suffered more than the Satsuma, for the latter continued to enjoy respectability under the patronage of the Shimazu clan in the Satsuma district of Kyushu. The headquarters of the school moved from Kyoto to Satsuma about the time of the great shogun Yoritomo (1147–99). This school continued to flourish until the general deterioration of the clan system in the Edo period. One must not think, however, that the Shimazu clan was a twelfth-century house of Esterhazy. These men were warriors and as such were more alert to warfare than to art. They discovered in the association of blind musicians a ready-built spy ring, for these priests had their own nationwide organization rather like the old Society of Jesus in Europe. They were free to travel all over Japan in a manner that few other men could do. Under the Shimazu aegis, they soon developed a good ear for news as well as for music.

These musical spies were not the most important development in biwa music of the Kamakura period. Rather, it was the founding of the great narrative tradition, *Heike-biwa*, that is remembered best. The stories of the battle between the Heike and Genji clans were already well known to the warriors of the bloody Kamakura period. They served as an inspiration in battle and a consolation in defeat. These stories had probably been told many times by a variety of storytellers, but it was not until the establishment of a biwa version that *The Heike Story* became an important literary and musical genre.

The origin of Heike-biwa is open to debate. The best-known story of its creation claims that it was first written by a court official named Fujiwara Yukinaga (circa 1189). This man had always prided himself on being an excellent gagaku musician and dancer. One day he was asked to perform a dance of seven sections. He started off in confidence but forgot two sections before he finished. The jokes made at his expense must have been bitter indeed, for tradition relates that he finally left the court and retired in shame to the mountain monastery of Hieizan. There, under the encouragement of a Buddhist priest named Jichin, he proceeded to write the story of the Heike clan and their decline. This story was then taught to a blind-biwa priest named Shobutsu, who, in turn, went about the country singing this new style of music.

Exactly how much truth there is in this story will probably never be known, but it does point out nicely the three main streams of music from which Heike-biwa evolved: gagaku, Buddhist shomyo, and blind-priest biwa music. More will be said of this in the second part of this chapter.

The popularity of Heike-biwa was immense. Both the court and the war camp found this music novel as well as germane to their own times and problems. Loyalty and bravery in battle, beauty and fidelity at home, a Buddhist acceptance of the evanescence of life; all these moods are found within *The Heike Story*. It was an apt artistic medium for a strife-torn period. It also provided a new source of livelihood for the tottering profession of blind biwa players.

The strains of Heike-biwa music drifted among the polished rafters of the rich man's mansion as well as the weather-beaten tiles of the temple gate. Each class enjoyed the stories in their own particular style, and many schools developed to meet the tastes of these various audiences.

As mentioned, the entire association of blind performers was organized on a nationwide basis. It was much like the modern musician's union. In fact, one could not perform without a license from the association headquarters. Within this political framework, however, there was a continual proliferation of differing musical styles. The two main schools of the Kamakura and Muromachi periods were the Ichikata and Yasaka. The Yasaka group claimed to use the original text, while the Ichikata music was based on a special edition which was supposed to have been given to one of their virtuosi by the emperor himself.

With the entrance of the shamisen and the many new styles of theatre music in the Edo period, Heike-biwa began to lose favor. The style remained static, while the times changed rapidly. Today a few old men in Nagoya are recounting, perhaps for the last time in history, *The Heike Story* as it was heard by the Kamakura warriors and the temple gargoyles.

As Heike-biwa declined and blind sutra singers nearly disappeared, other more timely biwa styles developed. The most important of these evolved among the Satsuma musicians under the patronage of the Shimazu clan. These men had done valuable service for the clan during the turbulent Kamakura and Muromachi days but by the sixteenth century their usefulness as spies was beginning to wane. Therefore, they were turned to a new task, that of "improving" the members of the clan with edifying music. In the previous chapter, many theatricals and other forms of popular entertainment which flooded the country in the Muromachi period were listed. It was the intention of the ruling members of the Shimazu clan to protect their warriors against the deleterious effects of overexposure to these supposedly vulgar musics. To this end, "popular" music was forbidden among members of the clan, and the cultivation of light classics was recommended. These consisted of three kinds of music: 1) music for a small type of vertical flute called a *tempuku* (Plate 50), 2) music for a special form of warrior dance called *samurai-odori* or *heko-odori*, and 3) new forms of narrative Satsuma-biwa music. Through these three artistic pursuits they hoped to build a clan of modest but sturdy soldiers.

The success of this interesting experiment in music propaganda is open to debate, but the musical results are very definite. From the sixteenth century on, a new style of narrative music can be said to have come into being. At first, the pieces were carefully arranged as suitable for various ages and sexes, but eventually a repertoire evolved which consisted primarily of war stories. It differed from the Heike-biwa style in that the music was more in keeping with contemporary fashions and continued to develop as styles changed. This music eventually became popular among the common people as well, and its style became less pompous and more dramatic. By the Edo period it had spread all over the southern part of Japan and no doubt had some part in the styling of the music for the fast-growing arts of kabuki and the puppet plays.

One of the acts of the Meiji Restoration of 1868 was to abolish the exclusive privileges of the blind performers. This spelled the death for most of what remained of the old moso-biwa and hastened the demise of Heike-biwa. However, many of the men who played important roles in the early government of the Meiji period came from the provinces of Satsuma, and they brought to the capital of Tokyo more than just new ideas of statesmanship. They brought Satsuma-biwa. This music was now open to anyone, and many people took it up as a hobby. Emperor Meiji was a great fan of such music and is said to have taken practice himself by means of phonograph records.

In the twentieth century this music has changed greatly. Many new schools have appeared of which the Kinshin and Nishiki are the most famous. The latter was founded by a woman, Suito Kinjo, and is highly influenced by shamisen music.

In the late nineteenth century the term Chikuzen-biwa appeared once more. The old sutra-singing Chikuzen music had died out long before.[2] This new style was created out of a mixture of narrative biwa, Satsuma-biwa, and shamisen music. It took the name of Chikuzen because it began in the Chikuzen district of Kyushu and because it used, at first, a small biwa like the old blind-priest Chikuzen-biwa. The style, in its classic form, has a certain grandeur that the more melodramatic schools lack. Unfortunately, being less showy, it is less suitable for presentation on the stage. The beauties of Chikuzen-biwa can best be heard in a small room, while the power of Satsuma-biwa is quite striking on stage. In an age of the microphone, Satsuma-biwa seems to be faring better. However, both forms are comparatively young and open to improvement. Contemporary attempts to infuse Western techniques (such as biwa "orchestras") have been rather disastrous, but there have been certain very effective dramatic works in which koto and flutes have been added as mood music. The biwa has always been eminently suitable for the accompaniment of storytellers. As long as it does not lose sight of this dramatic orientation, it should have a future.

III. The Instrument and the Music

Over the centuries the biwa has been subject to many modifications in construction. Certain features, of course, have had to remain constant in order to retain the biwa's characteristic tone. The most important of these is the relation of the frets to the strings. On a Western guitar the strings are very near to the finger board so that when they are pressed down against the frets a definite pitch is produced. It is impossible,

[2] When I say a form has died out I mean that it has ceased to be of any musical or historical significance or influence. It is characteristic of Japan that as soon as one says that a certain art form has disappeared, an old artist is discovered in some out-of-the-way village. Such persons are the hope of research scholars and the incubus of general survey writers.

44. One of Japan's earliest musical instruments, the biwa was popular among the court nobles of the Heian period. This is a scene from the famous illustrated scroll of *The Tale of Genji*. See page 134.

45. A Satsuma-biwa performance by a priest in the style of the old blind-priest tradition, though he is not blind. See pages 135, 146.

46. The beauty of Chikuzen-biwa music is best heard when played in a small room by a master such as Maestro Hirata.

47. Three kinds of biwa: (from the back) gaku-biwa, Heike-biwa, and moso-biwa. See pages 134–36.

48. The body of the biwa is carved out from one piece of wood. The biwa is not as popular as before, but a few artisans continue to make them in the traditional manner. See page 143.

however, to push the strings of a modern biwa down to the neck as they are set very high above it and the frets themselves are more than an inch high.[3] This method of construction makes two different playing methods possible. First, one may simply press the strings down on the top of each fret. This produces a definite pitch but the number of pitches available is limited to the number of frets. This is the system used on the gaku-biwa. The second method is to push the string down between the frets. In this manner a variety of pitches can be produced depending on how hard one presses down on the string. This method stretches the string and is only possible with a string of some elasticity. Such a long, elastic string (made of gut or silk) has a very "twangy" sound much like that of a rubber band. When this sound is amplified by the body of the instrument, it produces one of the most characteristic elements of the biwa's tone, its *sawari*, or "rattle." Strange things were done to the neck of the shamisen in an attempt to capture this same quality.

The shape and size of the body of a biwa are also open to great variation (see Plate 47). In general, it is made of two pieces. The back is a solid piece of wood that has been hollowed out to make a sound box. A covering is then glued over this cavity, usually with two crescent-shaped sound holes. A special strip of wood, cloth, lacquer, or leather is sometimes placed across the body to protect it from the blows of the plectrum. The interesting aspect of this so-called *bachimen* is that only the older style biwa are played in such a manner that the plectrum actually strikes at this place. The present-day Satsuma and Chikuzen schools play above this spot. However, tradition has prevailed and the cover remains below while the plectrum continues to chip paint off the biwa some six inches higher (Plate 46).

One of the most important factors in the tone of a biwa is the placement of the tail piece, that is, the piece of wood to which the strings are attached. Depending on the thickness of the sides of the biwa, the tail piece may be attached either over solid wood or over the hollow section. The "correct" placement is entirely a matter of taste, and there is a great variety within each school of biwa music. Other features like the number of strings and frets and the kind of plectrum used also vary within each school as well as between local branches. Therefore, such differences will be mentioned as the specific music styles of these schools are discussed.

The gaku-biwa and its music have already been studied (see page 94). As can be seen in Plate 23 it has four frets and four strings. It is plucked with a small bone plectrum

[3] The frets of the biwa became progressively higher as the instrument evolved. The gaku-biwa frets are just slightly higher than those of a Chinese p'ip'a, the Heike-biwa yet a bit higher, and the Chikuzen and Satsuma frets are quite high.

(*bachi*), and only the pitches produced by pressing directly on the frets are used. This is the instrument that is said to have been primarily a Chinese development.

The Heike-biwa is somewhat smaller than the gaku-biwa (see Plate 47). It has four strings and five frets and uses a larger, wider plectrum. The instrument and its manner of playing seems to have been influenced by the blind-priest biwa. For one thing, the strings are played between the frets unlike the gaku-biwa.

With the topic of Heike-biwa music we come to one of the fundamental influences in Japanese music over the last seven centuries. The instrument was basically of gagaku origin, but the music grew out of two traditions, early blind storytellers and Buddhist chanting. There is a controversy among scholars as to how *heikyoku*,[4] that is, the singing of *The Heike Story*, was first performed. Some believe that at first only a fan was used to beat out a rhythmic accompaniment to the narration. Such fan rhythm (*ogi-byoshi*) is still used by street musicians in Japan (Plate 13). The truth is probably that both the biwa and the fan were used during the formative period. From the standpoint of music history, however, the development of the biwa accompaniment is more important.

The common biwa version of *The Heike Story* is organized into two hundred verses which are in turn divided up into phrases. Each of these phrases is assigned a stereotyped manner of singing, and between the phrases other standard melodies are played by the biwa. The choice of these melodies depends on the length of the phrase and upon its mood. In the thirteenth century there were thirteen of these patterns, but since then as many as twenty-three patterns have appeared. As a rule, the voice patterns and the biwa patterns are not played simultaneously. Though some of the same names are used to designate them, their music is quite different. The characteristic style of Heike-biwa is for the biwa to sound the beginning pitch, the voice to sing the phrase, and then the biwa to re-enter with either the pitch for the next phrase or some melodic pattern that reflects the mood of the text.

The influence of Buddhist chanting is most noticeable in the vocal style and in some of the terminology. In addition, the vocal line has long sections of narration set between

[4] The term *heikyoku* refers to all music dealing with *The Heike Story*. However, in this book it refers only to the biwa music, as the earlier forms are not discussed.

notes a fourth apart plus a few wavers of a second (Figure 12). These remind one greatly of Buddhist styling. There is an interesting tendency for the tonal center of longer patterns to move a fourth or fifth lower.[5]

Fu ri ni ke ru i wa no ta — e — ma — yo ri

FIGURE 12. A Heike-biwa vocal section from the "Shiori Kudoki"

Returning to the terminology of heikyoku, the close intertwining of influences between Buddhist music, noh music, and heikyoku can be seen in such terms as *ageuta, sageuta,* and *kudoki*, which appear in all three. It really was not until the advent of the shamisen that a new musical nomenclature was created along with new meanings for the old terms.

The patterns for the biwa are not particularly melodic. The Heike-biwa has a rather percussive sound, and its music is replete with fast arpeggios and drones. Perhaps the most interesting feature of its music is that the frets are not the same distance apart on all the instruments. The tuning of the four strings is usually G, B, D, and G, but if the frets are placed in different positions, the actual scales produced might vary considerably. Of course, since the tones are produced by stretching the strings behind the frets, one can compensate somewhat for these discrepancies. The frets of the Heike-biwa, however, are much lower than those of later biwa. Thus, the exact pitches of the biwa music are flexible. This is but another example of the fascinating lack of concern for specific tonal relations between parts which was noticed in Buddhist chanting and in the music of the noh flute. Experiments with this type of orientation were hardly known in the West until the twentieth century.

Heike-biwa music, while rather simple sounding, is internally highly organized. The tonal tendencies, tempo, mode, and meaning of each musical phrase is severely regulated. As these phrases are applied to specific texts they are subject to modifications, but the over-all organization is ever-present. To the modern ear Heike-biwa sounds rather dull, but to the ears of the audience for which it was originally written it had great novelty and power. One often reads in the history of Western music of the tremendous reaction audiences had to the first violin tremolos in opera or the first or-

[5] A convenient summary of the tonal tendencies of the major Heike-biwa patterns can be found in ref. 6, IX, 217. This article also shows many vocal melodies and a few of the biwa patterns.

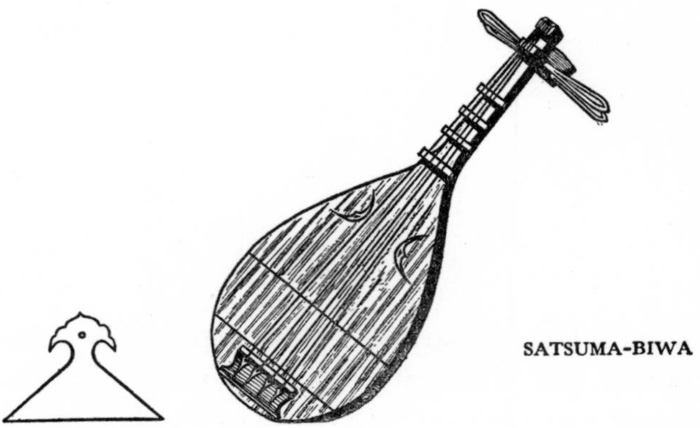

chestral crescendos at Mannheim. One need only take a similar historical perspective to realize what an important role Heike-biwa played in the development of Japanese narrative music.

The Satsuma-biwa is narrower than the Heike-biwa but has a much larger scroll (Plate 45). The ancient blind-priest Satsuma-biwa is said to have had three strings and six frets, but the most common Satsuma-biwa has four strings and four frets. These frets are very high. One of the characteristics of Satsuma-style frets is that there is a large gap between the first and second one. However, the most spectacular element of Satsuma-biwa is the plectrum which is a very wide, thin piece of wood (see Plate 45). This plectrum produces a resounding whack when hit against the body, an idiomatic sound in Satsuma style. The string can also be given a twist by a back stroke with the plectrum. This produces a very twangy sound without the usual precedent percussion. The finger technique of the left hand uses alternations of single fingers and two fingers together. The latter are used when several different pitches are produced from the same finger position by means of pressing down the string. A wide vibrato and a left-hand pizzicato are also common. The typical tunings for the Satsuma-biwa are shown in Figure 13, A and B. They differ with the various branches of the school. Tuning C is used by the Nishiki branch for their five-stringed, five-fretted biwa.

FIGURE 13. Biwa tunings

Musically, the Satsuma-biwa style is related to its Heike predecessor. Stereotyped melodies for both the voice and the instrument are used. The "edifying" Satsuma style created for the Shimazu clan is said to have been quite stately, but the style that developed through the support of the townspeople is more flashy. It is this latter style that prevails in the Satsuma-biwa of today. The influence of popular theatrical music is great. Though historically the modern Chikuzen-biwa is given credit for incorporating shamisen techniques into biwa music, these techniques can now be said to belong equally to both schools.

An important difference between the modern biwa schools and the Heike-biwa is that the voice and biwa parts are no longer always separated. While in present-day biwa music there are many sections of narration in which only the reciting tone is given with short biwa interludes as in the Heike, there are also many parts in which the voice and biwa are performing together. Because of this one often sees performances in which there are separate singers and biwa players.

Since the voice part is restricted to given patterns, the major development in the vocal line centers around the embroidering of these lines with turns and melismas (see Figure 14). Much like the old opera singers, these Satsuma (and Chikuzen) virtuosi delight in prolonging important phrases with special unwritten vocal peregrinations. As in opera, the passages where such opportunities exist are known by the fans, and well executed melismas are greeted by shouts of approval from the audience. One of the charms of modern biwa music is to observe the manner in which the audience and the performer work upon each other's enthusiasm.

The biwa accompaniment is also organized into specific patterns. These units, however, are often more melodic and extensive than those used in Heike-biwa. The Satsuma-biwa music is the most showy in this respect, and some of the patterns can produce quite a dramatic effect. A typical Satsuma example is *kuzure*, which is used during war scenes. This fast alternation between a low string and a very high note is the biwa equivalent of the violin tremolo or the sudden diminished chord in old-time movie thrillers.

The twentieth-century Kinshin branch of Satsuma-biwa has been the most bold in experimenting with new forms. On the whole, when straight shamisen styles have been imitated the results have not been very good. However, there has been some effective work done in borrowing the dramatic styles of more popular shamisen narrative musics like *Naniwa-bushi*. The music may not be very profound, but it is undeniable that when little sister has been lost by the river during a typhoon, the biwa can whip up one of the most effective storms in all Japanese dramatic music.

Another musical specialty of the Kinshin school is the singing of *shigin*, Chinese poems done in Japanese style. These poems were first created in the late Edo period and have no direct connection with the old Heian-court roei Chinese poems. The original shikin were sung unaccompanied or in concert with a shakuhachi. After the Meiji period, they were used to accompany a type of posturing sword dance called *tsurugi-mai*. This is said to have made them more rhythmical. Later they began to appear on biwa con-

CHIKUZEN-BIWA

certs and eventually the biwa was used for accompaniment. They were particularly popular during the days of the Russo-Japanese War.[6]

Biwa music in general is replete with heady melodrama, and contemporary Satsuma-biwa has made an honest attempt to capture the common audience without completely losing its more aristocratic origins. How well it has succeeded is a matter of personal opinion. Since there are still performers alive who represent all the major styles of Satsuma-biwa, one still has a choice for a while.

The Chikuzen-biwa in its classic form is the smallest of the existing biwa (Plate 46). It is said to be more directly related to the Indian form of lute. It also bears the closest resemblance to the old blind-priest biwa (compare with Plate 47). Two types of Chikuzen-biwa are common; one with four strings and five frets and another with five strings and five frets. Since modern Chikuzen music developed more directly out of shamisen music, the biwa itself is held sideways like a shamisen, unlike the upright position of the Satsuma school. Actually, the original biwa playing position was to sit cross-legged and place the biwa in a guitar position. The upright position developed in the Meiji period. The Chikuzen plectrum is unlike the usual biwa bachi. It is thick and blunt in the style of a Gidayu-bushi plectrum. However, in classic Chikuzen style, the percussive sound of the plectrum on the body of the biwa is not used as much as in the Satsuma school. One must keep adding the word "classic," as many contemporary Chikuzen players borrow both the instruments and plectrums of various Satsuma traditions. The fingering technique of Chikuzen-biwa is essentially the same as that already described. The standard Chikuzen tuning is shown in Figure 13, D. The tuning of the five-stringed biwa is the same as the five-stringed Satsuma instrument.

The music of Chikuzen-biwa incorporates features of the other biwa styles plus those of narrative shamisen music. The influence of the music for the puppet plays (Gidayu-bushi) is particularly strong. The Chikuzen-biwa is most effective in lyric sections. Its intimate tone lends itself more naturally to such music. While some of the most typical Satsuma music occurs during the biwa interludes, one finds in *nagashimono*, the music for biwa and voice together, a more representative Chikuzen music (Figure 14).

[6] Japan's first wide-screen movie was about Emperor Meiji and this war. Throughout the plot the emperor's emotions were expressed through the singing of shigin.

FIGURE 14. A Chikuzen-biwa nagashimono section

The individual melodies of Chikuzen-biwa are given picturesque names. Some are named after seasons, though their use in compositions does not always relate to the season in question. Other sets of melodies are simply numbered, for example, there are some fourteen *ban* (*ichi-ban*, *ni-ban*, *san-ban*, etc.), fifteen *go*, and twenty-five *cho*. In the notation they are marked only by number. Certain patterns are named after birds and animals also. Such a naming process is found in Satsuma-biwa and in Gidayu-bushi as well, though the specific names and their meanings may be different. The frets of the biwa are sometimes named after the elements (wood, fire, earth, metal, water). Perhaps this is a reflection of the biwa's Chinese origin.

The old ballad singer of the West belongs to the same tradition as Japan's biwa musicians. The *Illiad* and the *Odyssey* were preserved for centuries on the lips and lyres of Greek musicians. From the nordic *Kalevala* to the tales of Barbara Allen, it has been the singers who have kept the old tales alive and fresh. Such a tradition is fast dying under an irresistible barrage of celluloid dream worlds and radio tubes. This fate may be the inevitable price of scientific progress. Fortunately, in Japan the narrative tradition has risen far enough above the folk level to be able to take advantage of the advances of modern technology without being destroyed by them. Biwa music, though subject to new and very strong competition, is still an element in the over-all picture of Japan's musical life. Much of its storytelling function has been usurped by radio, television, and films, but it still retains that rare combination of music and drama that only narrative singing can offer. The setting and society may have changed, but the biwa bards of Japan continue to capture the imagination with tales of love and adventure.

Japan's drama-loving audience is large enough to support many different narrative forms. The temple fairs still exist in competition with the black markets, and biwa music can be heard over the radio. Perhaps few other countries have Japan's talent for knitting the old and the new into one multicolored tapestry.

CHAPTER

SIX

THE SHAKUHACHI

I. The History of the Shakuhachi

One of the easiest ways to approach the music of another culture is through its flute literature. There seems to be something in the tone of the flute which has a universal appeal. This catholic quality is amply illustrated by the example of the shakuhachi. Foreigners of the most diverse nationalities consistently point to shakuhachi music as one of the first forms of Japanese music for which they developed a liking. The plaintive tone of this simple vertical stalk of bamboo is one of the many romantic elements of a tourist's evening in Kyoto. Thus, the shakuhachi deserves a separate chapter by virtue of its popularity as well as its rather interesting history.

Like most Japanese instruments, the shakuhachi is of Chinese origin. However, there are some theorists who trace it all the way back to ancient Egypt. According to Dr. Tanabe Hisao (see ref. 16), its origin is found in the Egyptian *sabi* which, though much longer and thinner, had a similar mouthpiece. He further imagines that this instrument spread through the Iranian plateau and India via the Mohammedan Empire until it reached China and eventually Japan. Whatever may be the ancient origins of this instrument, it is the Chinese shakuhachi with which the Japanese model has the closest connection.

Actually, there are three distinct kinds of shakuhachi in Japan. The first is the gagaku shakuhachi (Plate 23). This is believed to have been brought over in the Nara period along with all the other gagaku instruments. While there are shakuhachi teachers mentioned among the court musicians, it does not appear that the instrument was used in the orchestra. Its soft tone made it more suitable for solo music.

This instrument may have evolved from the old Chinese pitch pipes. In ancient China, the proper tuning of the imperial music was of great importance to the maintenance of earthly and celestial unanimity. Every new emperor required a remeasurement of the pipes used to tune the court orchestra. A band of such pipes, called a *hsiao*, became part of the orchestra itself. In Plate 21 one musician can be seen industriously blowing on a Japanese version of this instrument. This type of panpipe was eventually disassembled, and each pipe was fitted with five holes so that melodies could be played upon it. This *t'ung-hsiao* (in Japanese, *dosho*) is said to be the origin of the Japanese

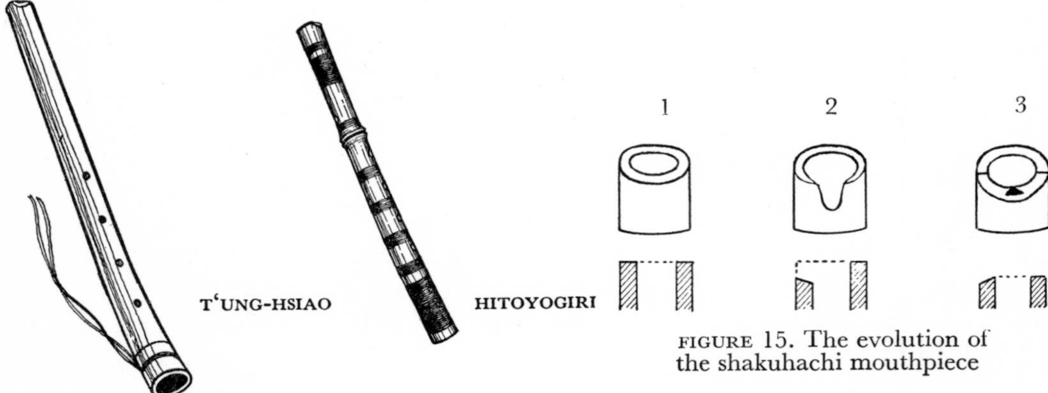

FIGURE 15. The evolution of the shakuhachi mouthpiece

shakuhachi. The term shakuhachi is believed to be a corruption of the Chinese measurement for one such instrument which in Japanese pronunciation is "*isshaku hassun*" (one *shaku* and eight *sun*, approximately twenty-two inches). The length of these early shakuhachi, however, varied considerably.

The major difference between the tubes of the panpipe as used together or separately and the structure of the early shakuhachi can be seen in Figure 15. The original pipe was merely blown across the top just as children do on a hollow reed or a bottle. When the pipes were used separately, a niche was cut in the edge and the end was covered by the lower lip of the player or was closed by a node in the bamboo (see Plate 50, the left-hand instrument). This type of mouthpiece can still be seen in modern Chinese vertical flutes, though they are longer and thinner than the ancient Chinese forms. The shakuhachi is unique in the manner in which its mouthpiece is constructed. It is cut obliquely outward, directly opposite to the Chinese manner (see Figure 15). This is believed to be a Japanese innovation. Much later, a small piece of ivory or bone was inserted so that the playing edge became finer and less susceptible to wear.[1] This insertion was called a *tsuno*. Its shape varies. Figure 15(3) shows its most common form.

The gagaku shakuhachi was still built after the Chinese model and produced the Chinese pentatonic scale (see Figure 2). It flourished during most of the Heian period and is mentioned often in the literature of the time. Afterward it died out and since then has never been revived with particular success.

One reason for its demise was the appearance in the Muromachi period of the second main type of Japanese shakuhachi, the *hitoyogiri* (Plate 50, second from the left). It is this instrument upon which is seen the new type of blowing edge. The inserted piece, however, was not added until the appearance of the modern shakuhachi. The hitoyogiri is similar to the modern shakuhachi in its arrangement of the finger holes. There are four on the top and one behind. The scales it was able to produce were Japanese folk scales. Being shorter than the modern shakuhachi, it sounded higher.

There are legends that the hitoyogiri also may have come from China or even southwest Asia. However, all that is known for certain is that during the Muromachi

[1] For a detailed account of how this is done see ref. 40.

period, beggar priests appeared playing this instrument. Part of the meager baggage that these beggars carried on their wanderings was a straw mat, which served as their bed. Therefore, they became known as rice-straw priests, *komoso*. These are the predecessors of the more famous *komuso* to whom we shall come presently.

The sweet, high tone of the hitoyogiri was pleasant but transitory. A majority of its music disappeared with the decline of the beggar-priest tradition, and by the nineteenth century the music was all but forgotten.[2] The narrowness of the instrument made its tone rather thin, and it could not compete with the more full-bodied tone of the modern shakuhachi. It was used occasionally as an addition to lighter shamisen music such as *kouta*, but twentieth-century attempts to revive it have been isolated, and it seems unlikely that the hitoyogiri will ever come into general use again.

The modern shakuhachi is the product of a very different age. There are legends that speak of a Heian origin or the importation of modern shakuhachi music from China via the Zen priest Chosan. However, significant shakuhachi music is a product of the Edo period. It is difficult to form an accurate picture of how this music evolved, as faking historical documents was a favorite pastime of Edo writers. One thing is certain: the main figure in the growth of this music was the *komuso*, a new kind of wandering priest (Plate 51). These basket-hatted men can still be seen on the streets of modern Japan. From behind their wicker visors, they have viewed the flow of Japanese life from the seventeenth century to the present. However, theirs was not always a passive interest in the daily affairs of the townspeople. It is believed that their name is a corruption of the word *komoso*, but their function in society was far different.

The ranks of the komuso were not drawn primarily from the seekers of Buddha's paradise. Rather, they were filled with *ronin*, masterless samurai who had lost their original rank and privileges during the violent clan struggles that marked the late sixteenth century. These men sought satisfaction more in earthly revenge than in heavenly rewards. It was from such ranks that many of the early Christians were drawn. When the Christian movement was halted by the slaughter of Shimabara (1638), many of these ronin felt their entire class would fall victim to the paranoid vengeance of the shogun government.

It is believed that one group of these desperate men formed a komuso group in Kyoto called the *Fukeshu*.[3] They secretly purchased a building which was associated with one of the larger Buddhist temples, in hopes that the shogun would not view their

[2] One hitoyogiri piece is recorded on Nippon Columbia LP–BL 5005.
[3] The following account is based on the incomplete research of the late Chikuzen Nakatsuka. A resumé of his work can be found in ref. 16, 224–28.

group as a Christian revival. This headquarters they named the Meian Temple. However, they were subjected to suspicion from other ancillary temples. In addition to their dislike of the ronin's unsavory background, these other temples probably felt an Edo-style fear of guilt by association.

In order to secure their position, the Fukeshu faked a number of papers claiming their historical origins as coming from China via the above-mentioned priest Chosan. They also produced a copy of a license from the first Edo shogun, Ieyasu, giving them the exclusive right to solicit alms by means of shakuhachi playing.[4] Armed with these documents, they finally notified the authorities of their existence and asked for official recognition of their temple and their rights. When the government received this request, they immediately demanded the original Ieyasu document. The Fukeshu claimed that it had been burned years earlier. It seemed certain that this group was destined to be short lived when one of the shogun's wiser advisers suggested that they be granted their request. His reasoning was that to destroy the group would be to scatter and further embitter already vengeful men. It would be wiser to grant them their much coveted security and preferment on condition that they act as spies for the government and keep track of the goings-on of all the other ronin. Such a proposition was made and accepted.

To facilitate the exchange of information as well as control of the organization, the komuso headquarters was moved to Tokyo, the seat of the shogun's government. Their "religious" headquarters was established in the Ichigatsu and Heiho temples outside Tokyo, while their "business" center was located in Asakusa, in the heart of the entertainment district. From there, they could fan out along the avenues and back alleys of this famous pleasure district, playing a few soft melodies and overhearing equally intimate conversations. Though the Meiji Restoration abolished this organization, one finds today that the wandering komuso of Tokyo still have many acquaintances on the police force. Whether one is dealing with the vendettas that fermented in the back streets of old Edo or the machinations that whirl through the modern Tokyo underworld, there is great need for "stool pigeons."

With the discussion of the so-called Fukeshu shakuhachi, we enter for the first time into the colorful life of old Edo (Tokyo). While shakuhachi music was not one of the great influential forms of music during the Edo period, the komuso who played it were a constant figure in the genre painting and novels of the times. We find in the tales of the komuso one of the myriad reflections of Edo life by which we vicariously savour the spice and danger of the period. For example, take the instrument itself. The

[4] An excerpt from this document can be read in ref. 4, II, 1027.

49. Shakuhachi performances are still frequent in Japan.

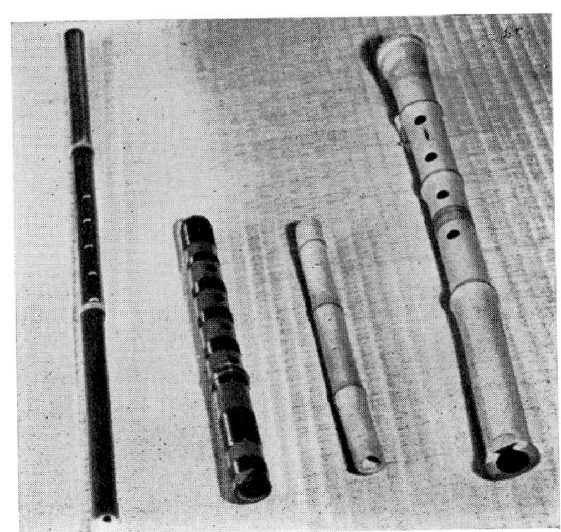

50. Four end-blown flutes: (from the left) dosho (or *t'ung-hsiao*), hitoyogiri, tempuku, and shakuhachi. The first three are predecessors of the shakuhachi. See page 152.

51. The komuso musician was originally a musical spy, his identity hidden in his basket hat. See pages 153–54.

SHAKUHACHI

hitoyogiri was a small, narrow bamboo tube with the playing edge taken from the root end of the tree. The shakuhachi, by contrast, was longer, much thicker, and used the trunk of the root end for the bell of the instrument. The explanation for this extreme change in design is found in the violence of the age. When these ex-samurai became wandering priests, they were denied the protection of their double swords. Therefore, they redesigned the shakuhachi so as to make it a formidable club as well as a musical instrument. This is perhaps the only instance in music history in which the practical necessity of self-defense was a major factor in instrument construction. Plate 75 shows several actors carrying shakuhachi in their sashes as part of the traditional costume of the *otokodate*, the "chivalrous commoners." The shakuhachi signify their refinement and also served, along with their swords, in their task of defending the weak.

The seventeenth and eighteenth centuries in Edo have a ribald quality that often reminds one of Boccaccio and fourteenth-century Europe. For example, there is a tale in an Edo-period jokebook (see ref. 4, II, 1026) concerning a gentleman-about-town by the name of Otori Ichibe. This man seems to have had no profession whatsoever and his only talent was an alacrity for telling "strange things to young people." He also had a flair for adventure and dangerous enterprises. On one occasion he got into an argument with a komuso while enjoying the hospitality of a local wineshop. In the heat of the debate Ichibe grabbed the komuso's shakuhachi and, his mouth being full of wine, played it with his most insulting orifice. In one of the greatest understatements in Japanese literature, the following sentence says that this is the first known instance of anyone of his class playing the shakuhachi.

Obviously, the shakuhachi music of this period was not very Buddhist. Popular theatre tunes and folk songs were more appropriate, and the pieces from that period reflect the more melancholy forms of such music. Although, legally, no one was allowed to play the shakuhachi without a license from the komuso headquarters, it gradually began to appear in the country and within the geisha quarters. The komuso costume, with its *tengai* basket hat, became a favorite device for anyone wishing to travel *incognito*. A variation of this hat is seen frequently in kabuki dramas, especially when the police inspector calls.

The original Kyoto komuso group became known as the Meian school of shakuhachi. The teachers of the Tokyo center called their school the Kinko. In the early Meiji period, a third main school appeared devoted to teaching the general populace. This was the Tozan school. As the two priest schools had lost their preferment in the Meiji reforms, they also turned to teaching pupils of all classes.

In the late Edo period, the shakuhachi had begun to be used as a secular solo instrument as well as in koto ensemble music (see *jiuta*). This precedent saved shakuhachi music from a sudden demise during those dark days of the early Meiji period when all Japanese music was considered uncivilized and worthless. As the mood of the times became more temperant, the schools of secular shakuhachi flourished. Even the Western-oriented university students found that playing the shakuhachi added an old-world charm to their terribly serious personalities. The use of the shakuhachi as shigin poetry accompaniment was mentioned in Chapter V.

As one of Japan's more Western-sounding instruments, it also was used extensively in the experiments of the new Japanese music movement in the 1920's and 30's. Perhaps the most famous and successful composition of this movement is the late Miyagi Michio's koto-shakuhachi duet, "Haru no Umi." This piece has been heard in every combination from violin and piano to the Philadelphia Symphony. For all its arrangements, it still sounds best in the original, as Miyagi made excellent use of the characteristic melodic style of the shakuhachi. Unfortunately, many composers are still obstinately trying to match the sound of the symphony by forming massed Japanese bands. The theory that ten shakuhachi sound ten times better than one is typical of the kind of traps into which much of modern Japanese music has fallen. To equate volume with quality is the worst kind of misconception of both Japanese and Western music. Fortunately, there is still a large segment of modern shakuhachi music which is devoted to solo or chamber-music literature. An occasional komuso can still be heard, but the real future of shakuhachi music is to be found now in the home and the intimate concert salon.

II. The Instrument and the Music

In the history section many details about the characteristic properties of the shakuhachi were given. Some of these features are: 1) the oblique blowing edge with its bone or ivory insertion in the center, 2) four holes on the top and one on the back, and 3) the bowed line of the instrument and slight tapering away from the bamboo root which forms the bell. The latter quality is not always found in natural bamboo so the shakuhachi makers many times must improve on nature and bend the wood until it has taken on a more traditional and aesthetically pleasing shape. The forte of many

Japanese artists has been their ability to subject nature to man-made laws of form without making the results seem artificial. Such an approbation can likewise be applied to the shakuhachi artisan.

Although the outside thickness of the instrument varies, the inside diameter is very carefully regulated by judicious cutting with special rasps and files. In the Meian-school shakuhachi one often finds that the ridge of the node in the bamboo is retained on the inside.[5] In most shakuhachi, however, it is removed. Looking down the barrel of a shakuhachi, one sees a skillfully rounded, lacquered tube with a deceptively simple line.

The length of the shakuhachi varies. The standard length is 54.5 centimeters. There are also seven- and nine-holed shakuhachi. There were two twentieth-century experiments which tried to combine the qualities of a flute with those of a shakuhachi. The first consisted of a horizontal shakuhachi. It really amounted to a bamboo bass flute, as the fingering and embouchure were, of necessity, different from that of a shakuhachi. The other experiment retained the all important shakuhachi mouthpiece but added a flute-like key system to the body so that Western chromatic scales could be played. This so-called Okura-aulos (it was invented by Okura Kishichiro) was unsuited for the traditional music and a new literature especially written for it never appeared. Nevertheless, it is an excellent example of the experimental spirit of the twentieth-century Japanese traditional musicians and their fervent desire to make some compromise with Western music. Like most of the Western experimental pieces of the 1920's, these works have fallen by the wayside. In the West, such music was a catharsis which cleared the way for the finer products of contemporary composition. One can only hope that a similar result will occur in Japan. So far, there have been few signs.

While the five holes of the standard shakuhachi produce the tones D, F, G, A, D, there are a host of other tones available by the process known as *meri-kari*. This is a system of combining half-holing (only partially covering the hole with the finger) with changes in embouchure in order to produce many different pitches from a single hole. Theoretically, there are three levels of highness (*kari*) and three of lowness (*meri*) for each fingering. These differences, however, do not represent Western half-step movements but more often very slight changes of a quarter tone or less. Such a technique was noted in the discussion of the noh flute. In shakuhachi music, however, it is exploited to a much greater degree. It is one of the characteristic qualities of the shakuhachi playing technique.

Another important refinement in shakuhachi music is the execution of the ending

[5] It is the Meian shakuhachi that has the differently shaped ivory insert also.

FIGURE 16. An example of shakuhachi music

of each breath phrase. In Figure 16 one can see that every such phrase has a final grace note. A correct performance of the proper grace note for each melodic situation is considered the mark of a true professional. Stylistically, this use of ending graces in contrast to the more common Western technique of precedent ones is another typical feature of shakuhachi music. The final techniques to be noticed in Figure 16 are the constant use of dynamic swells and the free rhythmic structure of the piece.[6] One of the main purposes of these swells is to allow the performer to display the different tone qualities available on the shakuhachi. From a whispering, reedy piano, the sound swells to a ringing metallic forte only to sink back into a cotton-wrapped softness, ending with an almost inaudible grace note, seemingly an afterthought. It

[6] This is basically a description of the Kinko-school shakuhachi style. The Meian-school phrases are shorter and more "breathy." However, the account given above concerns what is considered to be the typical playing style.

is a combination of all these musical idioms that produces feelings of vagueness and melancholy in the minds of many a listener.

One must not be misled into believing that the form of the music is equally as vague as the mood it evokes. While shakuhachi music is one of the freest in Japan, it still has discernible formal principles at work in every composition. The main distinction is that these principles have not been formalized into a written theory such as was seen in most of the Japanese music studied so far. In pure shakuhachi music, there is no explicit concept of dan sections or the application of the jo-ha-kyu theory, though a detailed analysis of many such pieces might reveal the existence of both. Such an exhaustive analysis has not yet been done, and the comments that follow concerning shakuhachi form are based on the study of only a fraction of the repertoire. Hence, they should be considered as general observations and not as definitive statements on the structure of shakuhachi music.

The music for the shakuhachi is divided into three main categories: 1) *honkyoku*, the original pieces, 2) *gaikyoku*, outside pieces, and 3) *shinkyoku*, new pieces. In the first category are found the basic pieces said to have been composed by the school founders and other early masters. Of course, the pieces vary with each school, but there are three compositions, "Kyorei," "Mukaiji," and "Kokureibo," which are considered as the classic foundations of all shakuhachi music. Legend claims that these pieces were brought from China with the first teachers and have been passed down through the komuso tradition. The melodic style and scale structure of the present-day versions, however, date from the Edo period.

The characteristic scale used in old shakuhachi pieces can be seen in Figure 16. This scale is known as the *in* scale. The *in* scale and the *yo* scale (see page 63) plus their permutations are the basis of most of Japanese art and folk music of the Edo period. The musician will notice that one characteristic of the *in* scale is the emphasis on a half-step upper neighbor (E flat) and a whole-step lower neighbor tone (C).[7]

Shakuhachi pieces vary in length from a few minutes to half an hour. In general, the music tends to follow a rondo-like form, that is, there is an alternation of one basic melodic idea with sections of new music. For instance, Figure 16 is the first section of

[7] A discussion of the many aspects of this scale and the *yo* scale as seen in Figure 4 would be interesting but unnecessary in this book. The music analyst will see for himself other features, while the nonmusician would not be in a position to appreciate the significance of a detailed explanation. However, I cannot resist footnoting one provocative idea that can be noted in both examples. Figure 16 is the first phrase of a composition whose final pitch is D. Figure 4 is a complete folk composition. In both cases, the music begins on A. Viewing the entire piece from which Figure 16 is taken, A seems to prevail throughout. It might prove very enlightening to forget the Japanese classic theory of *yo* and *in* scales and reanalyze Edo music on the basis of scales built on what is now considered to be the dominant pitch.

the piece "Hi-fu-mi Hachi Kaeshi." If we call this section A, the form of the entire composition could be represented by the scheme A-B-A-C-A.[8] The returns of the main theme are not exact. As in noh-flute music, the melody is subjected to constant variations of a highly subtle nature.

In addition to the rondo form, there is a tendency for shakuhachi pieces to begin in a low or medium register, build to a high climax, and then drop back to quieter music. These climaxes appear most often in the new-music sections of rondo-type pieces. It is in such sections that one finds the more angular melodic lines with many skips. These sections also tend to be longer than the returns to the main theme. The final statement of section A is usually quite fragmentary. One factor which adds to both the appearance of thematic germs and to the sense of wandering is the limited range of shakuhachi melodic styling. The various melodic germs do not have definite names as they do in biwa music and some of the other forms studied. Nevertheless, one becomes aware of very specific melodic types in shakuhachi music. Depending on how they are used and how familiar one is with the style, these tend to create a feeling of unity in the music or enhance the more common reaction to such music, the impression of aimless wandering. Perhaps the shakuhachi composers have done in music what the artisans have done in constructing the instrument. They have managed to give the illusion of a sound as natural as the wind blowing in the pines while covertly subjugating this sound to the artificial laws of music form.

The second category of shakuhachi music, *gaikyoku*, represents all music either borrowed from or played in concert with the shamisen or the koto. In the middle of the nineteenth century, many shakuhachi solos were based on famous shamisen pieces. It reminds one of the way in which early Western keyboard music often was derived from existing choral works. In both cases, a new form sought its base in an already established idiom and then gradually developed an independent style quite different from the original. In the case of the shakuhachi, the form of such pieces remained basically that of the original, and the only difference of note is in the instrumental styling.

The most common combination of the shakuhachi with the koto occurs in jiuta. This form, as it evolved as a koto genre, usually involved a koto, a shamisen, and one other instrument. Sometimes it was the bowed *kokyu* (see page 179). At other times it was

[8] This same form can be seen in the complete transcription in ref. 11, 18, 221. Figure 16 was transcribed by the author from a tape recording and is available only in native notation (see Appendix II, Figure 35). In both cases, the tonal center of the music continually fluctuates between tonic and dominant. Only in section C is there a modulation to dominant of dominant. Many more pieces must be analyzed before this tendency can be said to be idiomatic.

the shakuhachi. By the late nineteenth century, the shakuhachi became the most common addition. Its function in such music is to play a melismatic version of the basic koto line. The form of this music will be discussed in the koto chapter. Since the shakuhachi is subservient to the style of the original piece in music borrowed from the shamisen repertoire and acts only as a reinforcement of the main melody in koto music, neither of these gaikyoku forms can be considered to be a truly independent shakuhachi form.

The shinkyoku category covers all the pieces written since the "old days." When this period ends is a matter of school and clan. The form and style of these new pieces cover a wide range, including a great many Western-style experiments. Perhaps the most unfortunate of these are the massed shakuhachi bands mentioned earlier. It is really quite sad to hear the subtle beauties of the shakuhachi disappear in a gust of sound emanating from twenty or thirty instruments of varying intonations. Some new pieces attempt to use Western forms, but on the whole, they tend to keep to the traditional forms and scales and do not offer anything really original. Shakuhachi music has a pleasant static quality. Unfortunately, this same lack of movement seems to have enervated the contemporary composers of shakuhachi music.

There are a few old pieces which use shakuhachi ensembles. In some Buddhist temples, a small group of shakuhachi may be used to accompany the service. There are also shakuhachi pieces which are to be used as aids for Buddhist meditation. Edifying texts are printed along with the music notation. One of the loveliest ensemble forms of shakuhachi music, however, are the few classic duets. The best known is called "Shika no Tone," "the distant sound of the deer." It represents the mating calls between a buck and his doe. The two shakuhachi play divergent melodies which gradually become more alike until they are one. The symbolism may be somewhat crude, but the music is quite lovely. The titles of shakuhachi pieces are replete with such picturesque images that bespeak of romantic ideas and old customs. For instance, the title of the piece transcribed in Figure 16, "Hi-fu-mi Hachi Kaeshi," means "one, two, three, return the bowl." It refers to the journey of the beggar's bowl from his hands to the house-owner's and back to the beggar priest. For the largess contained therein, such music was performed by the ancient komoso and komuso shakuhachi players. In recent years, the remnants of this profession play much shorter pieces in return for a drink at back-street Tokyo bars.

Shakuhachi music today rests primarily in the hands of professional teachers and their secular pupils. There is only a scrap left of the religious traditions of shakuhachi music. Fortunately, most of the great works in the shakuhachi literature were created in a basically secular situation so that the finer products will survive as long as there are competent teachers and a sufficient number of amateurs to support them through lessons.

The shakuhachi is an introvertish instrument. With a modicum of materials, the player can reap a harvest of quiet pleasures. In a crowded and busy world, such simple means of refined musical recreation and tranquilization are to be coveted by any culture. Perhaps this is one of the most important secret appeals of the shakuhachi today.

CHAPTER SEVEN
KOTO MUSIC

I. Introduction

While much of the repertoire of the biwa and shakuhachi is a product of the Edo period, it is the music of the koto and the shamisen which represents best this very musical era. The shamisen belongs to the world of the theatre and all the turbulent excitement which the entertainment districts of Edo represent. The koto, by contrast, developed out of a court tradition and gradually entered the home as an accomplishment for the daughters of the rising commercial class as well as those of the nobility. The koto's harp-like tone added a gentler hue to the generally gaudy picture of Japan from the seventeenth through the nineteenth centuries. This gentility helped koto music survive during Japan's Westernization. It met the approval of Victorian taste and did not suffer from the unsavory past or un-Western sound of the shamisen. Since then, it has maintained a position in Japan somewhat analogous to that of the parlor piano in America. It is a sign of an attempt at good breeding in the home. For the upper- or middle-class Japanese girl, playing the koto is a valuable premarital asset.

Today, perhaps the most important function of the koto is as a bastion for the defense of an artistic Japanese home life. It stands together with the Western piano in the battle of homespun art against ready-made entertainments. In both East and West, the best one can hope for in this struggle is some kind of truce. At present, however, our concern is not with the battle but with the description of Japan's main defending champion, the koto.

II. The History of the Koto

Originally, the word *koto* was used generically for all kinds of stringed instruments so that even the biwa was known as a type of koto. The practical use of the word in Japan, however, refers to any one of the various horizontal plucked chordophones. In China, this type of instrument came in two basic forms, those with bridges and those without. It is this first form that became most popular in Japan.

Two members of the koto family have already been mentioned, the wagon and the gaku-so. The wagon had six strings which were tuned by means of six high bridges

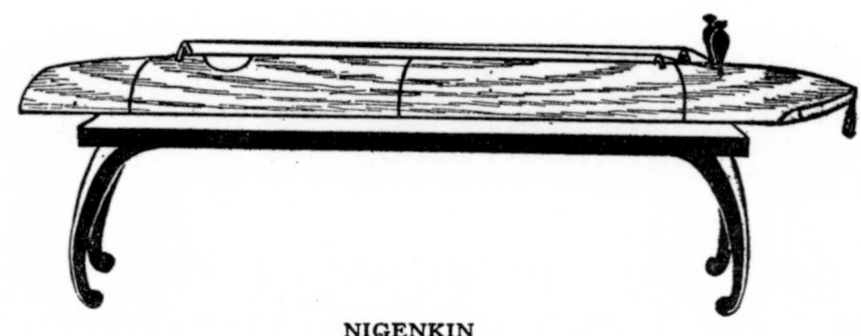

NIGENKIN

made of twig forks. The gaku-so was more closely modeled after the Chinese forms with twelve or thirteen strings and firmer bridges of ivory or wood.[1] The full-bodied tone of the court koto made it more suited for solo use.

Tradition claims that Fujiwara Sadatoshi first brought the solo koto music tradition of China to Japan in the ninth century. There is little chance of proving this musically, as all the solo koto literature of the Nara and Heian periods seems to have been passed on in the form of secret pieces. In the turbulent Kamakura days that followed, the music disappeared in the chaos of crumbling imperial power.

While we cannot view this music firsthand, we can receive many vicarious impressions of its beauty via the literature of the period. In *The Tale of Genji* alone, there are no less than fifteen different occasions when either the koto or the wagon are an important part of the story. For example, when Prince Genji is in exile in Akashi,[2] he consoles himself with the playing of his koto. He is joined by a retired courtier with whom he reminisces about the music and other pleasures of the court in Kyoto. True to the romantic theme of the book, the old man has a daughter who also plays the koto. However, it is not until Genji is about to return to the capital that he induces her to play for him. Upon parting, he leaves his own koto with her with the promise that he will be as constant as the middle string of the koto, which is always tuned the same. The prince left more than just his koto behind. Eventually, the lady of Akashi and the baby are brought to the environs of the capital. When Genji first rides out to see her, he hears the strains of his own koto being played in the same tuning as the one in which it was set upon his departure.

Finding beautiful ladies by means of their koto music seemed to be a favorite *deus ex machina* among many Japanese writers. In the biwa saga, *The Heike Story*, a trusted warrior is sent to find the emperor's recently lost paramour.[3] Her hiding place is unknown but her koto playing is so beautiful that the warrior has only to ride through the suspected district until he hears her play. The system worked and the girl, Kogo, is

[1] The best-known bridgeless koto in China is the ch'in. It is said to have been a favorite of Confucius. It was used sporadically in Japan. The only major Japanese developments along this line were the one- and two-stringed koto (*ichigenkin* and *nigenkin* or *yakumon*) which flourished in the late nineteenth century. Nothing matching the grandeur of the Chinese ch'in tradition, however, ever appeared in Japan.

[2] See Lady Murasaki, *The Tale of Genji*. op. cit., Vol. I, 255ff.

[3] See A. L. Sadler, *The Heike Monogatari*. Tokyo: Kimiwada Shoten, 1941, p. 265.

returned to the emperor. However, the story has a typical Heike-style ending. After a child is born of this union, the enemies of Kogo at court ambush her and commit the twenty-three-year-old beauty to a nunnery. Soon thereafter, the emperor died.

Many a courtier and warrior met a more violent death in the struggles that marked the end of the Heike dominance. Musically, it is the survivors of these blood baths that are of the most interest. From the twelfth century on, a steady stream of court women fled to the relative security of Kyushu. Though refugees, they still traveled with a baggage train proper for a person of their standing. Thus, we read that the remnants of solo koto music could be found in northern Kyushu long after it had disappeared from the capital.

This was not the first koto music to appear in the provinces. There is some reason to believe that popular Chinese koto music came directly to Kyushu much earlier. Unfortunately, only the legends concerning this importation have survived, and there is no music with which to test the hypothesis. The music brought by the refugees was believed to have been based on the style of imayo, roei, and saibara, the three main vocal genre of the court. Whatever may have been the basic source of this early Kyushu music, the present-day survivals stem from a sixteenth-century school known as Tsukushi, the name of a district in Kyushu. This so-called *Tsukushi-goto* was founded by the priest Kenjun. It is interesting to note that the traditional first piece of this school, "Fuki," is based on etenraku-imayo, one of the favorite court forms of music (see page 90). Kenjun is said to have composed ten pieces using a form known as *kumiuta*. This form consists of a group of short poems, usually with no topical connection, which are set to music and sung in a given order. The form originated in shamisen music, but it also is the starting point of popular koto music.

The music of the Tsukushi school stands on the border line between present-day popular koto music and the old court koto tradition. Unfortunately, this style never regained the protection of the court. It had to fare for itself among the priests and Confucians of Kyushu. The teachers kept an aristocratic aloofness from their environment. For example, the rules of the guild specified that Tsukushi-goto could not be taught to blind men, and even women were barred from playing this music for some time.[4] The latter prohibition seems strange since the distant origins of the music were brought to Kyushu by female minds and fingers. The irony of the edict, however, is the fact that the only remaining performers of Tsukushi-goto today are two women.

4 From our study of biwa and shakuhachi music we know that most blind musicians were merely beggars. Much as in the West, the social status of musicians in general remained extremely low until the twentieth century.

Out of the original repertoire of secret and "most secret" pieces, only a fraction is remembered. Today, this music is performed in a slow, languid style somewhat like that of the imayo from which it may have developed. However, it is difficult to tell how much the style has changed over the past three hundred years. As it stands, Tsukushi-goto music has an old-fashioned grace and leisurely pace which are pleasant but anachronistic. Fortunately for the music historian, the tape machine has saved this tradition from complete oblivion. A detailed analysis of this music and its history may give us a clue as to the style of those ancient koto pieces that drifted through the gardens of the Heian palaces. The court koto tradition escaped the ravages of war only to succumb to the inevitable death march of time. We can only be thankful that Tsukushi-goto managed to hold on so long. Perhaps the final irony of the situation is that one of the most efficient executioners of traditional music, the radio tube, should also become the final repository of its remains.

History is usually written with a polemic. Music history is no exception. The explanation of how popular (in Japanese, *zoku*, or "vulgar") koto music developed out of Tsukushi-goto is a good case in point. It is said that a student of Kenjun named Hosui went to Kyoto to perform. He played poorly and was not accepted at court, so he traveled on to Edo. There he met a blind shamisen player to whom he taught the basic songs of Tsukushi-goto. When the Kyushu headquarters learned that he had instructed a blind man, Hosui was expelled from the school. However, the damage was done. This blind musician took the name Yatsuhashi Kengyo.[5] He went to Kyoto and there began the Yatsuhashi school of popular koto music. The exact innovations of Yatsuhashi are uncertain. We know that he borrowed the original kumiuta of Tsukushi-goto and rearranged them to suit more popular tastes. Some claim that he knew the pieces only incompletely and was influenced by his shamisen background. One interesting change can be noted in the case of the above-mentioned piece "Fuki." The tuning for the Tsukushi piece is one of the old gagaku modes while that used for the same piece in the Yatsuhashi school is in the folk *in* scale (see page 160). One of the early names for these blind koto players was *insei*, which could be translated as "singing in the *in* scale." Perhaps the same historian who claimed that Hosui taught in Edo because he failed in Kyoto also chose the Chinese characters which appear in old texts for the word *insei*. These translate "a lewd voice."

It may be that Yatsuhashi composed no original pieces himself. Until 1957 there was even serious doubt as to whether Yatsuhashi-koto had ever really existed as a separate

[5] The term *kengyo* is a title bestowed on blind musicians of great talent. It is somewhat analogous to the Western term "maestro."

school. In that year an old Yatsuhashi teacher was discovered in Nagano, complete with music and a genealogy chart. The full significance of this discovery has not yet been ascertained. However, the fact that the early seventeenth century saw the flourishing of popular koto music is undeniable.

One of our best sources for information on koto, shakuhachi, or shamisen music of the early Edo period is the *Shichiku Shoshinshu* by Nakamura Sosan, printed in 1664. Among the pieces credited to the Yatsuhashi school in this book are such famous classics as "Rokudan," "Hachidan," and "Midare." There are some opinions that at least the first composition may have been of ancient Chinese origin. This theory is based partially on the fact that the same piece exists in the koto music of the Ryukyu Islands, but in a Chinese tuning.[6] There are also Ryukyu pieces called "Ichidan" and "Nidan." *Ichi* means one, *ni* means two, and *roku* means six. Therefore, there may have been a series of dan pieces before the creation of the surviving "Rokudan."

In addition to the flourishing of a new koto solo literature, the seventeenth century also saw the koto used as dance accompaniment and in special ensembles. It was not until the end of the century, however, that something truly new occurred in the field of koto music. At that time, a teacher named Ikuta Kengyo founded a new style of koto music based on existing shamisen forms, particularly jiuta. This term originally meant the shamisen music of Kyoto in contrast to that of Tokyo. It did not come to mean a special form until Ikuta used the term to designate his new-style koto music. His big innovation was to combine the koto with the shamisen and to develop a music that emphasized the instrumental part more than the vocal. Up until his time, the koto had been primarily a vocal accompanying instrument. The jiuta ensemble was called *sankyoku*, or "music for three" because a third instrument was usually added (see Plate 52). It was either the kokyu or the shakuhachi. By the end of the Edo period, the shakuhachi had taken precedence. Greater detail about jiuta will appear in Part IV of this chapter. Suffice to say for now that the basic element of jiuta is an alternation of vocal sections with instrumental interludes.

At the end of the eighteenth century another koto teacher turned to shamisen music for the raw materials of a new style. Yamada Kengyo borrowed the style of various Edo narrative shamisen forms (Itchu-bushi, Kato-bushi, etc.). Under the influence of such music, the Yamada school developed a style in which the voice line was more important. The main distinction between the Ikuta and Yamada schools is still explained in terms of their respective instrumental and vocal orientations. At present,

[6] The Ryukyu Islands koto school is also called Yatsuhashi, but as yet, no historical connection has been established between this school and the Japanese group by the same name.

there is a basic repertoire of standard pieces which are considered their common heritage. The new compositions in both schools tend to be more instrumental. It is primarily in the products of the nineteenth century that this vocal-instrumental distinction is most noticeable.

In the early nineteenth century, Yaezaki Kengyo of Kyoto further developed Ikuta jiuta by the addition of a second koto, which played a melody independent from that of the main koto. This compositional technique, called *danawase*, will be explained in Part IV. The style was known as *kyomono* because it came from Kyoto. It became a basic technique of the Ikuta school. Although both schools spread out over the country, the Ikuta school is generally considered to be a Kansai-district phenomenon while Yamada koto is said to be a product of the Kanto district. In the twentieth century, these regional distinctions have lost much of their significance. However, the stately geisha dance form of Kyoto known as *kyomai* is still accompanied with the Ikuta jiuta trio (Plate 52).

In the twentieth century, koto music has been the most successful of all hogaku forms in its attempts to build a new style of music based on Western ideas. The man most noted in this field is the late Miyagi Michio. His untimely death in 1957 (a blind man, he fell from a speeding train) ended a truly brilliant career. Miyagi was one of the few creative artists able to provide compositional backing for the credos of the pamphleteers who clamored for a new Japanese music. From the mass of Japanese compositions created in the last fifty years, only a few works of Miyagi and his Yamada-school counterpart, Nakanoshima Kinichi, have survived. They proved that new hogaku could sound as well as Debussy. Miyagi's death marks the end of that era. It is now time for someone to approach Japanese music from the standpoint of the age of Bartok.

III. Japanese Music Teaching

Piggott in his book on Japanese music (ref. 9) describes a typical koto lesson at the turn of the century. What he said concerning koto teaching methods probably applied to other instruments as well. The account of the contemporary system given below is also applicable in principle to the other popular forms of Japanese music. A comparison of the two descriptions may point out some of the constants and variables in the music-teaching tradition of Japan.

A teacher's home is usually his or her studio. Here, on certain days of the week and for a specified number of hours, he is available for lessons. The problems of lesson scheduling do not bother the Japanese traditional teacher. In Japan, it is a matter of first come, first serve. This has an advantage in that you are never late for a lesson. It also means that to complete your day's lesson it may take twenty minutes or three hours. It all depends on how many students are waiting ahead of you. Usually, the students wait in an adjoining room where they may talk or follow the course of the piece in progress. In winter, a knot of pupils can be found huddled around a table which is set over a sunken charcoal pit. One can idle away pleasant hours in quiet conversation waiting for a lesson while dangling one's toes in such a pit (shoes are not worn in a Japanese house).

The lesson itself consists of a twenty-minute playing of the particular composition under study that week. Usually the teacher plays also. There are some students who do not read readily the notation and learn the entire piece by imitating the teacher. To assist in this rote teaching method, a special solfège, which the teacher sings as he plays, is used if there is no special vocal part in the piece. The order in which one learns the repertoire of a particular school is set. It is very difficult to learn a piece out of order and impossible (openly) to learn a composition belonging to another school. Before the extensive use of printed notation, one had to pay a special fee to learn certain pieces. Today, this system has deteriorated, though certain compositions are still considered as sacrosanct. There is something to be said for the refusal to let a student learn a certain piece before he is qualified to play it. However, the special fee system in Japanese teaching became more of a means of increasing the teacher's income than of protecting the purity of the school. Average teachers today receive three dollars a month for giving two twenty-minute lessons a week. Therefore, one cannot blame them for trying to augment their incomes.

Though the business of paying for special pieces is less popular than in Piggott's time, there is still a good market in bestowing professional names (*natori*). After one has completed a certain number of compositions, one is allowed to apply for a professional name. The difficulties involved vary with the school and the type of music being studied. One factor is constant, it costs money. In certain professions all newcomers must pay the head of the entire school in addition to their own teacher in order to acquire a professional name. In most schools, one must also be able to play, and rigid performance tests are administered before one is granted the privilege of buying a name. However, there are a few less reputable groups who specialize in bestowing professional names to young ladies anxious to have such diplomas as assets in the matrimonial market.

The choice of a professional name is also regulated. One takes the school name, for example, Yamada or Ikuta, and then creates a title which includes part of the teacher's name. The custom is quaint but it makes for much confusion when meeting a group of professionals from one school.[7]

While the teaching method is uninspired by Western standards, the student recital life is laudable. Every teacher has a full-scale recital at least twice a year. These are endurance contests for both the audience and the teacher. It is not unusual for the teacher to appear in every number from the concert's beginning at eleven in the morning until the finale around eight o'clock in the evening. The audience is not expected to show an equal amount of tenacity. One comes and goes freely with ample time off to enjoy the presents received. Japan is one of the rare places in the world where the audience is given a gift for coming. Bean cakes and candy are the usual fare, though coin purses, key chains, and even sake wine are not unknown. The secret to the finances of these programs is that every student pays to perform. In koto recitals this may cost each student approximately ten dollars a composition. In Japanese dance recitals, the bill is more often fifty to eighty dollars. For this reason, student recitals seldom have many solo numbers.

An important element in the Japanese teaching system is the formation of an in-group. While the lessons may be mechanical and somewhat impersonal (though not unfriendly), the weekly waiting for lessons with a group of one's peers develops a sense of companionship between the students. The fact that one is not allowed to study outside the school reinforces this sense of belonging. Student-teacher parties and outings are common. The fortunes and misfortunes of each individual are theoretically the concern of the entire group. The relations between the myriad branches of the same school are tenuous, but within the closed group there is an interrelationship not unlike that found in a good church social club in the West. Like church youth groups, there are parties and games for the children. The adult students, however, usually enjoy a more robust evening than would be tolerated by most churches.

As a social unit the hogaku teacher and his students form a strong link with the customs of the feudal past. As a teaching method, hogaku instruction seems unnecessarily tedious. The rote method, as used in Japan, is constantly in danger of producing musical automatons.[8] It is only the most inspired teacher who can surmount the endemic difficulties presented by traditional teaching techniques. This system originated

[7] On one occasion, I met a number of drummers who were named respectively, Tanaka Sadenji, Tanaka Sakiji, Tanaka Sataji, Tanaka Sashichiro, and Tanaka Satojuro.

[8] In learning the noh flute, my teacher would illustrate each note of the melody on the edge of his closed fan. When all the notes had been learned in order, the rhythm was added. The entire melody was never played beforehand so that one did not have any idea of the over-all sound of the piece. This is an extreme but not atypical case of Japanese rote teaching methods.

52. Jiuta music is sometimes used as dance accompaniment. The basic jiuta ensemble of koto, shamisen, and shakuhachi can be seen in this picture. See page 170.

56. An early print showing types of Edo-period street musicians: monzen-kokyu players, above, and a yotsu-dake castanet player. See page 179, also Plate 13.

KOTO

in a period when notation was almost unknown and many of the students were apprentices who had committed their lives to the learning of the repertoire. Today, such pupils are rare. Young would-be professionals attend the hogaku department of the University of Fine Arts in Tokyo. The modern teachers must depend on amateur students who only have a limited time to spend on committing long traditional pieces to memory. Notation was developed to meet this new situation. Even with that, one is constantly amazed at the Japanese amateur's ability to retain a vast number of pieces. However, the teaching method is still in great need of repair. While it is a tacit tradition of private teachers all over the world not to give out information too fast, there has been considerable growth in the West of the concept of creative teaching. Teaching methods and music are often very intimately connected. It remains to be seen if creativity can be injected into Japanese music teaching without destroying some phase of the music or the social structure, which is such an important ancillary to the system.

IV. The Instrument and Its Music

There is a legend that the shape of the koto originated from that of a crouching dragon. If true, the dragon must have had a very pleasant demeanor to inspire the creation of such a lovely sounding and physically attractive instrument. The modern koto has thirteen silk strings and a body made from two pieces of paulownia wood. One piece of this wood is hollowed out to form a sound box. The other piece is used as a plank to cover the bottom. There are two sound holes in the ends of this plank which also make it possible to restring the instrument easily. The average Yamada koto is six feet in length. The Ikuta koto is longer and narrower. A seventeen-string koto of proportionately larger dimensions has been in frequent use since the 1930's. It was invented by Miyagi Michio for use in his new compositions.

Two factors are important in the construction of a good koto. One is the manner in which the wood is cut from the tree. An excellent instrument will always show sharp parabolic designs on the surface created by the rings of the tree. The other factor is less evident. In the inside of the koto, special patterns called *ayasugi* are carved in order to improve the tone.

It was said that a distinctive feature of the Japanese koto is its use of moveable bridges (*ji*). In addition to wood and ivory, they are sometimes made of plastic. By adjusting these bridges, any thirteen-note scale can be produced. In practice, the number is limited. The gagaku koto uses six tunings. Tsukushi-goto borrowed one tuning from gagaku and added another in the Edo period based on folk scales. The popular koto schools developed a host of different tunings. Some became standard while others were used only for certain compositions.[9] The two most common tunings, *hira-joshi* and *kumoi-joshi*, are shown in Figure 17. Notice that they are in the *yo-in*-scale system. The court koto and the early Tsukushi-goto kept to the *ryo-ritsu*-scale tradition of gagaku.

FIGURE 17. Koto tunings

Besides the notes available through the adjustment of the bridges, there are also pitches that can be produced by pushing down on the strings with the left hand. Such a movement stretches the strings so as to produce whole or half steps as needed. This technique is typical of popular koto styling. There are many other special techniques available. Normally, the strings are plucked with ivory picks (*tsume*) attached to three fingers of the right hand (Plate 54). The shape of these picks varies. The Ikuta picks are square and the Yamada picks are parabolic. Because of this, the Ikuta performer sits at an oblique angle to the instrument, while the Yamada musician sits at a right angle.

There are many varieties of upstrokes, glissandos, and tremolos which greatly extend the tonal range of the koto, In addition, the strings may be played with the bare fingers of the left hand. In modern works harmonics are used much as they are in Western harp music. A more unique playing method is the twisting of the string with the left hand. This produces an extremely subtle change in the pitch and tone of the string. Another interesting method of playing is a sweep down the length of one string with

[9] For a list of koto tunings see ref. 1, 382.

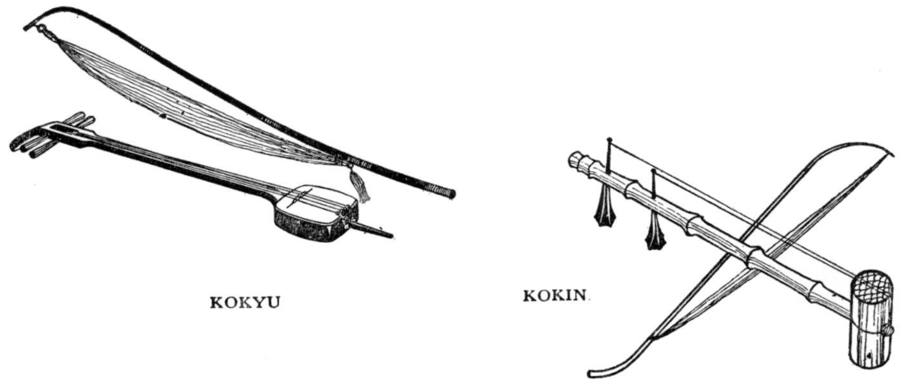

KOKYU

KOKIN

two fingers. This produces a strange swish. In recent years, many other techniques have been added to the playing of the koto. The devices mentioned above, however, are considered the basic koto techniques.

Before passing on to the music itself, one should make note of the other instrument used in koto ensembles. The kokyu (Plate 55) deserves mention by virtue of the fact that it is Japan's only bowed instrument. Varying in size, the average length of the kokyu is sixty-nine centimeters. It has been used with two, three, and four strings. In the case of the four-string kokyu, the top two strings are in unison. The normal tuning for the kokyu is in two fourths (*san-sagari*), though there are rare pieces using a tuning of a fifth and a fourth (*ni-agari*). The common shamisen *hon-choshi* (a fourth and a fifth) is not used. The three-string kokyu, originally a Chinese instrument, appeared in Edo around 1720. The creation of the four-string kokyu is credited to Fujiue Kengyo, later in the eighteenth century. He is also said to have made the bow longer.

Besides its use in the koto trios, the kokyu was popular as a dance accompanying instrument. In prints of the Edo period one can see an ensemble of several shamisen and one kokyu accompanying a veritable chorus line of dancing girls who are performing for the delectation of a group of affluent customers. In addition to its use in these Edo-style night clubs, the kokyu found a place among the off-stage instruments of the theatre. It is still in common use in the puppet plays (bunraku), especially during sad scenes. Finally, the kokyu should be mentioned as another instrumental accoutrement of the wandering street musicians (Plate 56) and village beggar priests (*yamabushi*). Shamisen, kokyu, and drum trios can be seen walking through the pleasure districts of Tokyo. Lately, the saxophone has tended to usurp the kokyu's position in these trios.

When well played, the kokyu sounds similar to the violin, though it has a smaller dynamic range. As can be seen in Plate 55, the bow is quite loose. When playing, the hairs are pulled tight by grasping them with the ring and little finger of the right hand. The bow is held in the manner of a pair of chopsticks. Another interesting aspect of the kokyu is its very high, arched bridge (*koma*). Because of this arch, one must turn the instrument in order to play on different strings. To facilitate this, the instrument is set on a peg which is placed between the knees. It is quite fascinating to watch an expert kokyu player spin his instrument back and forth as he performs.

The kokyu is played with a wide vibrato. This type of string tone is found all over the orient and produces one of the distinctive tonal elements by which we identify oriental bowed instruments. With the introduction of the Western violin, the kokyu lost its popularity. Today, its solo literature is all but forgotten and its use in koto ensembles is rare. Outside the theatre sound-effects room, there seems to be no place in modern Japanese life where the kokyu can find patronage. Perhaps it will fall victim to the same fate alotted to many old Japanese biwa and become an unplayed wall decoration in modish Western homes.

The shamisen used by the Yamada school in its koto ensembles is the standard nagauta shamisen (Plate 73). The Ikuta school, however, uses a slightly larger instrument. The plectrum also is quite different. It has a very thin edge. When this is combined with a heavier bridge, the tone produced is much softer than that of the normal shamisen. This tone is felt to blend more easily with that of the koto. In theory, it should be simple to distinguish between the Yamada and Ikuta koto trio performances because of this difference in shamisen. In modern practice, there is often much borrowing of plectrums, bridges, and instruments so that such distinctions should not be taken doctrinarily.[10]

Now that all the instruments have been discussed it is possible to investigate the music itself. The generic term for koto music is *sokyoku*. This music can be divided into two types, that with singing and that with none. The oldest type of vocal koto music, kumiuta, has already been mentioned. In the early Tsukushi-goto kumiuta each set consisted of several poems. The singing of each poem is considered a *dan*, or "step." This term is the keystone to any discussion of koto music form. The Tsukushi-goto dan were sixty-four beats long. The Yatsuhashi kumiuta used a similar form except that each dan was one hundred and twenty beats long. It is interesting to note that each poem was sung in four phrases, a method common with the performance of court imayo. Kumiuta composed after the middle of the eighteenth century tend to have shorter dan.

The main type of instrumental koto music is *shirabemono*. Under this term fall all the strictly instrumental pieces. The piece "Rokudan" is a classic example of this form. Such music is usually composed along the same lines as that of the noh-flute pieces discussed earlier. That is, a basic theme is presented and with each successive dan it

[10] When a Yamada ensemble is playing an Ikuta instrumental interlude, the shamisen will often use a specially wide bridge called a *daibiro*, which is meant to produce a sound similar to that of the Ikuta shamisen.

is subjected to variation while new material is interpolated between the phrases of the original theme. The main difference between this technique as used by the noh-flute and the koto is a matter of degree. The koto pieces are much longer. The interpolated sections are more extensive and often interrelated. Sometimes they act as substitutes for original phrases. Thanks to Sir Francis Piggott,[11] the West became aware of this compositional technique very early in the twentieth century. However, it is only one method of organization among a variety of techniques found in Japanese music.

The most important form of koto composition is the *jiuta*. It is a hybrid form, combining the techniques of both kumiuta and shirabemono. This music is sometimes called *tegotomono*, because its important contribution to koto music is the use of *tegoto*, instrumental interludes. Its innovation is the addition and extension of the instrumental transitions occurring between the songs of kumiuta-style pieces. In its simplest form, it consists of three parts; a fore song (*maeuta*), an instrumental interlude (*tegoto*), and an after song (*atouta*). As this form evolved, it became longer. Thus, one can find pieces which consist of an instrumental introduction, a song, an interlude, a song, and an instrumental close. Obviously, one could go on indefinitely splitting songs and interludes into further songs and interludes. Normally, such music does not extend beyond a six-part form: introduction-song-tegoto-song-tegoto-song. As a rule, there is no thematic connection between the various interludes.

The normal contemporary jiuta ensemble consists of a koto, shamisen, and shakuhachi (Plate 52). In jiuta nomenclature, the shamisen is called the *sangen*, an older term for the same instrument. In such an ensemble the koto plays the main melody, while the shamisen and shakuhachi follow the general contour of this melody, adding small variations as they go. The shakuhachi is the most melismatic of the group, but even its simultaneous variations (heterophony) are rather simple. The Japanese say that the koto is the bone, the shamisen the flesh, and the shakuhachi the skin of a jiuta composition. The analogy is picturesque but not quite appropriate, as the affinity of the instrumental parts is closer than that of the anatomical ones.

The basic ensemble can be expanded. If a second koto is added, it may be used to further embellish the melody, especially during the instrumental interludes. During the song sections the accompaniment is more subservient to the vocal line. The most unique technique involving two koto occurs in the instrumental interludes when *danawase* or *dangaeshi* are used. Danawase refers to the compositional process in which the basic koto (the *honte*) plays the original melody while the second koto (the *kaede*) plays

11 For Piggott's transcription and analysis of "Rokudan" see ref. 9, pages 94–95. This analysis was the first of its kind in Japanese music.

a completely independent melody. Obviously, this is possible only with songs in the same tuning. Sometimes the superimposed song must be altered in order to fit. Nevertheless, in the technique of danawase we see once more the common Japanese tendency to use the same melodic material in more than one composition.

Borrowing melodies is common in Western music also, but, except for the Renaissance quodlibets and early polyphony, one seldom finds the simultaneous use of unrelated tunes. However, the real difference between the Eastern and the Western techniques is not so much the frequency of use as the manner in which it is applied. The rules of Western counterpoint tie the disparate melodies together into a single polyphonic unit. The use of danawase in koto music, by contrast, produces more the effect of a free obligato. This is due, in part, to the fact that the tunings of the koto-form chords are reminiscent of those used by the French impressionists. Therefore, when two koto are playing different melodies within such an unchanging harmonic structure, the effect to the Western ear is that of two arpeggios being played on one chord.

It is almost impossible not to play a melody on the koto. By merely improvising on the strings in some rhythmic frame, one can produce something that would pass for a tune, albeit a wandering one. Perhaps this is one reason why the koto was particularly successful during the early years of experimentation with Westernized Japanese music. It had a ready-made harmonic frame which was familiar to the West and thus, a priori, was able to produce melodies pleasing to Western tastes. In the early days, this was a godsend but later it proved to be a stumbling block.

Modern koto composers are still loath to face the problem of modulation. Tunings are changed within many koto compositions, but the basic enervating quality of the static harmonic field in which koto music is set has never really been challenged.[12] The problem is peculiar to the koto because only the koto has such a harmonic tendency inherent in its musical style. The day koto composers decide to break out of their self-imposed trap, we may hope to see a truly new and exciting form of koto music.

The technique of dangaeshi differs from danawase in that material from the original melody is superimposed upon itself. This is possible because of the sectional (dan)

[12] Of course, there have been attempts to use new scale structures. The Western major scale became *oranda-joshi* in honor of the Hollanders who introduced it. There was also the use of the Chinese pentatonic, which was called *kankan-joshi*. This name came from the title of a piece played by the lovers of Ming Chinese music (*Minshin-gaku*) during the late nineteenth century. These innovations, however, did not attack the basic problem of static tonality. Large koto orchestras have been used, but as yet few have experimented with the use of several koto in different tunings, preferably nontraditional ones. There are still great untapped resources in koto music. It will take someone with a thorough knowledge of both contemporary Western music and traditional Japanese music to break through the mental block that presently surrounds koto composition. The recent compositions of Mamiya Michio may show the way to such a new koto movement.

organization of koto music. One may take the second dan of an instrumental part and perform it simultaneously with the exposition of the first dan. To a certain degree, this is "paper music," for it is impossible to recognize a variation on a theme before you have heard the theme. However, dangaeshi represents one of the most Western-like forms of Japanese traditional composition.

Though the shamisen normally follows meekly after the koto melody, there are times when it has an independent part. Sometimes two shamisen are used in which case one may play an ostinato or drone. Though both the Yamada and Ikuta schools grew out of a shamisen tradition, it is still the koto that is the center of any jiuta ensemble.

In contemporary performances any one of the above-mentioned techniques may be heard. For example, the famous koto piece "Chidori" is set in a four-part jiuta form (introduction-song-interlude-song). However, it can be heard as a solo piece, a koto duet, or with one of the other ensembles mentioned above. The music of the koto is always open to rearrangement. "Rokudan," though officially a shirabemono, can be heard with a jiuta ensemble. Actually, the term jiuta represents today more a manner of performance than a group of specific compositions.

Several random comments on contemporary koto music have already been made. There have been koto concertos with Western orchestra and others with special Japanese ensembles for accompaniment. The invention of the seventeen-string bass koto has proved very useful in the forming of new koto ensembles. I have already stated my admiration for the spirit behind contemporary koto composition and my prejudice against most of the results. I would need to write a very technical and specialized book to do justice to the accomplishments of these pioneers in new Japanese music as well as to point out in detail what I consider to be their errors. In this book the comments of the past few pages must suffice. In the rather static world of traditional Japanese music, the koto composers stand out among the most forward-looking musicians.

The skin, meat, and bones of koto music are not instruments, they are principles. The Japanese composers must learn to distinguish between a superficial understanding of both Japanese and Western music and the fundamental laws which control the articulation of their musical musculature. The epidermis of music can produce only sensations and titillations. A musician must draw from the very marrow of music in order to produce significant composition. Koto music has a great tradition behind it. Let us hope it has a brilliant future as well.

CHAPTER
EIGHT

THE SHAMISEN AND ITS MUSIC

I. The Instrument and Its Background

Of all the traditional instruments of Japan, the shamisen undoubtedly has the greatest variety of uses. It is the backbone of kabuki music, a vital ingredient in every party, a social grace in many homes, and the vehicle for a host of folk musics. The shamisen repertoire of art music is one of the great cultural legacies of the Edo period. At the same time, the shamisen's sharp but slightly wistful tone still pervades the atmosphere of modern Japanese life.

Tradition claims that the shamisen was first introduced into Japan around 1562 at the port of Sakai near Osaka. The particular instrument that appeared at that time was the *jamisen* of the Ryukyu Islands (Plate 70). Like its Chinese ancestor, the *san-hsien*, the jamisen had three strings, a small wooden bridge, a snakeskin covering, and was played with a pick somewhat in the same manner as a banjo is strummed. This instrument was considered primarily a musical novelty toy until it passed into the hands of some biwa players. These men found that playing the instrument with their biwa plectrums greatly improved the tone. They also discovered, however, that the snakeskin would not hold up under the blows of this larger plectrum, so they cast about for a more suitable covering. When catskin was tried they found not only a more durable material but also one capable of a completely new world of sound. This new instrument (by then called the *samisen*) underwent a whole series of further changes until it finally evolved into what is known in modern vernacular Japanese the *shamisen*.

Plate 73 shows the most common forms of shamisen used today, that is, the instrument used for nagauta music and that used for Gidayu-bushi. As there are many different styles of shamisen music, there are also many variations in shamisen construction. These individual variations will be mentioned as specific types of music are discussed. Certain features, however, are basic to all shamisen.

The body of the shamisen is made of four pieces of wood, preferably red sandalwood, mulberry, or Chinese quince. Concert models are carved inside with a herringbone pattern known as *ayasugi*, which is said to improve the tone greatly. The body iscovered on the top and bottom with catskin or, in cheaper models, dogskin. To protect the top skin from the blows of the plectrum, a small half-moon of skin (*bachigawa*) is

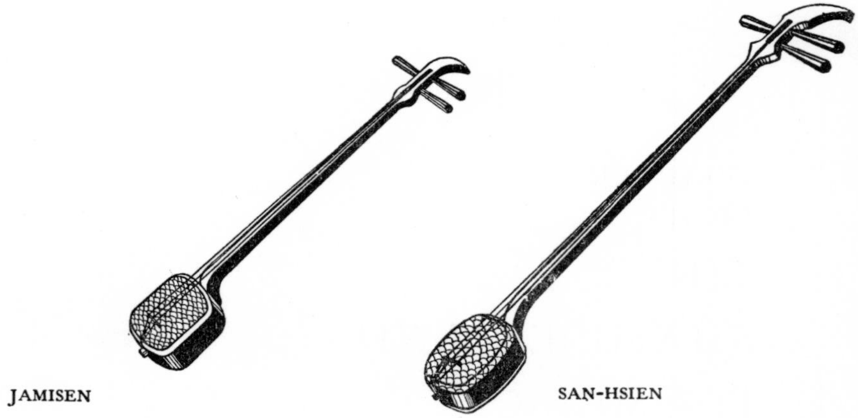

JAMISEN SAN-HSIEN

added at the top and center. The long neck of the shamisen is made of three pieces of wood which can be disjointed for convenience in carrying. The thickness of this neck, varies with the type of music performed as does the gauge of the three twisted silk strings used on the shamisen. Nylon strings are also being used now. The strings are attached to a rope tailpiece (*neo*) at the lower end and to three large pegs (*itomaki*) above. These pegs are made of ivory or wood.

Because of the sensitivity of the skin, the shape, weight, material, and placement of the bridge (*koma*) are very important to the tone of the shamisen. The most common bridge is made of ivory, though plastic and wood are also used. The plectrum (*bachi*) also varies in size and shape. Plate 73 shows three of them. From the left they are the jiuta plectrum, the nagauta one, and finally one for Gidayu-bushi. The concert plectrum is made of ivory, while the practice models are made of wood. These wooden plectrums are ingeniously constructed of three different kinds of wood so that the rear and center portions have greater weight for balance while the striking edge has resiliency for tone.

The tone is the most unique aspect of the shamisen. In addition to its sweet-sour resonance it has a drum-like snap and, in the lower register, a twangy hum somewhat like that of a jew's-harp. The drum effect is caused by the snap of the plectrum as it hits both the string and the tight catskin at the same time. The reverberation (*sawari*) is created by a small cavity and an extra metal bridge at the top of the neck. The lower string does not rest upon this bridge, while the other two strings do. This causes the lower string to vibrate against this cavity, while the other strings, being raised, pass over it. The sound created by this novel device is actually an attempt to imitate the much stronger reverberation of the biwa strings, for the biwa was the original instrument of the first experimenters with the shamisen.

There are a dozen little accessories for the shamisen, but the only one that need be mentioned here is the *yubikake*, or the "finger hanger." This is a small knit device that is put between the thumb and first finger of the left hand in order to make it easier to slide the hand up and down the back of the neck. Modern civilization has infringed

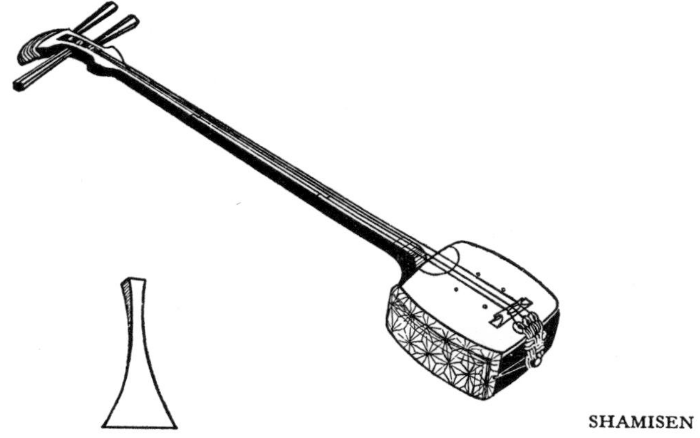

SHAMISEN

upon this traditional piece of equipment, and yubikake may now be bought in various shades to match milady's kimono. There is even a nylon "stretch" variety.

There are three basic tunings for the shamisen shown in Figure 18. The first is *hon-choshi*, or "original tuning," which consists of a perfect fourth and a perfect fifth. The second is *ni-agari*, or "raise the second," which is a fifth and a fourth, and the last is *san-sagari*, or "lower the third," which is two fourths. There are other tunings but they are all constructed from hon-choshi.

FIGURE 18. Shamisen tunings

Since shamisen music is primarily vocal music there is no fixed basic pitch to which the instrument is tuned. It varies from G to D, B being used most commonly in transcriptions. It must be remembered, therefore, that the pitch of any transcription of shamisen music is arbitrary or, at the most, represents only the tonality of the one particular performance from which the transcription was made. Thus, there is no set pitch for a composition such as a song in B flat major or a symphony in D minor. There is, however a concept of "happy" and "sad" tunings which is found in our major-minor concept in the West. Specifically, hon-choshi is said to be best for solemn music, ni-agari for gay, and san-sagari for melancholic or serene music. The practical application of this theory is nebulous, yet the concept must be mentioned, as it forms part of the psychological outlook of the more traditional-minded musicians.

II. The History and Construction of Shamisen Music

The first shamisen players were converted storytellers from the biwa schools of the Osaka-Kyoto district. Naturally, then, the first music for the shamisen was also of a narrative nature. There are records of its early use as accompaniment for folk songs, but the most important form as far as the development of Japanese music is concerned is the narrative form called *joruri*. The word joruri is an abbreviation of the title of a story called *Joruri-hime Monogatari*, which translates picturesquely as "the story of Princess Lapis Lazuli." Actually, it is the tale of the early years of the great Japanese military hero, Yoshitsune, who figured so strongly in *The Heike Story* mentioned earlier. The original music of this first-known shamisen saga of his life has disappeared, but the dozens of imitations and elaborations that exist today attest to its popularity.

The word *joruri* soon came to mean any one of a dozen different types of narrative shamisen music utilizing any subject matter from ancient to modern times. Such music also goes under the general term *katarimono*, which means songs primarily concerned with narration as distinguished from *utaimono*, songs primarily concerned with melody. The main distinction between the words joruri and katarimono is that joruri is a historical term while katarimono is a word imposed on narrative music by later scholars for the sake of contrast with utaimono. The difference between katarimono and utaimono is much like the distinction that is often made between French opera, with its orientation toward the words, and Italian opera, which emphasizes the voice and melody. While in practice, the distinction is often not clear in either the Japanese or European case, such categories do serve, nevertheless, as most convenient devices for the division of the study of a many-faceted style of music.

KATARIMONO - NARRATIVE SHAMISEN MUSIC: One of the earliest forms of narrative music of which there are remnants today is *Naniwa-bushi*. It is the main inheritor of the dramatic storytelling tradition of uta-zaimon mentioned in Chapter II. The uta-zaimon artist spun his tales of love before a crowd of common folk, gathered in the shrine compound. Naniwa-bushi also has kept this contact with the peasants. It is comparable in appeal to the hill-billy music of America, though the topics and style of delivery are more highly developed.

Contemporary Naniwa-bushi, though commercialized, still retains the basic quality of what is believed to be the original narrative style. Its formal elements are the common denominator of storytellers all over the world. They are: 1) a short instrumental overture, 2) a scene-setting song, 3) straight dialogue set in a light background of mood music, 4) occasional songs at crucial points in the plot, often commenting on the emotions or fates of the characters, 5) instrumental interludes, particularly at points of action or scene changes, and 6) a final song summing up the plot, often with some moralizing thought to end the story. Within this framework one can set storytellers from time immemorial whether they be European, African, or oriental. The differences lie in the types of morality injected into the stories by the society in which they function and in the particular musical idiom employed.

In the case of Naniwa-bushi the music is quite explosive, a thick-necked shamisen being played with a blunt plectrum to produce sudden sharp sounds interspersed between much lighter passages played on the highest string. This gives the extremely rough-toned, almost-primitive vocal line a rhythmic drive which it could not have alone. Before the advent of the shamisen, storytellers beat out an accompaniment on their left hand with a closed fan or with various percussion instruments (see Plates 13 and 56). This early accompaniment might help to explain the sudden spurts of sound which are so typical of Naniwa-bushi. One must mention also as part of the style the equally violent shouts of the shamisen player. These cries fill nearly every rest in the music. Though originally signals to the singer and perhaps teaching devices, they have now become an important dramatic element of the music, much like the noh drum calls mentioned in Chapter IV.

Perhaps the most unique aspect of Naniwa-bushi is that one can find almost no reference to it in any Japanese music book written in the twentieth century despite the fact that Naniwa-style music is heard on the Japanese radio daily. The explanation of this peculiar intellectual boycott is found in the following story.

In 1911, a famous Naniwa-bushi singer named Tochuken Kumoemon made a recording and soon thereafter recorded the same piece for another firm. A civil lawsuit charging violation of the copyright laws followed. When the case came to court, the defense brought up the question of whether Naniwa-bushi was really music. If it were not, then his client could not have violated any music copyright. In order to settle this problem, a group of music experts were brought in and after due deliberation, the decision of the court was handed down: Naniwa-bushi was *not* music – case dismissed. Ever since that time, no Japanese music scholar has deigned to write on this subject since it was now, by official decree, "not music." One must add that there had always been a strong feeling among scholars that it was too low class for serious study.

Perhaps this singular musical anathematization is due to the heavy narrative emphasis of Naniwa-bushi or to its commercial popularity, for it is one of the few forms of traditional music that has managed to keep abreast of the times. The broadcasts of Naniwa-bushi music are complete with sound effects, soap-opera theme songs and guitar backgrounds mixed in with shamisen mood music. Between long sections of straight dialogue, one can hear a completely traditional singing voice declaiming, "She takes the streetcar and transfers at Nihombashi." Thus, singers continue to entertain a large following, blissfully ignoring the fact that, legally, they don't exist. Meanwhile the scholars naively ignore the fact that they do exist. In any event, everyone's face is saved, and those who enjoy Naniwa-bushi would rather listen to it than read about it anyway.

The number of schools of shamisen music which fall into the category of katarimono is enormous. Only someone seriously interested in the problems of Japanese narrative music could hope to unravel the complicated threads of interrelations and influences. In general, one can say that a new school was formed whenever a pupil deviated enough from his teacher's style to cause distinction or friction. The guild system, even today, has a firm grip on Japanese arts, including the modern arts. If one wants to change the way of doing things, the only recourse is to leave the guild and found a new one. Therefore, we find in music a host of schools named after the founder of their style. For example, *Kato-bushi* was founded by Kato Masumi (1684–1725) and *Bungo-bushi* was founded by Bungo Miyakoji (died 1740).

To the Westerner there may seem to be no discernible difference between the various schools, but the differences are there, and a connoisseur can spot them easily. Often the distinction lies in the type of text chosen. For example, many musics, such as Kato-bushi, make a specialty of domestic tragedies. In these stories the brother-in-law is often the villain, and the hero is beset with the age-old mother-in-law problem. One can well understand why such forms would find popular support and sympathy regardless of their musical qualities.

Bungo-bushi (now almost extinct) is another example of a "bushi" with a special story style. Bungo created such vivid descriptions of love affairs, usually ending in double suicides, that it is said that the government issued a ban on his music in order to arrest the alarming rise in double suicides by musically inspired lovers. Since double suicides have been rather a national pastime for centuries, another less romantic explanation gives the real story of the demise of Bungo-bushi. It seems that Bungo's music was in direct competition with Kato-bushi, which happened to be a favorite among certain members of the governmental army. When Bungo-bushi showed signs of winning the struggle, the Kato musicians did some eighteenth-century lobbying, and Bungo-bushi was banned. Such cases as this show that a study of Japanese music is not without its social and political ramifications. Unfortunately for Japanese music, the "battle of the bushi's" has continued to the present day. The bitterness of the fight seldom is engendered by any musical considerations.

While text differences were the distinctive features of some schools, others differed in the style of singing or playing. Anyone who has heard the fantastic flights of a *Shinnai-bushi* singer can never confuse these vocal peregrinations with any other style. This music, created by Shinnai Tsuruga (1714–74), earned the rather unique distinction of being banned in the Yoshiwara district of Tokyo, a place euphemistically called "the nightless city." The story behind this banning is quite different. The madames and owners of the various houses within the Yoshiwara district found that after prolonged exposure to Shinnai-bushi, their "employees" tended to fall in love and in many cases run away, both of which acts were bad for business. Despite this prohibition, or perhaps because of it, Shinnai-bushi can still be heard today.

Shinnai-bushi uses a shamisen style somewhat like that of Naniwa-bushi, and the instrument they use is also rather thick necked. The plectrum, however, is not so blunt. In Shinnai, there is often a second shamisen which continues to pluck away at a light, high obligato. This adds more sweetness to the over-all tone of the music. When Shinnai is used to accompany theatrical performances the voice of the singer is quite penetrating and intense, while in concerts the intensity is retained but the volume is reduced. The most characteristic quality of Shinnai music is a tendency to start main phrases at a terrifically high pitch and then flutter down in tight, short arabesques until a reciting tone is reached. The formal outline of Shinnai-bushi pieces is similar to that of Naniwa except that there are very few dialogue sections. The pieces that are sung today also tend to be shorter than those of Naniwa.

Shinnai-bushi has developed groups of amateur practitioners, for it is not so blatant in its emotional display as Naniwa and yet it has managed to retain enough eroticism to be appealing. Shinnai-bushi can best be heard and appreciated in one of the smaller Japanese theatres in which everyone sits on the mat floor. Here one may smoke, eat, or drink while casually savoring the melancholy of an old love tale sung with great passion – but not too much of it. Perhaps this is the real secret appeal of Shinnai-bushi.

Tokiwazu-bushi, founded by Tokiwazu Mojidayu (1709–81), is one of the forms of narrative music often found in the kabuki theatre. It also has a good following among amateurs and shamisen-concert devotees. It differs from the styles described above in that it uses a much less intense vocal style and has a less percussive shamisen part. Both the neck and plectrum are not so thick, though the tone of the shamisen is definitely more heavy and throaty than the lyric-style instruments to be described later. A wide-based bridge helps to produce this "alto" sound in the shamisen family.

The stories of Tokiwazu are typical of those found in all the narrative shamisen forms.

To get some idea of what these stories are like, let us look at the plot of the nineteenth-century ballad, "Gompachi," one of the favorites in the Tokiwazu repertoire today.

The story is divided into two parts. In the first half, the hero, Gompachi, has been arrested. Earlier he had fled from his native prefecture to the anonymity of the Yoshiwara. He was forced to do this because he had seriously wounded a man during an argument. He soon found that his money did not last very long in the Yoshiwara and resorted to robbery for a livelihood. For this crime he was now being led away to execution. As he traveled to his doom, his mistress, Komurasaki, appeared and begged the guard to let her exchange a cup of water with her lover as this was the customary ceremony performed by a doomed man and his friends. The guard consented, and as they began the rite, Komurasaki whipped out a knife and cut Gompachi's bonds. At this dramatic point in the story we find Gompachi waking with a start. It has all been a bad dream.

The second half of the story shows that not all of the dream was unreal, for Gompachi is worrying over the reputation of his mistress. He is afraid that her association with him will ruin her business as a geisha in the Yoshiwara. He vows to leave her out of love for her, but as they weep and pledge eternal love, they become aware of suspicious activity outside. It is too late, the police have surrounded the house! There is only one solution left in a pure-style joruri piece, which is, of course, a double suicide and a long, tearful scene of slow dying. An added bit of pathos may be noted in this particular tale, for the graves of Gompachi and Komurasaki are said to be visible today in Meguro Fudoson, a temple in Tokyo. Though the story of their actual death has been considerably altered for the sake of the drama, their green-mossed memorial pillars are evidence that many of these romantic tales have a foundation in genuine human tragedies.

The resemblance between this story and an Italian opera libretto only points up the fact that both countries have a great love of melodramatic music dramas. As a matter of fact, there is a theatricality to everyday life in Japan which might be likened to that of Italy, though some would say it is a bit more pompous. The itinerant salesman of Japan has an innate sense of dramatic timing, and often his sales talk is really an aria, with banging sticks for accompaniment. All life seems to be lived as if it were on a stage. The very seasons can be marked by a series of songs that are sung by the goldfish man, the bamboo man, the junkman, or any one of a host of seasonal food sellers. In such a country, it is no wonder that the dramatic and musical arts have become so firmly entrenched.

The piece "Gompachi" described above originally belonged to a style of music called

57. The Gidayu singer and the shamisen accompanyist of the bunraku puppet theatre sit on a rostrum placed on the stage-left. The Gidayu singer, who alone portrays all the characters of a play from child to grandmother, represents one of the most highly developed narrative music forms in Japan. See pages 199–203.

58–69. The intense concentration and the almost overwhelming expressions of the Gidayu singer are clearly revealed in this sequence of photographs showing Takemoto Tsudayu during a performance at the puppet theatre. See pages 199–200.

70. This Ryukyu jamisen is the predecessor of the Japanese shamisen. See page 185.

71. Nagauta, one of the main components of kabuki music, is among the most developed music forms in Japan. A full nagauta concert ensemble produces an orchestral effect. See pages 205–8.

72. The Gidayu shamisen, plectrum, and costume of the musician all add to the grandeur of Gidayu music.

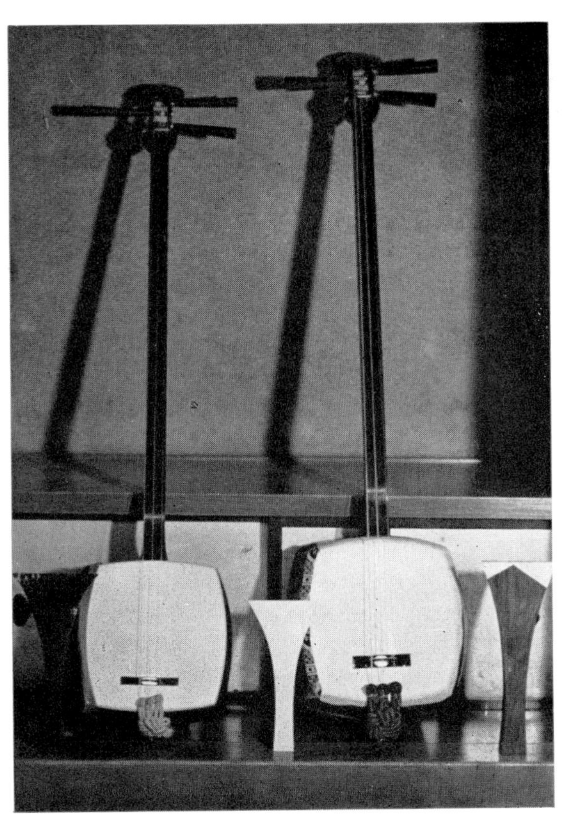

73. The Gidayu shamisen is built much heavier than the nagauta shamisen. The three plectrums shown (left to right) are used for jiuta, nagauta, and Gidayu.

74. A geisha nagauta ensemble playing for the famous "Miyako-odori" festival in Kyoto. The inclusion of the noh hayashi is one of the distinctive features of the nagauta ensemble. See page 206.

Kiyomoto, founded by Kiyomoto Enjudayu (circa 1814). This form, though listed as a katarimono, stands on the border line between the lyric and the narrative styles of shamisen music. The voice part is very high, and falsetto-like tones are used much more than in most other styles. To aid this quality the shamisen, plectrum, and bridge are all built thinner. The tunings are generally higher also. All these factors do much to delete the normal percussive quality of the shamisen from the music of Kiyomoto.

Returning to the vocal quality, it should be noted that the general tendency in the voice part of shamisen music is to force the voice "naturally" into the musical stratosphere. Any Western-trained voice would find such attempts most unnatural. Actually, this technique is unnatural only in the sense that it involves a completely different kind of preliminary training. The same can be said, for example of Western opera singing.

Kiyomoto, because of its high, light tone, has been termed as very sweet and is found as the accompaniment for many love scenes on the kabuki stage. In addition to its firm place in the theatre, it also has become quite popular as a form of home music. Many an afternoon meeting of Japanese women is rounded out with a few selections from the Kiyomoto repertoire.

GIDAYU-BUSHI - THE MUSIC OF BUNRAKU: During this discussion of narrative shamisen music no mention has yet been made of the giant of them all, Gidayu-bushi. Founded by Takemoto Gidayu (1651–1714) in the booming commercial city of Osaka, it has all the bluster and drive of the merchant class to which it was directed. At one time, the thoughts and speech stylings of Osaka merchants were guided by Gidayu songs in much the same manner that some Americans are cultural by-products of the *New Yorker* magazine. Together with the famous playwright, Chikamatsu Monzaemon, Gidayu created one of the great traditions of the Japanese theatre. Much of present-day kabuki is nothing but a humanization, if you will, of the puppet plays of Chikamatsu. Likewise, the singing of Takemoto Gidayu was so powerful that from his time onward, the music of Gidayu-bushi was considered to be the epitome of narrative shamisen music.

The Gidayu musicians at a bunraku puppet performance are placed on a rostrum to the left of the stage.[1] From this position, the singer invokes life into the magnificently handled puppets by violent onslaughts of the most intense range of vocal expression. His extravagances match perfectly the puppet's gestures, which must themselves be bigger than life in order to compensate for the puppet's nonhumanity.

Look at Plates 58–69. They show clearly that Gidayu singers are as much actors as

[1] Stage-left is left facing the audience. Down-stage is at the footlights and up-stage at the back.

musicians. By connecting these pictures with the following description of a performance, those who have never seen a Gidayu singer in action may have some small idea of the excitement of such an occasion.

After a shamisen prelude, the singer begins with a deep rumbling hum somewhat like the sound of a two-ton truck in low gear. Slowly his lips part and a rough but very open vowel sound floats over the stage to awaken the puppets and the audience to the electricity that lurks heavily in the atmosphere. The story begins to unfold in a simple monotone with the shamisen restlessly making short tonal comments between phrases. Gradually, the tension mounts, the shamisen interrupts more frequently, and the voice becomes part singing, part speaking, and part an indescribable mixture of the two. At the same time, the singer's entire body becomes possessed by the characters he is portraying. His legs seem bound to the cushion, but his trunk, head, and arms become a mass of writhing emotion – and his face! Look again at Plates 58–69. Picture the scarlet, perspiring face and the bulging veins of the neck and temple. It is as though the singer were trying to infuse great passions into his wooden counterparts on stage by the sheer heat of his own emotions. The music-stand in front of the singer is a heavy, squat affair and it needs to be, for it is pounded, thumped, and crawled upon as the crises mount ever higher and higher.

A lone singer can portray every character on stage from the smallest child to the warrior and the old grandmother. But never did a villain growl more ferociously nor a heroine simper in such a squeaky, humble tone, for in Gidayu things are black and white. The confusing greys of many Western dramas are not often found in bunraku plays. Right is right, wrong is wrong, and death is the only solution for a single transgression. Thus, no one has ever cried as hard nor laughed as heartily as the characters presented by the Gidayu singers.

When the midway point comes in the series of crises, the singer solemnly closes his book, touches it to his forehead, and the rostrum suddenly revolves, revealing a fresh pair of artists, a shamisen player and a singer, who begin all over the same process until the plot is brought to its conclusion.

Gidayu is considered by many to be the most difficult of all Japanese music forms, for the singer must possess a voice of great stamina, be a good melodramatic actor, and be able to coördinate with the stage action and the shamisen accompaniment at the same time.

The problem of stage direction itself is actually in the hands of the shamisen player who must keep an eye on the pace of the drama and by grunts and musical signals knit the entire production together.

The shamisen used in Gidayu is quite different from other shamisen (see Plate 73). The skin is thicker and the general structure of the instrument is heavier. The plectrum, in turn, is very narrow and blunt. The net result is a deeper, harder tone which matches admirably the forceful expression inherent in the entire drama.

The music of Gidayu-bushi is constructed in a manner similar to that of the biwa music studied earlier. That is, the music consists of many stereotyped patterns strung together. In Gidayu-bushi this technique is more highly developed than in most biwa music. Actually, Gidayu is the basis upon which many present-day biwa styles are founded. For instance, the transcription of a biwa section in Figure 14 also resembles Gidayu music. In Gidayu, the various standard patterns are used more freely. Like biwa music, there are narrative sections in which only the reciting tone is used, but the number of instrumental interludes is greater and the dialogue sections are in a completely independent style.

Each Gidayu piece has special musical features which must be learned by the apprentice musician through rote methods. As noted before, this slow, mechanical process is typical of Japanese teaching methods. It does have the advantage that the resultant performances are practically automatic conditioned responses. This is particularly convenient in Gidayu-bushi, for the musician must also contend with the coördination of the music with the events on the stage. One big disadvantage of the rote system for the researcher is that detailed notation is not used (see Appendix II). Hence, the death of every old-time Gidayu musician means a further loss in the repertoire of that performer's special numbers. The tape machine, if used properly, may be able to minimize this loss in the future.

The structure of the dramas of Gidayu-bushi is organized into five main parts, or *dan*. While the music also follows this outline, the classic joruri form is usually further subdivided. The music sections in their usual order are: 1) the *oki*, 2) the *michiyuki*, 3) the *kudoki*, 4) the *monogatari*, 5) the *uta*, 6) the *odori*, 7) the *miarawashi*, and 8) the *chirashi* or *seme*.

There is considerable flexibility to the manner in which these eight sections fit into the larger five-part scheme of the drama. All the sections may not necessarily appear in one play. The character of each of the eight sections, however, is more definite. The oki is always a section of mood or scene setting, while the michiyuki is used to introduce the various characters. The kudoki is a lyric section usually devoted to the laments of the heroine, while the monogatari is the section in which the story is progressed to a crucial point. The uta, or "song," and the odori, or "dance," are the musical high points of the drama. The latter also gives the puppeteers an opportunity to show their skill to best advantage. The miarawashi is the point at which the central problem of the plot is brought to a head, and the chirashi is the solution of the problem, in Japanese theatre, usually by tragic means. The psychological build up of this form is admirably supported in the music. Once this structure is realized, Gidayu music has a formally satisfying effect. The reaction of a Japanese familiar with this structure is equal, for example, to a Westerner's reaction to an A-B-A form. The fact that Gidayu music is always connected with a drama makes the need for thematic repetition and other such elements of so-called pure music less important. As in architecture, form follows function though, of course, there can be no satisfactory function without form.

This so-called joruri form has influenced all the narrative styles of shamisen music, but it is most highly developed in Gidayu-bushi. However, from a musical standpoint, it is most important for its influence on the structure of the more lyrical form of *naga-uta* to be discussed presently. For the beginning listener to Japanese music, the characteristics of Gidayu music to be noted are the melodramatic violence of the singing, the extremely deep tone of the shamisen, the almost brutal snap of the blunt Gidayu plectrum, and the aphoristic comments of the shamisen during the recitative sections of the drama. With such a series of masculine characteristics, it may be surprising to learn that there are also female practitioners of Gidayu-bushi.

Usually, shamisen players and singers team up and work together for years so that their coördination is perfect. Gidayu is not always performed by two people, however, and certain numbers require four or five singers and several shamisen. This is more true of contemporary pieces.

Perhaps the most interesting new production of recent years is *O-Cho Fujin*, better known to Westerners as *Madame Butterfly*. It is not only the Japanese theme that caused the bunraku people to choose this play, but also the fact that it contains all the essential ingredients of any bunraku play, that is, several tearful scenes, preferably with a child about somewhere, frustrated love, a sense of obligation, a tragic death, preferably suicide, and more tears. Once again, one is forced to call attention to the close connection between the spirit of joruri and that of Italian opera.

The bunraku version of *Madame Butterfly* opens with "Auld Lang Syne" being played on an off-stage violin mixed with the Japanese folk song "Sakura" from the Gidayu shamisen. The play ends with the famous death scene and the Gidayu singer weeping, "Pinkerton-san, Pinkerton-san!" By that time there is many a maudlin tear in even a Western viewer's eyes. To appreciate the honest, heart-on-the-sleeve melodrama of Gidayu-bushi one needs only a little orientation (in this case, a familiar story). With further listening and a modicum of preparation, any sensitive listener can discover for himself the truly excellent theatrical qualities of this king of Japanese narrative music, Gidayu-bushi.

Looking back over the entire field of katarimono music, one can see several distinctive styles classified under this one category. Naniwa-bushi presents the roughest style with a vocal quality that is highly nasal and almost shouted at times. Gidayu-bushi is next in roughness of tone, but the vocal and shamisen techniques are much more developed and the entire structure of the Gidayu compositions is more evolved. Shinnai-bushi comes next in line with a tense but more restrained style accompanied by a much softer shamisen part. Bungo-bushi is out of the picture today, and Kato-bushi is rare, its style being much like Tokiwazu. Tokiwazu is markedly less violent in its vocal technique as well as the shamisen sound, while Kiyomoto is the highest and least percussive of the narrative musics. In order to recognize more specific distinctions between the various musics, one must simply hear each type many times. The results are well worth the effort.

UTAIMONO - LYRIC SHAMISEN MUSIC: Previously, the early use of shamisen for accompanying folk songs was mentioned. This use might be called the beginning of *utaimono,* the lyrical music for the shamisen. Out of this style developed many ditties which were collectively known as *kouta,* literally "short songs." These songs were combined into sets known as *kumiuta.* It was shown earlier how this form affected early koto music. The general style of these songs is quite simple and unassuming, while the poems tend to be wistful and romantic. For example, here is the translation of two poems by Rosai Ryutatsu, an early-seventeenth-century composer of kouta.

I.

The longer I live in this world,
The more I think of my love.
I'd like to disappear with the moon
Behind the ridge of the mountains.

II.

I can't seem to write
The letter I have in mind,
So let this piece of white paper
Give you my message.

The sentimentality of the words and the intimacy of kouta performances made them ideal for geisha parties. The net result was that every geisha and brothel district (there is a difference sometimes) began its own style of kouta. Another type of short song called *hauta* also appeared, reaching its greatest popularity in the nineteenth century. Nowadays this term is used somewhat generically for all short songs with shamisen accompaniment, as hauta do not have any strong stylistic traits. Kouta usually refers to the gayer party-music tradition, though there is little consistency in the Japanese use of these terms. Some say that hauta often tell a story while kouta do not.

Under the aegis of various brothel employees one can well imagine that the delicate imagery of the earlier kouta songs began to deteriorate. The natural punning ability of the Japanese language was overworked to the point that the play on words was lost and the erotic meaning became too direct. For instance, here is a kouta text that was found on a woodblock print of the late seventeenth century.

Indeed, indeed! With all their hearts sharing love's pillow:
Stroking her Jewelled Gate, and taking
The girl's hand and causing her to grasp his Jade Stalk:
What girl's face will not change color,
Her breath come faster?

Since the era of such excesses, kouta has gone through several reforms. The most noteworthy of these was the nineteenth-century form, *utazawa*, which attempted to add dignity and grace to the music and to use less erotic words. Today kouta is considered a light form of party music, and the erotic references in the words are more indirect. The intimate quality of kouta is enhanced by playing the shamisen with the finger tip instead of a plectrum (utazawa, however, uses a plectrum). This finger strumming produces a softer tone. In addition to the many female practitioners of kouta there are a number of businessman kouta singers with whom kouta has become a social fad. Many a kouta concert will show a comely female shamisen player accompanying a slightly rotund gentleman in a somber business suit who has rushed from the office in order to be on time for the performance. One might say that kouta meetings are now the Japanese equivalent of American barbershop-quartet clubs.

Kouta, utazawa, and hauta re-create the atmosphere and thoughts of the Edo period in much the same manner as do the famous *ukiyoe* woodblock prints. Kouta represents to many Japanese the "good old days," much as "Bicycle Built for Two" conjures up nostalgia for the supposedly gay Gay Nineties in America. As long as there is room in the world for a little unashamed sentimentality, there will be room for kouta.

NAGAUTA - THE HEART OF KABUKI MUSIC: If Gidayu-bushi is the king of the narrative branch of shamisen music, then nagauta is the ruler of the lyrical domain. Nagauta, or "long songs," are a product of Tokyo in the same way that Gidayu is a product of Osaka. Though the term nagauta was applied earlier in history to a different form of music in Kyoto, this older music is now designated as *kamigata*(upstate)-*nagauta*, while the giant of whom we are going to speak now is called *Edo-nagauta* or simply *nagauta*.

The growth of nagauta is intimately connected with the evolution of the kabuki theatre in Tokyo. When the shamisen was first used in the kabuki, probably sometime before 1650, the music played was a type of kouta. These short songs, however, were found to be insufficient for the extended dances that were being developed. Longer pieces were written, and by around 1740 a new, mature form of nagauta was created which had all the lyricism of the shorter forms plus the sustaining power of the more narrative music. After the time of the first Kineya Kisaburo (early eighteenth century), many of the earlier forms of kabuki music and the older styles of nagauta were absorbed into this one form. The fame of nagauta and the Kineya clan of musicians spread side by side through all the theatres of Tokyo. To this day, the head shamisen performers in the major theatres are members of the Kineya school. At the same time, nagauta has become one of the mainstays of kabuki music and has also developed an independent concert life. It is now quite popular as a type of home music, and there are even expurgated versions of certain pieces for use in family circles.

FIGURE 19. Ozatsuma patterns

What are some of the features that make nagauta so unique? First of all, it is the synthesis of all the lesser forms which have since disappeared. Within the nagauta repertoire one can hear influences and many times direct borrowings from other musics. One of the best examples of this are sections known as *ozatsuma*, which appear with great regularity in nagauta pieces. These melodic fragments are all that remain of a form of music once known as *ozatsuma-bushi*. In this particular group of melodic patterns, unlike most such borrowings in nagauta, each melody has a separate name just as was the case with the Gidayu and biwa music mentioned earlier. They are known collectively as the forty-eight *ozatsuma-te* and form the basic accompaniment for many introductions, cadences, and recitatives in nagauta. Figure 19 gives several patterns used in recitatives. Notice how they tend to imitate the curve of dramatic speech.

These types of melodic patterns serve as convenient signals to the enlightened listener, indicating sectional changes as surely as an "amen" cadence indicates an ending to Western-trained ears.

Perhaps the most unique element in nagauta is the addition and use of the noh hayashi, the drums and flute of a noh drama (Plates 36 and 74). Since kabuki itself grew out of the noh tradition, it is only natural that kabuki music should borrow the instruments from the same source. In keeping with the gaudier tradition of kabuki, the number of drums, however, is often increased (Plates 71 and 74). When the shamisen and singers were added, a real type of orchestral ensemble was formed with voice, strings, percussion, and winds all represented.

The value of this ensemble is not in its instrumentation but in its use. In order to understand this one must first review the basic premises upon which Western music is built. Simply stated, Western theory says that music consists of three elements: melody, harmony, and rhythm. The melodic element is the center of the music, the thought to be conveyed or the logic to be expressed. Rhythm enhances the exposition of this melody by either supporting the accents of the melody or providing contrasts against them. The function of harmony is basically to color the melody and force it to move by providing tension or help it come to a halt by means of chords consonant with the melody and its tonal context. The melody alone creates tensions and releases, but harmony intensifies or mollifies these inherent drives in the melody.

In the nagauta ensemble, the voice and the shamisen provide the basic melodic element. Sometimes a seven-holed bamboo flute (the take-bue or shino-bue) is added to this melodic unit. Two of the noh drums, the o-tsuzumi and ko-tsuzumi, usually play a supporting rhythm.[2] The normal noh-style drum patterns are also used sometimes. However, the distinctive feature of the use of the o-tsuzumi and ko-tsuzumi in kabuki is the prominence of rhythmic patterns directly related to the rhythm of the shamisen line. These rhythms are known collectively as *chirikara-byoshi*. The title comes from the rhythmic mnemonics by which the parts are learned.

It was mentioned in the noh chapter how closely the music of the noh flute and the

[2] Since these two instruments are used together so much of the time, they are often known collectively as the *dai-sho*. The word comes from another pronunciation of the Chinese characters for "o" and "ko," large and small. "Tsuzumi" means drum.

taiko drum are related when they are playing together. This affinity is retained in the nagauta ensemble. Though one is a melodic instrument and the other rhythmic, they can be considered as one functional unit as far as their relation to the entire ensemble is concerned. Thus, the taiko can be heard playing rhythmic patterns unrelated to either the shamisen or the other two drums except for the use of a common over-all rhythmic frame. Meanwhile, the flute plays a melody both tonally and thematically unrelated to the shamisen. Actually, it is an independent melody oriented to the entire ensemble only through its relation to the taiko. It can be thought of as an added color, which indeed it is. Its purposely indistinct melodic style blurs the outline of its line so that it does not clash too strongly with the basic shamisen line. This adds to its coloristic effect. However, when one views the flute and taiko as one unit and analyzes this unit in relation to the rest of the ensemble, it seems to be more than just a coloration device. This unit is, in fact, a third force.[3] Through its contrary rhythmic phrase lines and independent melodies it sets up tensions which drive the composition forward in the same way that harmony pushes Western music to its cadences.

The theory of tension and release is more basic in music than harmony, melody, or rhythm. We may do without one or two of the latter elements, but without the building of tensions there can be no musical movement. Oriental music has succeeded in producing many excellent musics which are basically static as against our Western concept of dynamism. The Javanese *gamelan* has been cited as an example. However, even within this seemingly aimless music, there is a tight formal structure and germs of accoustical discontent which force the music forward to its climax.

One of the favorite clichés about oriental music is that it lacks harmony. Certainly in nagauta there is little of this element except for the occasional two-note chords on the shamisen or the sound resulting from differences between the various melodic instruments. This is not conscious harmony in the Western sense. However, the unit of the taiko and the noh flute serve the same *function* as harmony does in the West. It produces tensions which find release only at the cadences. Of all the music techniques studied so far in this book, perhaps this one is the most original. The tonal independence of the noh flute predates the bi-tonal experiments of the modern Western compos-

[3] The reader must be warned that this theory is the author's own and needs further analytic data before it can be stated with certainty. However, its exposition, even as a tentative explanation of Japanese music, should provide other researchers with a fresh approach to a fascinating and as yet unexplained music. At present, I am willing to extend the theory only to nagauta and only when the o-tsuzumi and ko-tsuzumi are playing chirikara-byoshi and the flute and taiko appear together. Further expansion of the theory must await future research.

ers by centuries, and the use of a separate rhythmic-melodic unit in lieu of harmony has scarcely been exploited outside the orient. Further research may show that this compositional device is one of the major Japanese contributions to the general theory and practice of music.[4]

Another important feature of nagauta is its development of form in Japanese music. It was influenced by the earlier joruri form and evolved side by side with the art of kabuki dancing. These two elements set its basic form, but when nagauta began to be used in concerts outside the theatre this joruri-dance form was expanded. This growth of a concert form out of a dance form has a parallel in the history of form in Western music.

Nagauta based on kabuki-dance form has six standard sections: the *oki*, *michiyuki*, *kudoki*, *odoriji*, *chirashi*, and *dangire* (compare this arrangement with the joruri form on page 201).

The oki of nagauta is introductory in nature and devoted to setting the scene. Musically, it is often rather recitative in quality and many ozatsuma patterns may occur. In some pieces the atmosphere is set by an instrumental prelude. For example, in the piece "Azuma Hakkei" (the eight views of eastern Japan) the oki is said to represent a lovely spring day in old Tokyo.

The term michiyuki was used in the noh drama for the section of the play in which the actor moved onto the stage. The music of the nagauta michiyuki accompanies the same action. In kabuki, the actor often arrives via the *hanamichi* (Plate 75), a ramp that extends from the back of the theatre to the stage. The music of the michiyuki varies with the personality of the character and his manner of entrance (walking, running, through a trap door, etc.). In general, it is marked by an instrumental interlude and the use of the drums.

The kudoki in nagauta as well as in Gidayu-bushi is generally very soft in style. In kabuki, this was originally designed as the dance section for the female impersonators. For this reason the drums seldom appear in the kudoki and the shamisen part is quite restrained and simple.

The odoriji is a contrast, for it is livelier. The drums often reappear and, in fact, this section is sometimes called the taiko-odoriji because the taiko drum is exploited frequently in such sections. This points up the relation between the kabuki dance forms

[4] By calling this a compositional device I do not mean to imply that it is a conscious technique used by nagauta composers. On the contrary, it is a culture-conditioned reaction. One proof of this is that this theory is written here for the first time in any language. It was derived from analysis, not interviews or books. Contemporary nagauta experts are completely inarticulate on the subject. They simply know what sounds right and feel no compulsion to explain further.

and that of the noh drama, for the taiko is important during the dance sections of noh plays also.

A change of shamisen tuning is also common at the beginning of the odoriji. If it goes to ni-agari (a fifth and a fourth), the bamboo flute may be added. Since this flute follows closely the contour of the shamisen line, it is built in seven different sizes to match the particular intonation of each performance. One occasion comes to mind during which the flute player calmly performed the entire odoriji a whole step higher than the accompanying shamisen. The effect is better imagined than experienced.

The chirashi means the "scattering" and that is what happens. The pace may vary but eventually it quickens and one feels a definite sense of a finale approaching. This section is the most free, like the development section of a sonata (though I hasten to add that there is no development of any theme as such in nagauta). Since it is freer, it is harder to make any general statement about all chirashi sections.

The dangire is the finale. All the instruments appear, and the final pose (*mie*) or tableau is struck by the dancers. The types of final cadences are so well known that the audience starts to applaud the moment they appear. Hence, the last few bars are completely lost in the din. This habit is sometimes carried over into Japanese concerts of Western music with discomforting results for foreign listeners.

This, then, is the basic form of nagauta. Superimposed over this structure and over the joruri form as well, one can find the aesthetic concept of jo-ha-kyu discussed in the noh chapter. As was explained, jo is the introduction, ha the breaking apart, and kyu the climax. There is some disagreement over its application to nagauta form. There are certainly variations among specific pieces, but in general, it can be said that sections one and two are the jo, three and four are the ha, and five and six are the kyu. It must be remembered that as the form developed its ramifications became very broad. Just as many a sonata is only nominally in sonata form, so many a nagauta uses the above-stated formal outline in a very free manner.

All nagauta do not follow this form. This is especially true of pieces composed for concert performance only, the so-called *ozashiki-nagauta*. Among the most common non-kabuki dance form systems of organization is the structure of jiuta discussed in the koto chapter (page 181). That is, there are some pieces that are basically an alternation of vocal sections with instrumental interludes.

The instrumental interludes (called *ai-no-te*) are a study in themselves. Many of them are clever imitations of other styles of music, representations of weather conditions, or sometimes even imitations of natural sounds. In "Aki no Irokusa" (the colors of autumn foliage) there is a delightful interlude which represents the chirping of insects in the pine trees. In another piece, "Shiki no Yamamba" (the four seasons of Yamamba) there is a very droopy, lazy interlude that pictures quite well the feeling of a Tokyo summer.

In such interludes one often has an opportunity to hear an *uwajoshi-shamisen.* This is a shamisen to which a small nut (*kase*) has been added so that it plays an octave higher than usual. It is used to embellish the basic melody or to play a drone against which the main line can be set.[5]

Nagauta, like Gidayu, makes extensive use of a series of stereotype melodic patterns. Their use in nagauta, however, is much freer. They are rather like the technique used by Baroque composers in Europe in which certain standard types of melodies depicted certain emotions. Their use can be good or bad depending on the composer (Bach used them frequently). In this light it is unjust to say, as some have said, that nagauta composition is not composition but merely arrangement. The technique of using stereotype patterns, often of known emotional implications, is, after all, the basic idea behind the Wagnerian leitmotiv. Perhaps the difference between the Japanese and Western use is primarily one of degree. Certainly it is overly condescending to brush aside the skill of shamisen composers simply because they have limited their material. This, in truth, is a basic principle of all creative activity. The beauty of much of Japanese painting and poetry is derived from the extraordinary skill with which the artists operate within a carefully prescribed range. To do the same in music does not seem to be necessarily less artistic.

One other feature of nagauta composition should be noted which may seem strange to Western musicians. After the shamisen and vocal line are completed, the music is handed over to a drummer who puts in the hayashi part separately. There are conferences on the placement, but still it is an interesting manifestation of the strength of the guild system in Japanese music. A similar technique was mentioned in the case of noh music.

The problem of the relation between words and music is a bit beyond anyone but an accomplished Japanologist. In general, we can say that the poetry itself is full of subtle allusions, which in many cases are reinforced by equally subtle reactions in the shamisen part. A good illustration of this interaction can often be found in sections in which cold weather is mentioned. It is common during such phrases for the shamisen to borrow the melody of a jiuta piece called "Yuki" (snow). As in Wagner's *Ring*, a

[5] Playing an uwajoshi part is not as simple as it seems. The tuning is always different from that of the basic shamisen (the *honte*). For example, if the honte is in hon-choshi, the uwajoshi will be in ni-agari. Thus, the musician must learn to play each piece in an entirely new set of fingerings.

considerable amount of preperformance knowledge is necessary to appreciate fully the many reactions to the text that are found in the music.

Another interesting observation is that the texts of nagauta seldom tell complete stories. Rather they are more in the nature of tableaus from famous stories or simply scenes from nature. In such cases, the words are used like the Latin texts of many Gothic motets, that is, they are a series of sounds serving primarily as vehicles for the voice. In narrative music, by contrast, the voice serves as a vehicle for the words. In sum, the best approach when first hearing nagauta is not to worry about the meaning of the words but rather to enjoy the beauty of the music and the mastery of the performers.

The thematic and developmental techniques of Western composition are not commonly found in shamisen music. Instead, a more fruitful avenue for understanding the form of nagauta would seem to be a study of its repertoire from a psychological point of view. Given subdivisions of rather definite emotional characteristics and a series of melodic patterns which to some extent are also indicative of sectional changes, it is possible to conceive of a perfectly satisfying form that completely ignores the developmental principles so dear to modern Western music. Western vocal music and much of early choral music also manifest this type of aesthetically satisfying but nondevelopmental techniques. One need only learn how to apply such principles to oriental music to realize that there is organization there also.

In summary, there is manifested in nagauta a sense of progression within formal bounds, a restriction of thematic material, a premeditated psychological planning, an awareness of the value of changing tone colors in the ensemble, and attention to the general mood of the text. In short, nagauta shows all the major characteristics by which one judges Western music. Because of its theatrical origins, it is capable of producing exciting and dramatic moments, but at the same time, its basic orientation is toward lyricism. Thus, it stands at the crossroads of the myriad shamisen music forms while also displaying qualities admirable to the West.

Nagauta is the most independent shamisen form. Not only have the instrumental interludes been developed to the greatest extent, but the texture of the music has been enriched by the use of drums and flute. We have seen how this addition has created unique manifestations of the law of tension and release. This addition also gives nagauta an orchestral aspect lacking in much of Japanese music. If a very general comparison is made, it can be said that Gidayu resembles romantic opera, jiuta is like chamber music, kouta compares to a Schubert song, and nagauta is like a song with orchestral accompaniment.

Nagauta is a popular and virile music and it offers great pleasure to anyone who listens to it and also learns what to listen for in it. By understanding some of the history, aesthetics, and formal principles of such music, one can develop a real respect for those Japanese musicians who created it. For those who embark on an active listening campaign, their efforts will be amply rewarded by the opening of wide vistas of new musical experience and enjoyment. From any point of view, the shamisen and its many musics have served and still serve vital functions in the very core of Japanese music.

CHAPTER NINE KABUKI MUSIC

I. The Components of Kabuki Music

The basic components of kabuki music have already been discussed. It remains for us to tie these elements together and show more precisely how they are used in the theatre. However, first it might be wise to learn something about the history of kabuki itself.

Kabuki is the great theatrical contribution of the Edo period. As such it is the inheritor of all the varied forms of theatricals that preceded it. Tradition claims that kabuki began in 1596 on the bank of the Kamo River in Kyoto with the performance of a Shinto dancer named Okuni of Izumo. She is said to have danced *nembutsu-odori*, a form of Buddhist exorcist dance (see Plate 13). However, her performance was decidedly secular. Indeed, the early use of the word *kabuki* carried distinct connotations of the lascivious.[1] When kabuki went on tour, a troupe was formed from the ever bountiful supply of city prostitutes. This female kabuki was eventually banned and all-male troupes came into existence. These troupes also found governmental resistance strong until they reduced their more obvious homosexual tendencies. The colorful, complicated history of kabuki thereafter shows a continuous struggle against prohibitive regulations throughout its formative years until it became a mature theatrical form and the very center of Edo social life.

The crowds that appeared daily in the theatre district were comprised of members from every social class. The government had ossified society, but the theatre surreptitiously dissolved some of the social restraints that were felt by every man in every rank. Perhaps this is one of the major reasons for the popularity of kabuki. In a highly restricted society, it provided a safety valve through which some of the pent-up energy of the people could be dissipated. The adulation accorded actors was in excess even of that given to modern movie stars and popular singers. Speech, clothes, and morals were guided by the kabuki actor. Under the pressure of modern communications and propaganda methods, mid-twentieth-century civilization shows a similar concern with fads. However, in that microcosmos of frustration known as the Edo man, one finds this fixation for fads even more intense. Perhaps without the theatre, Edo civilization

[1] The present Chinese characters for the word *kabuki* mean song, dance, and acting.

would have fallen apart sooner, but that is a problem for the sociologist. What concerns us here is the music of this famous theatrical tradition.[2]

Old scroll paintings show that kabuki first used a standard noh hayashi, a noh flute and three drums, for accompaniment. In fact, early kabuki was performed on noh and kagura stages. Such performances were particularly popular during public benefit performances (*kanjin-noh*) put on by various ruling houses. As kabuki developed its own form of architecture, it also added more instruments. For example, a large drum (the o-daiko) was installed in the kabuki theatre in a tower over the entrance. If the audience became too rowdy, the drum was used to signal soldiers to come and pacify the customers. Eventually, this instrument was used to signal the opening and closing of the theatre. As will be shown later, it also became a mood-creating device in the plays themselves.

When the shamisen made its appearance on the kabuki stage (sometime between 1620 and 1650) the main genres of shamisen music were kumiuta and kouta. As was mentioned in the previous chapter, the kabuki found such music too short for dance accompaniment. This led to the creation of Edo-nagauta, the core of present-day kabuki music. I have spoken of its unique combination with the noh hayashi to form the typical stage ensemble of kabuki. Tokiwazu, Gidayu, Kiyomoto, and Shinnai-bushi also found a place in the kabuki theatre, but nagauta remained the basic musical accompaniment.

The nagauta ensemble, when it appears on stage, is called the *debayashi*. This group is usually placed at the back of the stage and set on tiers (Plate 78), with the singers and shamisen above and the drums and flute on the floor level. Because of this, the hayashi are known as the *shitakata*, the ones below. When a piece is derived from a puppet play, it is common to see the Gidayu singer and shamisen player seated at the lower stage-left (see page 199), as they are in the puppet theatre. However, sometimes they are placed in a special alcove above the stage-left entrance or in an off-stage room at stage-left. In such cases, they may be hidden from the audience by a bamboo curtain. This set of Gidayu musicians is known in kabuki as the *chobo*. They perform in a manner similar to that used in the puppet theatre, except that their use is more restricted. In the puppet plays, these musicians are the life-giving element in the drama. They propel the plot with their music and narration. In kabuki, however, the chobo functions more as a commentator. Musically, it is similar to the chorus in ancient Greek drama though theatrically it is different. In addition to commenting and scene setting, it can

[2] Those wishing greater detail on the history and technique of kabuki should read Earle Ernst, *The Kabuki Theatre* (see ref. 57).

75. The kabuki stage has a ramp (called the hanamichi) extending all the way to the back of the theatre from the right of the stage (shown here in the background). Occasionally, as in this case, another ramp is added on the stage left. The off-stage music room is behind the windows of the stage-right flat. See page 221.

76. In the finale of *Momiji Gari* the hero corners the demon in a tree and assumes a classic pose as the curtain closes. The musicians on the stand by the pine tree are the nagauta musicians, while the Tokiwazu musicians are placed on the dais downstage right by the foot of the hanamichi. See pages 228–33.

77. The michiyuki section of *Momiji Gari* brings the actors on stage via the ramp from the back of the theatre. The Tokiwazu musicians can be seen at the foot of the ramp.

78. The kabuki stage during the play *Kanjincho*. Notice the placement of the nagauta musicians. See page 214.

79. Behind the bamboo blind the off-stage musicians provide all kinds of special music and sound effects. See page 222. Shown here is a noh hayashi, often used during plays derived from the noh repertoire.

be used to express the thoughts of the actor. However, such functions are not the exclusive domain of the chobo, and other forms of music may serve the same purpose.

The use of Tokiwazu or Kiyomoto is most frequent in romantic scenes. When they appear on stage, they are usually placed downstage right. The placement of any group of musicians on stage, however, is flexible and will vary according to the scenic requirements of the play. As Earle Ernst (ref. 57, 125) has pointed out, the physical presence of all these musicians on stage is in keeping with the presentational (vis-à-vis representational) attitude of the kabuki theatre. That is, kabuki plays do not try to hide their theatricality, but rather exploit it through a thorough stylization of the various contributing elements. One feels a symbolic rather than a realistic presentation of these elements whether they be music, scenery, or acting. The use of such communicable abstraction is one of the major contributions of kabuki to the world of the theatre.

Not all kabuki music comes from the stage. The most fascinating kabuki music emanates from behind the slates of a window in the downstage-right scenery flat. On the other side of the bamboo curtain that screens this room from the eyes of the audience are the performers of *geza-ongaku,* the off-stage music of the kabuki (Plate 79). This room is called the *kuromisu,* or "black curtain," in memory of the black flat that used to be placed before it. The name *geza,* "lower place," comes from the original position of this room which was below the second-floor chobo room at stage-left.[3]

From the semi-darkness of this room, the geza musicians peer out upon the stage and the ramp leading to the back of the theatre (the hanamichi) (Plate 75). Their task is to provide all the necessary music, noise, sound effects, and signals not covered by the musicians on stage. For this purpose, the geza musicians have a battery of percussion equipment and many other instruments. A study of such geza music can best be divided into two sections: the melodic music of the geza and the use of the battery.

Although the koto, kokyu, and shakuhachi are required in certain plays, it is the shamisen which dominates the music of kabuki, off stage as well as on. As it is used off stage, it functions primarily as an indicator of atmosphere. This can be a reminder of a period, place, time, or mood. For example, the melody called "Shinobi Sanju" is played off stage to set the atmosphere of a very dark, mysterious scene. To further this effect, the opening phrase of the shamisen music imitates the call of the summer cicada insect. Thus, to the sensitive listener this melody evokes both the time and mood of the scene.

If the shamisen plays "Kangen" (see Figure 41, Appendix II), it is indicating that

[3] In the Edo period this word was also written 外座, which meant an outside place referring to their placement off stage. However, the present writing of the word, 下座, is more common.

the scene is laid in olden times at the court, as the word *kangen* means the orchestral gagaku music. A good example of a shamisen piece that indicates place is the tune "Tsukuda." Tsukuda is the name of an island at the mouth of the Sumida River in Tokyo. Across from this island was a large geisha district. In order to accommodate their would-be customers, the owners of these houses provided boats to carry the patrons to and from the district. As they passed by Tsukuda Island on the way to their pleasure, they were entertained on the boats by shamisen-playing geisha. The geza melody "Tsukuda" is reminiscent of these boat songs and is used whenever the Sumida River figures in the plot of a play. Kabuki tradition is rather rigid, for this tune cannot be used to indicate any other river except the Sumida.

The geza shamisen music comes from two sources, borrowed music and original music. In many cases, pieces that are thought to be original geza melodies may actually have been derived from one of the many defunct forms of Edo shamisen music. Although the geza musicians were originally nagauta men, they play all kinds of music. For example, the melody of the koto piece "Rokudan" is used during the kabuki play *Sukeroku*. The only reason given for this is that both pieces have the word *roku* in their titles. Usually, the reason for using a piece is more directly related to the requirements of the drama. Mention was made earlier of the jiuta piece "Yuki" (snow) that is used during winter scenes.

Since geza shamisen often underlays dialogue or action, it is purposely rather wandering. There never seem to be strong cadences or extremely virile rhythms. This enables such music to accommodate itself easily to the pace of the action on stage. Because of its general background function it does not often use singing. However, a form of nagauta known as *meriyasu* does appear in certain scenes in which the actor is meditating on some gentle subject. These songs are quite short and simple and seem to be remnants of the older kouta used in the kabuki. On rare occasions a solo voice will be heard coming from the geza room. This is highly effective in quiet melancholic scenes.

The other two main melodic instruments of the geza are the noh flute and the bamboo flute. The noh flute is heard most often as a reminder that a certain play is an adaptation of a noh drama. It is used particularly at the beginning and ending of a play. At other times, it is used to indicate court music because its sound resembles that of the court flute (the ryuteki). The bamboo flute is seldom used alone though it appears in many combinations, especially those imitating folk festival music. Since there are no full-time shakuhachi players in the kabuki company, the bamboo flute is used when the sound of the shakuhachi is desirable.

Like the sound-effects equipment of the radio studio, the percussion department of the geza has an eternal fascination to the outsider. In addition to the standard taiko and o-tsuzumi and ko-tsuzumi, there are many other types of drums, several sizes of gongs, chimes, and bells, and a collection of miscellaneous instruments ranging from castanets to xylophones.

The king of the geza percussion section is the o-daiko. Like its temple companion (Plate 12), it is a large drum with two tacked heads. Different sticks are used to hit it, depending on the effect desired. The most common sticks are two long, tapered pieces of wood. These can be played on the tips or they can strike flatly in order to produce a much sharper sound. Occasionally one stick is held against the skin while the head is beaten with the other. This creates a dramatic rattle somewhat like that produced by the snare on a snare drum.

The o-daiko has a long tradition as part of the kabuki. Its use as a signal instrument in the watchtowers of the old kabuki compounds was mentioned. This tradition is maintained today. One hour before curtain time "Ichiban-daiko" (drum number one) is played on the o-daiko drum. Originally, this pattern was played early in the morning to indicate that there would be a performance that day. This was necessary because the financial and political position of theatres during the Edo period was such that a manager was never sure from one day to the next if his theatre would be able to continue. The government took a very dubious view of the popular theatre, and there were enough laws already on the books that a theatre could be closed with very little pretext. This, by the way, is one of the many reasons why one never sees a social or political protest play in the kabuki. The existence of kabuki was dependent on the favor of a highly paranoid government. The very fact that it did prosper is proof of the growing strength of the townspeople and the merchants as well as the cleverness of the theatre managers.

After the playing of "Ichiban-daiko" there followed "drum number two" and "drum number three." Then the dedicatory dance "Sambaso" was performed, and the kabuki day had officially begun. Today, only "Ichiban-daiko" remains. It starts with a gradually accelerating roll executed on the edge of the drum. This is meant to represent the sound of a heavy wooden bar unbolting the entrance of the theatre.[4]

The greatest use of the o-daiko is not for traditional signals but for the creation of atmosphere. For example, the sounds of wind or rain are common effects played on the o-daiko. The sounds used, however, do not directly imitate the sounds of real wind

[4] If this tradition is true, it must date from the latter half of the Edo period. Until that time, the entrance of kabuki theatres consisted of a "mouse door" which allowed only one person at a time to pass through while the guards checked tickets and weapons.

or real rain. Rather, the o-daiko patterns are a symbolization of the idea of wind and rain. Such abstractions are necessary in order that the music may blend with the nonrealistic acting style of classic kabuki plays. In keeping with this idea, these drum patterns are sometimes used when the element depicted does not figure in the play at all. On such occasions it is felt that the quality of that element is present rather than the thing itself. Thus, one may hear the pattern of the sound of the wind in a quiet night scene when a robber is peering surreptitiously into a house. The feeling of a chilling wind and the cold eye of the robber are enough similar in the kabuki musician's mind to warrant the use of the same music for both. One utilitarian use of the wind pattern should be mentioned. It is used between scenes while the stage is dark to keep up the tension and cover the noise of the scenery being moved.

It should be obvious by now that a large part of the appreciation of geza music depends on previous knowledge of the music and patterns used. In this respect it is similar to the leitmotiv technique of the Wagnerian operas. In Wagner, themes are used to indicate people and situations as well as ideas important to the opera. One may hear the theme of the Rhine maidens when they are not on stage. To enlightened listeners such a theme reminds them of the maidens' connection with the topic under discussion on stage at that moment. It is interesting to note how a similar technique developed in kabuki some one hundred and fifty years before Wagner. A complete appreciation of kabuki music, like an understanding of the Wagnerian cycle, is dependent on learning to recognize some of the music leitmotivs and their significance.

Some of this knowledge is simply intellectual fun. For example, when the o-daiko plays the sound of the ocean, the shamisen often joins in on the piece "Chidori," as the *chidori* is a bird (a sandpiper) commonly found along the shores of Japan. The knowledge of many other effects, however, is a true contribution to one's response to the entire production. For example, the drum pattern for rain can produce a convincing sensation of precipitation though no other stage effect is used to assist in the creation of this feeling.

After the o-daiko, the next best-known percussion instrument is the *hyoshigi*. These two rectangular blocks of wood actually are not part of the geza. Rather, they are used by a special stagehand called the *kyogen-kata*. By hitting these two sticks together he warns the entire theatre of the number of minutes before the curtain rises. When the curtain is opened it is accompanied by an accelerating series of clacks from the hyoshigi. Just before the curtain closes, there is a sharp report of the hyoshigi which calls the audience's attention to the final pose. As the curtain comes down (or is pulled across, depending on the play) the hyoshigi is once more used as accompaniment.

During fight scenes and other such rough-style (*aragoto*) acting, the hyoshigi are played on a wooden board placed on the apron of the stage at stage-left. The clatter of these beats adds greatly to the power of the fighting.[5]

The hyoshigi can be heard outside the theatre as well. An evening's stroll through Tokyo will be accompanied by two musics. One is the Arabic sound of the noodle peddler's shawm, and the other is the clack of the fire watcher's hyoshigi. If you stay in an old Japanese inn, you will often hear the sound of the hyoshigi reassuring the guests that the fire watch is patrolling the halls during their slumber. In the daytime these same hyoshigi become the signal of the *kamishibai* man. With the hyoshigi he calls the children of the neighborhood to his bicycle. After they have bought enough of his candy, he shows his paper slides in a small theatre box set on the back of his bicycle. These kamishibai paper plays are narrated with all the flourish of a country kabuki actor. Television has not yet destroyed this ancient children's theatre, but then television sets do not sell penny candy.

A complete list of all the instruments in the geza room together with their various uses would form a separate book and require voluminous photographs and textual illustrations.[6] However, to help the reader identify some of the sights and sounds he may experience at a kabuki performance, here is a brief description of the other major geza instruments.

DRUMS (membranophones):

Okedo, a folk drum with two heads lashed together. It can be seen in the lower-left-hand corner of Plate 24. It is played with one or two slightly tapered sticks. Used primarily in folk scenes.

Daibyoshi, a two-headed lashed drum. Unlike the okedo, these heads extend beyond the body of the drum (like a taiko head) and the binding ropes are lashed around the middle to create tension. Primarily a Shinto-music instrument, it is played with two thin sticks.

Gaku-daiko, a short-bodied drum with two tacked heads. Played with two thin sticks, it is meant to imitate the sound of the gagaku large drum and is also used in war scenes.

[5] In classic kabuki, stage fighting is highly stylized so that many times it appears to be stately dancing accompanied by fierce grimaces. In keeping with this, the shamisen–o-daiko piece, "Dontappo," used in fight scenes seems rather leisurely for the mood it is meant to represent. The kabuki explanation is that to put rough music behind such a scene would make it too rough. Following this same theory, kabuki will occasionally use happy music behind a sad scene to keep it from being too sad. However, this theory is not applied with any consistency.

[6] Photos of these instruments can be seen in ref. 6, III, pp. 172 and 274–77.

Uchiwa-daiko, the fan drum mentioned in Chapter II is found in the geza. Its use is not restricted to religious scenes.

GONGS AND BELLS (idiophones):

Hontsuri-gane, a temple-style bell hit with a large padded hammer (see Plate 79). In addition to its use in temple scenes, it is also a signal device like the o-daiko.

Dora, a gong with a knobbed center. Used in conjunction with the bell mentioned above in temple scenes and for signals.

Soban, a gong with a rough surface. In addition to its use in temple scenes, it is played at the entrance of various rough characters. Made of thinner metal than the dora, its tone is more percussive.

Atari-gane, a brass hand gong played with a small bone hammer on the inside of the gong (see Plate 4). Its use in folk music and festival hayashi groups has already been discussed. As a rule, its use in the kabuki is similar. It is played either held in the hand or suspended by a rope.

Hitotsu-gane, a small gong similar to the atari-gane but set on three legs and played on the outside. It was originally used in the performance of Buddhist rosaries and hence appears often in religious scenes. It is also used in festival scenes. A smaller version of the same instrument is called the *matsumushi* (pine insect) and is used to create the sound of these seasonal insects as well as being used in religious scenes.

Orugoru, a set of bells of varying pitches. Originally Buddhist-style Sanctus bells, they are used most often in kabuki to indicate lightness, for example, in scenes containing butterflies. Horse-sleigh bells (*ekiro*) are used also in certain dances and when a peasant effect is desired.

Rei, a Buddhist sutra bell. Used to indicate religious services or the entrance of a priest. Bell-ringing beggar priests are still seen around Japan. The *mokugyo* mentioned in Chapter II is also used in such scenes.

Chappa, a pair of small cymbals. Used for dance accompaniment and temple or Chinese music scenes.

Yotsudake, four short pieces of bamboo that are played like castanets (Plate 56). Used in certain goddess dances. This instrument is found in the old dances of the Ryukyu Islands also. The two-piece wooden clapper of the court (the *shakubyoshi*) is also used for scenes in which court music is needed, particularly if imayo is sung.

Mokkin, a xylophone with sixteen keys. The pitch of these keys is not important because it is played in a desultory fashion. The mokkin follows the rhythm of a piece rather than the melody. Borrowed originally from the Japanese societies for Chinese music (Minshin-gaku), it is used in kabuki primarily for comic dances.

HYOSHIGI
OKEDO
DAIBYOSHI
GAKU-DAIKO
DORA
SOBAN
ATARI-GANE
HITOTSU-GANE
REI
EKIRO
YOTSUDAKE
CHAPPA
ORUGORU
MOKKIN

This list is long but incomplete. However, it gives the reader some idea of the variety of sounds that come from the geza room. These instruments are combined in a host of different ways so that the ear is constantly assaulted by a kaleidoscope of sounds. The choice of these sounds, however, is regulated by the requirements of the play. The geza is not used without dramaturgical justification. In order to better understand this process, let us look at a specific example. Though each play has a variety of musical requirements, the detailed explanation of one production will provide a basis for the understanding of other performances.

II. The Texture of Kabuki Music

Momiji Gari (the maple-viewing party) is an example par excellence, for it uses nagauta, Tokiwazu, and Gidayu musicians on stage and virtually every geza instrument off stage.

The story revolves around the encounter of Taira Koremochi with the demon of Mount Togakushi. The exact plot line and production varies from year to year and troupe to troupe. The following account is based on the Kichiemon-troupe production for November, 1956. The music was arranged by Kawatake Mokuami, and the geza was created by Tanaka Zanzaemon.

The prelude to every play is the sound of the hyoshigi which cracks out the minutes before the curtain. When everything is ready, the noh flute begins a slow overture (in this case, "Issei," meaning "one voice." The small and large tsuzumi join in from across the stage, producing the effect of the introduction to a noh play. The reason for this music is that *Momiji Gari* is based on a drama from the noh repertoire. As the curtain rises, however, the deep, menacing tones of the o-daiko are heard, removing the noh-like serenity from the music and creating a sense of danger.

The first shamisen music heard comes from a group of Tokiwazu musicians placed on a dais downstage right (see Plate 76). They are followed by a comment from a quartet of Gidayu musicians placed in a separate niche just above the stage-left entrance. The next music comes from the nagauta musicians who are placed upstage and a little to the left in order to accommodate the tree that forms part of the set (Plate 76). There are no actors on stage at the moment. The music sets the scene, which is in the mountains in the fall. This section corresponds to the oki mentioned in the Gidayu and nagauta forms.

It is the Gidayu singer who begins the actual story by telling how the warrior Taira Koremochi has been sent by the emperor to kill the demon of Mount Togakushi.

From the back of the theatre Koremochi and two attendants suddenly appear and come marching down the ramp that connects with the stage. This is accompanied by the booming of the o-daiko, which gives weight and pomp to the entrance of the hero, while the flute is added again as a reminiscence of the original noh drama. This is the beginning of the michiyuki section of nagauta form. The ko-tsuzumi and o-tsuzumi take over in noh-drama style, while the Tokiwazu musicians continue the singing.

Finally, the actors stop at the traditional place just short of the stage and the dialogue begins (Plate 77). Beneath this dialogue the nagauta shamisen play a very light, slow melody. This backing of conversations with shamisen is usually the responsibility of the geza shamisen from off stage, but in this production it is done by the nagauta players, probably for economic reasons. At the same time that this music and dialogue are going on, one can hear the occasional beats of the ko-tsuzumi which are immediately answered by another ko-tsuzumi on the opposite side of the stage. This effect, called *kodama*, has been added to heighten the mountain setting by providing echoes bounding across the make-believe valley.

When Koremochi and his servants walk onto the stage proper, they are again accompanied by the o-daiko, while the Gidayu adds comments much like a Greek chorus or the chorus in a noh play. Suddenly, a young girl appears, and the music changes to the softer strains of Tokiwazu. The drums continue to echo across the valley as she informs Koremochi and his men that her lady is in the region enjoying the beauty of the maple leaves and would like to have them join the party. The girl leaves to bring her princess, and the Gidayu singers comment again, while the o-daiko lightly taps to mark her hurried steps out. During the argument about whether to remain, the nagauta shamisen play a soft background, and occasionally the singers come in with commentary. The valley echoes continue and the o-daiko is heard whenever the actors move about the stage.

Koremochi decides that he must not be swayed from his mission and begins to leave when a court lady appears (to the music of Tokiwazu) and tries to dissuade him. Gidayu music warns that the princess comes, and as she and her retinue appear the nagauta singers extol her beauty (she, by the way, is a he, as are all the actors of present-day kabuki). The bamboo flute and two medium-size drums are added, which give a processional sound to the entrance. Nagauta and Gidayu underline the ensuing conversation between the princess and the warrior. Once again Koremochi vows to leave, but one court lady tries to retain him in a comic pantomime dance done to Tokiwazu music. As another girl joins in the pantomime, the music switches to Gidayu, then nagauta, and finally back to Tokiwazu. In this way, the various sections of the dance are marked off by actual stylistic changes in the music. Koremochi is convinced he should stay by the princess, who says that their meeting in such a lonely place must have been predestined. The Gidayu makes note of this.

The bustle and preparation for the picnic are done to the accompaniment of Tokiwazu plus the taiko drum and occasional beats with a hard stick on the edge of a gong (the dora). This produces a very festive mood. Tokiwazu and nagauta are used while the warrior sits down with the princess, and wine is poured. When the flirtation begins, the more menacing sound of Gidayu takes over.

The party begins, and dance interludes interrupt the progress of the plot. First, one of the princess' attendants dances a lighthearted dance to the accompaniment of Tokiwazu, flute, cymbals, and two drums (the okedo and daibyoshi). Such an ensemble gives a bright, festive sound. When the dance continues with a flower and a little girl added, nagauta is used. The dance ends with Gidayu.

One of the warrior's men then gets up and does a balancing dance to a mixture of Gidayu and Tokiwazu. The percussion includes sleigh bells (ekiro) plus ko-tsuzumi and o-tsuzumi. When he changes to a fan dance, the music becomes nagauta and the sleigh bells stop.

His fellow attendant then dances in competition, the subject of his dance being a blind man. The music is Tokiwazu, and the percussion uses the o-daiko plus the edge of a cymbal and the xylophone (mokkin). These add to the gauche quality required.

The dancing stops, and rice wine is mixed with gentle conversation set in a quiet matrix of nagauta shamisen. In general, whenever there is dialogue in the play there is a shamisen background, though it may not always be mentioned in this description.

Finally, the princess herself consents to dance. In addition to the regular nagauta music, the geza provides a very clever imitation of a gagaku court orchestra. Small double reeds are blown to sound like the sho, while the daibyoshi drum plays in court style and the hand gong, noh flute, and another drum (gaku-daiko) add characteristic court sounds. When the music changes to Tokiwazu the gagaku imitation is dropped and a normal ko-tsuzumi and o-tsuzumi part is used.

The next section of the princess' dance is done to Gidayu plus noh flute, ko-tsuzumi, and o-tsuzumi. The style changes to the softer Tokiwazu, and the hayashi is silent as in a kudoki section. Koremochi begins to succumb to the lulling effect of wine, soft music, and gentle dancing. The princess dances on, watching him occasionally to see if he is asleep. The menacing roll of the o-daiko is heard as she dances closer to the warrior. Then suddenly, with a sharp bang on the o-daiko, he awakens and she quickly changes into a fast dance to nagauta, bamboo flute, taiko, o-tsuzumi, ko-tsuzumi, and the silvery-toned orugoru bells. When Tokiwazu takes over, she begins a Japanese fan dance, the hayashi continuing to keep the rhythm and the mood. Then Gidayu is played (without hayashi) as she uses two fans. Nagauta plus hayashi is used while she performs tricks by flipping the fans in various clever ways. The hayashi continue as the music styles change at a faster rate. During one of the Gidayu sections, Koremochi is discovered to be fast asleep. There is a little more dancing to Tokiwazu and taiko, and then a finale with all the shamisen joining with the hayashi and the piercing noh flute. There is silence as the princess hurls her final curse at the helpless warrior and dashes off stage to the sound of nagauta and the roar of the o-daiko. The roar subsides to a menacing rumble as the Gidayu singers provide a transition.

Next, there is a great banging of cymbals, drums, and o-daiko as a child messenger from Hachiman, the war god, appears on the ramp through a trap door. This is the usual music for the appearance of a god, especially if he arrives by way of the trap door, called a *seri*. The choice of instruments also shows the use of the ensemble meant to indicate temples. During the young messenger's dialogue and dances, the three main styles of shamisen music alternate, while hayashi is used throughout. The o-daiko becomes particularly loud whenever he tries to wake up the warrior. In his final dance, a whole host of drums are used, each played with two sticks to add weight to the sound. Cymbals and the noh flute are also present. Finally, he wakes Koremochi and his companions and informs them that the lovely princess is really the demon Kijo, the object of their mission to the mountains. The messenger gives Koremochi a sacred sword and to the terrific pounding of the o-daiko, the hero dashes off stage in pursuit of the villain.

While the o-daiko keeps up a steady rumble, the two male attendants do a comic dance to Gidayu as they find that their legs are not too steady after so much drinking. Finally, they too dash off stage, and a big blast on the o-daiko signifies the end of Act One.

Act Two begins with nagauta shamisen music taken from the ozatsuma music patterns. In Chapter VIII, I discussed these remnants of an old shamisen genre and their use as transitional material and for the backing of narrational sections. In this case, they form a very necessary flexible form of transition music used until the actors are ready to appear once more on the stage. Finally, there is a flash of lightning, the o-daiko is hit with one stick lying against the skin so as to increase the rattle, and the villain comes flying on stage, his face hidden by a veil and hotly pursued by Koremochi. An added effect to the lightning is the grating of a bronze hand gong over the rough surface of a much larger, thinner gong (the soban). This gives a real lightning "ripping" sound. It is also used when the villain reveals himself in all his horror and begins to twirl his long hair about by violently swinging his head.

The music for the big fight is mostly nagauta and hayashi with plenty of o-daiko mixed in. The villain blows blinding smoke into the hero's eyes. There is a sudden silence as the villain approaches his now-helpless victim. The shouts (*kakegoe*) of the drummers break the silence, the noh flute, taiko, and o-daiko join in, and a slow dramatic fight begins in which the magic sword keeps frustrating the villain by protecting Koremochi while he is recovering his eyesight. The fast fight begins once more with all the musicians and most of the percussion adding to the din of battle. At last, the villain mounts a nearby tree, spits a final load of flame and poses with fearsome grimaces as the curtain comes down (Plate 76).

While the actors make a dash for the dressing rooms to change and the set disintegrates under the hammers of the stage crew, the o-daiko, together with the noh flute and two taiko, bangs out the finale of the drama with the rhythm called "Uchidashi," the playing out.

This, then, is the way a kabuki drama is constructed musically. What general observations can be made? First, one should note that the music proper and the geza were arranged by two different people. Though there are separate pieces called *Momiji Gari* in both the nagauta and Tokiwazu repertoires, the particular version used for the kabuki play is a very special pastiche with different musical materials being used plus the addition of Gidayu. It is important to notice how this switch from one style of music to another usually indicates a change in action as well as helping to add variety to the color and pace of the drama.

The geza music of this play shows most of the characteristic uses of off-stage effects. Notice how the o-daiko music runs through the entire play serving many different functions. The geza shamisen music was produced on stage in this play, but its character remains the same. It wandered quietly beneath the drama in much the way of modern film music. Notice that the use of the other geza instruments indicated special situations but did not reproduce the exact sounds of these atmospheres. The ripping of the lightning flashes was not realistic but still very effective. The nearest this play came to direct imitation was the gagaku effect at the beginning of the princess' dance. Even then, the sound could never be confused with that of the real court orchestra. It gave a hint of the sound. As in most of Japanese art, it was up to the viewer to fill in the rest with his imagination.

The most important observation to be made concerning this play is that it shows a sense of over-all "orchestration." There is a constant awareness on the part of the producers of the need for varied tone colors and the proper psychological timing of theatrical effects. For example, there is the sudden switch to the rougher style of Gidayu when the dance of the princess begins to show menacing characteristics.

Even a cursory study of this one kabuki play shows that the full appreciation of kabuki music is more involved than it would appear on the surface. The use of leitmotivs, signals, varying musical styles, and sound effects has been coördinated in a manner little exploited in the West. Unfortunately, this aggregate of theatrical traditions is passed down from teacher to apprentice by rote methods. Until recently, books of geza music contained only titles and no notation. The few books of geza notation are considered the sacrosanct property of the various geza-music guilds. Hence, it is difficult, and sometimes impossible, for the researcher to see such materials unless he joins the guild and works his way through the repertoire at the slow pace regulated by the head musician.

For the normal kabuki fan, the process of geza-music appreciation requires no such arduous tasks. With a review of the materials given in this chapter plus a sharp ear in the theatre, one may savor that delicious sensation of being one of the audience who "knows." For those who may never attend kabuki, the understanding of kabuki music reveals another facet of the great theatrical tradition of Japan.

CHAPTER

TEN

FOLK MUSICAL ARTS

I. Introduction

The fishermen pulling in their nets, the farmer planting his crop, a wedding, a festival, a lullaby; these are the inspirations for folk music all over the world. Japan is no exception. The folk-song field worker need only visit any rural area in Japan and with patience he can uncover a full repertoire answering these same musical needs in peasant life.

Because of the long years of feudalism and relative lack of intercommunication, each area of Japan shows a surprising variety in its folk arts. The festivals and songs of one district may be quite different from those of adjacent territories. Thus, when we view all of Japan, we see a very rich tradition of folk music. There have been a few enthusiastic collectors of these materials, but as yet there has been little attempt to correlate and compare the musics of various districts nor have there been many studies made of the all-important relation between Japanese art music and the folk tradition.[1] However, in this short introduction to the subject one can discover some of the general musical characteristics and the typical forms which give Japanese folk musical arts their special appeal.

The study of Japanese folk musical arts can be divided into two major categories: folk songs (*minyo*) and folk theatricals (*minzoku-geino*). While these two are not mutually exclusive, they emphasize an important characteristic of the field. In addition to the usual folk-song tradition, there is extant in Japan, as in most oriental countries, a strong proclivity for folk theatricals. In addition to the charm and color of these folk *geino*, their study provides many excellent clues as to the origins and early styles of the more famous Japanese theatre traditions.

In order to have a well-rounded picture of the music popular with the folk of Japan, two additional items must be added to our discussion of folk music. One is the field of commercial Japanese-style popular music. The other is the music of minority groups and cultures contiguous with Japan. If the essential elements can be found in all these various areas, one will have a good understanding of the present condition and the rich heritage of the world of Japanese folk musical arts.

[1] Maps showing the distribution of various folk-music forms can be found in the front of ref. 63.

II. Folk Songs

The basic ingredients of the Japanese diet are rice and fish. Therefore, songs about rice growing and songs about fishing are two of the major genres of Japanese folk music. For example, one of the most widespread forms of folk song in Japan is the *taueuta,* the "rice-planting songs." The words of such songs are similar all over Japan. They concern the process of planting and estimates of the yield, to which is usually added a bit of local color. All the other acts of rice cultivation are accompanied by songs. Though the production methods may have changed somewhat, many of these songs live on and have become party songs instead of work songs.

This same evolution is found in the case of fishing songs. The famous "Soran-bushi" of Hokkaido was originally meant to coördinate the pulling in of nets full of herring. Now it is sung and danced all over the country by farmer, fisherman, and businessman alike. A different kind of evolution is found in the work songs of the lumbermen and construction workers. This music, known as *kiyari,* has since become a type of festival chanting so that it now serves both functional and ceremonial purposes. Despite the frequency of such changes, one can still hear many pure local work songs in the more remote villages of Japan.

A great majority of the old songs are meant for work or for ceremony. These tunes seldom use more than hand clapping for accompaniment, though the ceremonial pieces may add flute and drum. The entrance of the shamisen into the field of folk music did not occur until the sixteenth century. With it came the kouta tradition and a greater number of love and party songs. However, though there are many references to lost loves in old Japanese folk songs, one is impressed by the large number of unadulterated work songs that still exist in Japan. Of course, the party music is another matter. When the rice wine is poured, full license is granted. In the Japanese folk tradition, it is the old folks, particularly grandma, who are allowed to be the most bawdy. The radio is taking its yearly toll of lost folk songs, but in the work and play of the distant villages of Japan one can still find rich and relatively untapped treasures of folk music.

Whether work song, play song, love song, or lullaby, Japanese folk tunes have one thing in common, they are set in the *yo-in*-scale system. The basic forms of these scales were discussed before (see pages 63 and 161). In both folk music and shamisen music one finds that a piece can move back and forth freely between these two modes. Thus, a piece may start in the *yo* mode and switch to the *in.* Modulations to *yo* and *in* scales built on a note a fourth or fifth away are not uncommon. The use of modes built on

80. The colorful costumes of these folk singers and dancers are typical of the many folk festivals in Japan.

81. This is one of the more colorful of the various lion dances that mark many a folk festival in Japan. Note the large drums suspended in front of the dancers. See page 248.

82. These red-faced devils are also frequently seen in folk festivals. See page 248.

83. A devil fights off two lions in the "Oni-daiko" dance from Sado Island.

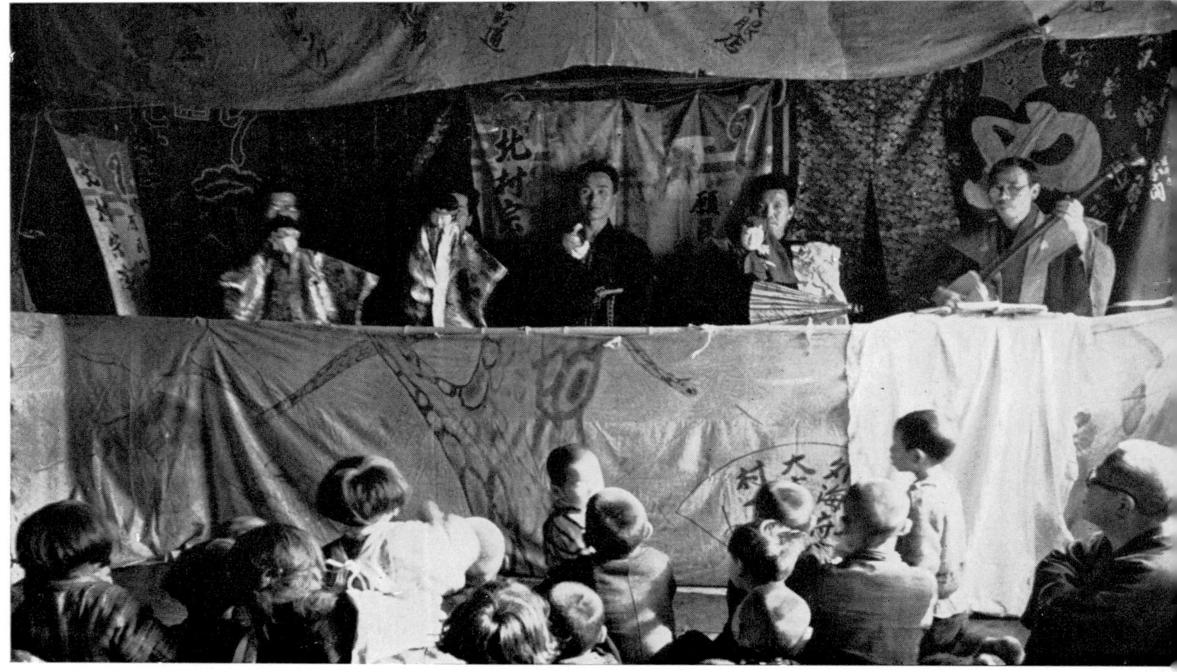

84. In this folk puppet play from Sado Island one man does both the singing and accompanying. See page 250.

85. A country-kabuki performance of the play *Chushingura* by villagers on Shodo Island. The theatre is open on three sides and is covered by a thatched roof but it has a revolving stage and an enthusiastic audience. See page 251.

86. The shamisen and taiko are used to accompany this "Yasuda-odori" from Shodo Island.

87. The women play the shamisen but the men wear the fancy hats and kimono as they travel through a village street in a folk festival.

88. The Ainu natives of northern Japan create strange effects by singing into each other's mouths. See page 246.

89. The Ainu tonkori is an instrument plucked with both hands. See page 247.

the fourth and fifth above the basic pitch of the scale are also frequent. That is, the same notes are used, but a different note is used as a tonal center.

With these possibilities plus various altered forms of the *yo* and *in* scales themselves, it is sometimes difficult to say definitely what the modulatory scheme of a certain composition is. For instance, Figure 20 could be considered as starting in the *yo* scale on G, changing to the *in* scale, and then returning to the *yo* scale. The first phrase could also be considered as centered on a different *yo* scale built on D, hence a modulation to the *in* scale on G and a return to the original scale of D. But these are problems for the music analyst.

FIGURE 20. An excerpt from the "Ise-ondo"

What the general reader need note is that Japanese folk music makes very free use of its tonal basis. As shamisen music became stronger, many tunes were changed from the *yo* to the *in* scale. In some cases the change was not complete, leaving a piece ambiguously perched between two tonal systems. One of the vital elements of folk music the world over is its refusal to be bound by rigid laws. Thus, if a Japanese farmer wants to alter the songs his grandfather taught him, he will do so with no feeling of being an iconoclast. In the Edo period such changes created the various *in* modes. In modern times it sometimes means the use of a Western major or minor or the addition of a Western accompaniment.

The form of Japanese folk music is usually quite simple. Binary (A-B) and ternary (A-B-A) are most common. In some cases ternary songs consist of three independent phrases (A-B-C). Longer forms appear in certain ceremonial pieces, especially in solo-flute folk parts, but the binary and ternary forms are the most usual. The poetry of this folk music is usually set in traditional 7-7-7-5 syllable lines.

Musically, one should note that there is a strong tendency in Japanese folk music to emphasize the notes just above or below the basic tone, the tonic, of the scale used. Japanese folk songs often do not begin on the first note of the scale, the second or fourth being common (see Figure 21). Many times the melody will emphasize the fourth and second below the tonic before one hears the basic pitch clearly (see Figure 4). The use of the so-called whole-step lower neighbor (C to D in Figure 4) or the half-step upper neighbor (E flat to D in Figure 20) is quite idiomatic of Japanese folk music. One often finds the third below the tonic used as a kind of leading tone (E to G in Figure 20), particularly in the *yo* scale.

Japanese folk music is usually in rhythms of two or four beats, though the internal division of each beat may be a triplet. However, this principle is not doctrinaire, especially in solo songs. The rhythmic accompaniment of old folk songs is quite simple (see Figure 4) though several different instruments are used. Various drums (Plate 5), rattles (Plate 8), and gongs (Plate 4) are used in a variety of combinations. It is only with the influence of theatre and art music that the folk percussion parts became more involved. The various festival hayashi groups mentioned in Chapter II were so influenced, though it was noted that there was a constant trading of influences between the folk and the art world.

Basically, Japanese folk rhythms are utilitarian and primitive. They serve only to coördinate movement and are seldom a means of expression in themselves. As in many cultures, the folk singer in Japan is more concerned with coloring the words and melody than adding variety to the percussion parts. Indeed, one of the great pleasures of such folk music is the enthusiasm with which these Japanese singers twist and turn about the basic melody.

In addition to rhythmic accompaniments, there are also two common melodic instruments used, the flute and the shamisen. It was mentioned that most Japanese ceremonial music uses the flute as the main melodic instrument. The flute or sometimes the shakuhachi are also added to vocal compositions. Folk flutes usually play a melismatic version of the vocal line. During certain dance accompaniments, however, the combination of the flute and voice is very different. As the dancers move through the many repeats of their figures, the flute plays certain standard melodies. From time to time the singers enter with various folk songs. However, there is often no tonal or melodic relation between these two parts. They are held together only by a common rhythmic frame and a common purpose. One wonders what connection this custom might have with the similar orientation of the noh flute to noh singing, especially since noh grew out of such a number of ancient folk theatricals.

A typical shamisen accompaniment to a folk song is shown in Figure 21. Note the use of upper and lower neighbors in the typical manner mentioned above. The strumming of an open string plus a fingered string reminds one of the similar hill-billy

FIGURE 21. Bon-odori music from Chiba

fiddler technique.[2] Notice how the shamisen keeps the melody rhythmically alive by playing variations on the vocal line. Measures ten through fifteen are good examples of this so-called heterophony. At other times the shamisen plays endlessly repeating drones over which the voice can improvise at will. Though this example is written in two-four time, such shamisen parts are often played as if they were in six-eight. This difference is similar to that found between jazz as it is written and as it is performed.

In the field of commercial music there is found a very interesting compromise between East and West. The classic *in* scale is used for a love song which is accompanied by a standard Western-style dance band plus a shamisen or, in its place, an electric guitar. The singers use a vocal style which ranges all the way from a pure Japanese nasal folk quality to the sound of a sultry blues singer. This popular music is known as *ryukoka*. The term also includes all the Western-style fox trots, mambos, and jazz pieces played in Japan. However, it is the pseudo-folk-song ryuko music that offers

[2] In folk shamisen, hon-choshi is usually used for pieces in the *yo* scale and ni-agari for pieces in the *in* scale.

the most interest to the student of acculturation. It is also this music that is hummed and whistled about the streets of modern Tokyo.

Though mass communications may eventually completely reorganize the structure of national musics, at present there is a difference between urban and rural music in most countries of the world. By definition,[3] the popular music of the cities is not folk music, but still it is a part of the over-all picture of the musical life of a nation that cannot be ignored. In the Edo period such short-lived music was known as *hayariuta*. These tunes floated through the streets of the city for a few months only to be replaced by a new flood of ditties. The hit parade was no more stable in those days than it is now. The present-day Japanese hit parade includes the latest foreign tunes plus a number of these ryukoka. Only the future will tell what effect these songs will have on the stream of folk music that continues to flow through all the eddies and currents of temporary music fashions.

In addition to Japanese folk music and commercial music there is another area to be discussed, the music of contiguous cultures. These groups are found at the two extremities of Japan. In Hokkaido in northern Japan, there are the Ainu, Gilyaks, and a few Orochon people, while south of Kyushu in the famous Ryukyu Islands are the native Ryukyuans.

The Ainu culture has been a fascination to scholars for many years. Early Japanese history is a long and bloody saga of the battle between the Japanese and these wild men of the north. Gradually, the Ainu were driven to Hokkaido where, like the American Indian, they were left to die out through cultural starvation. Ainu music reflects the non-Japanese origin of the race. It is strikingly similar to American Indian music, with many songs and dances imitating birds, bears, and other creatures. Most of the singing is done to the accompaniment of hand clapping. The most unusual piece in the Ainu vocal repertoire is a duet called "Rekukkara" (Plate 88). In this duet one singer carries the tune and the other creates a percussive accompaniment in her throat using the pressure of the incoming air from the other person's mouth.

Ainu dance songs and their choreography show a strength and rough humor alien to the Japanese tradition. The grunts of the male sword dance, the trills of the female bird dances, and the solemnity of the ritual bear sacrifice adumbrate a very ancient and primitive origin. For one trained in traditional Japanese folk music, the sound of an Ainu song comes as a real shock. It is like meeting a grizzly bear in a pet shop.

There are only two instruments of importance in present-day Ainu music. One is

[3] Folk music is presently defined as music which is passed on orally, has no known composer, and is subject to variation by the performers.

the *tonkori*, a two- to five-stringed plucked instrument (Plate 89). It is played as a drone accompaniment for singing or as a solo instrument. Only the open-string sounds are used, and it is plucked with both hands to create a basically rhythmic effect. The second Ainu instrument is the *mukkuri*, a type of jew's harp. Both these instruments are played by women. In ancient times, flutes were played by men, but today the flute tradition has nearly disappeared.

There is no future for Ainu culture. However, if one has a chance to hear the remnants of its music, one can tell that theirs was once a virile, primitive society.

The Gilyaks and Orochon peoples have almost become extinct as a pure race. Their origins seem to have been in Siberia and in the steppes of Manchuria. A few of these people are found in the Sakhalin Islands above Hokkaido and in Hokkaido itself. The remains of their music consist of certain short-phrased folk songs and chanted sagas. The jew's harp is found in both cultures and the Gilyaks use a one-string fiddle built much like similar Eskimo and Indian instruments. They also use a pan drum which resembles Eskimo drums. It is often used by female shamans who come to drive away evil spirits and cure the sick. These two peoples are not Japanese but their existence on Japanese soil should be noted as a special element in the study of folk arts in Japan.

To the south of Kyushu lie the Ryukyu Islands. In the study of Japanese culture, these islands play an important role as a bridge for the passage of Chinese culture to Japan. We have spoken of the transfer of the predecessor of the shamisen, the jamisen (Plate 70). This instrument is still the backbone of Ryukyu folk music. Plucked with a horn pick and usually tuned in the Chinese pentatonic, it provides accompaniment for the many folk dances and songs. Unlike the Japanese shamisen, it never developed a truly independent style and remains very subservient to the singing. The koto is also found in the Ryukyus. It is played much like the Japanese koto except that the tuning is usually Chinese.

Folk flutes and a taiko are also common. The most distinctive element of Ryukyu instrumental styling is the technique used on the taiko. The sticks seem to fly away from the skin rather than toward it. It is one of the liveliest folk techniques in the Far East. Many folk dances and old court and geisha dances still survive in the Ryukyus. For our survey all we need note is that both the choreography and the music show a strange mixture of Chinese, Japanese, and Southeast Asian influences. The scales, costumes, and foot movements are Chinese, the hand movements suggest Indonesian gestures, while the instrumentation reflects Japanese influence. As a commercial crossroads of the ancient orient, these islands offer a gold mine of information concerning the interchange of cultures in the Far East.

III. Folk Theatricals and Dances

The words *minzoku-geino* cover all the folk theatre arts as well as the field of folk dance. In the West, these areas of study are usually separated. However, the tradition of nonprofessional theatricals is so strong in Japan that it would be very difficult to say in some cases where folk dance ends and pure theatre begins. For example, the Yuki Matsuri described in Chapter II is replete with elements of both. For the purposes of this general survey, the word geino will be accepted as defined by the Japanese.

The greatest number of these geino occur during folk festivals. In Chapter II the ceremonials and entertainments for the gods which went under the title of kagura were discussed. Also, the famous community-dance form of bon-odori was mentioned. In addition to these, there are many kinds of circle and processional dances used during folk celebrations. One of the most widespread types is the *hanagasa-odori*, the dance with the flower hats. The early hanagasa dances were probably done with simple floral decorations on the farmer's broad-brimmed hats. However, eventually these hats grew in size until they covered the dancers' entire head and projected several feet in the air. Large umbrellas were also built with paper flowers festooned all around. These umbrellas and fantastic hats were the main props of the city furyu dances which were so popular in the fifteenth and sixteenth centuries (see page 107). They still remain in the folk dances of many districts of Japan.

In addition to these special hat dances, there are many forms of mask dances used in Japan. The most universally popular are the *shishi-odori*, the "lion dances" (Plate 6). Horse, cow, and deer dances are also common. However, the greatest variety of masks represent gods, devils, or creatures of imagination. The long-nosed *tengu* and various red-faced devils (*oni*) are particularly popular (Plate 82). Many of the folk masks are remnants of very ancient Chinese theatricals (gigaku) and old forms of noh masks. Through the preservation of these old folk traditions, the scholar is able to trace some of the techniques and props of Japan's early theatricals.

Another favorite form of ceremonial dancing is the *taiko-odori*, dances with a drum. Sometimes these drums are carried by the dancers and sometimes the dance is performed around one large drum. This is not a completely independent category, as drum-carrying dancers may wear masks or flower hats. Plate 81, a lion dance, is an excellent example of a combination of styles. Notice the large drum suspended in front of each dancer. This is quite typical. Actually, the importance of the drum as a center of many Japanese folk dances is little realized by the casual visitor to Japan.

A common characteristic in these various folk ceremonial dances is the accompaniment. Kagura, flower-hat dances, lion dances, masked dances, and those using the drum as a prop all use the flute and drum as accompaniment. Sometimes singing is included. As was said, the shamisen is found in community dancing but almost never in old folk ceremonials.

In general, Japanese ceremonial dances have props. There is a great liking for plumes, poles, and other appendages that tower in the air above the dancer. It is also common to hide the dancer's face in a mask or a flower hat. Finally, one should note that the choreography of such dances is conceived in relation to magic numbers, particularly three. This tertiary, left-right-left, orientation of such dances shows that they are basically religious in origin and not theatrical. What they lose in stage effect they gain in bringing the will of the gods in line with the desires of the community by means of magically significant repetitions of dances and movements within dances.

The field of nonceremonial folk dance is equally as varied. These dances fall primarily into two intermingled categories, work pantomimes and pure party dances. The great number of folk songs concerned with special forms of labor were mentioned above. It is only natural that there should be a repertoire of accompanying dances. While these work dances may have originally had magical significance, today they are used primarily as party dances. Some have become commercialized and are performed in dance halls and banquet rooms all over Japan. "Tanko-bushi," the coal miner's dance, is the best-known example of this type. Others are still the property of regional villages.

There has been a rise of folk-dancing societies in Japan somewhat like the growth of American square-dance clubs so that more of these country dances have been made available to the general public through instruction and music books (see ref. 67). However, the original forms of such dances are fast disappearing from the national scene. It may well be that only such party tunes as "Tanko-bushi" will remain to remind us of the many work pantomime dances of rural Japan.

Japanese parties are set in such a definite pattern that this form of dance will probably never die. Some of the lewder pantomimes may drop out, but the tradition of self-entertainment at Japanese parties is so strong that there should always be a businessman who will be able to wrap a towel around his head and stumble through the outlines of a country dance. The Japanese huckster as well as the peasant has a pride in knowing how to sing a folk song or perform a dance. The passive attitude of the West toward entertainment has not yet made sufficient inroads into Japanese life to endanger this tradition.

There is little artistry in most of these dances, but they are very gay. They offer an important emotional outlet and at the same time reaffirm a contact with the past which is still important to Japanese rural society. The fact that even urban business society requires that a well-bred man be proficient at a modicum of folk song or dance is further proof of the power of tradition. It remains to be seen whether the great pacifier, television, will be able to crush this tradition of socially acceptable exhibitionism. At present, amateur hours filled with such performers consume much of the time on Japanese radio and television.

To the theatre student, the most interesting part of Japanese folk music is the true folk-theatrical tradition. In addition to all the involved festivals and ceremonials already mentioned, there are in Japan folk puppet plays, noh dramas, and kabuki. The great puppet tradition of Japan is believed to have begun on the island of Awaji where one can still see amateur puppet performances. On some of the smaller islands of Japan, such plays are the only theatrical entertainments available. Stages are set up in a field or sometimes in special buildings. During slack times in the farming or fishing seasons, the village puppets are dusted off and the old plays revived. Some folk puppets are manipulated by two or three people like the professional bunraku, while others are one-man puppets like those used in the old Punch-and-Judy shows.

The puppet tradition is very old in Japan and hence has had ample opportunity to spread among the people. Prints of old Edo show traveling puppeteers performing in the streets. The kind of puppets used for such shows were extremely simple, consisting of a head placed on a stick with a cross piece for arms holding out the costume. These play puppets were designated *ayatsuri-ningyo* to differentiate them from ordinary dolls (*ningyo*). In some farm districts of Japan these primitive puppets are still used.[4] Whether the puppets are simple or complex, our main interest here is the music used to accompany their actions. In the more primitive cases the operator himself simply dramatizes the stories much like the kamishibai man mentioned earlier. In the more developed folk-puppet traditions, one finds local joruri singers shouting and gesticulating in imitation of their professional mentors. Through the media of folk-puppet plays many of the lesser-known forms of joruri have survived long after they have disappeared from the professional theatre world. The folk-puppet theatre is losing ground, but it is still an important factor in the country theatre life of Japan (see Plate 84).

Country kabuki is rather like amateur theatre and road companies in the West.

[4] In Aomori Prefecture of northern Japan dolls of this type called *oshirasama* have become household gods. A new layer of clothes is added to these dolls every year. Thus, one can trace the history of fabrics in that area as far back as one hundred years by examining the layers of cloth that cover these dolls.

It is essentially the same as the professional theatre as far as content is concerned. Perhaps the most significant difference in the case of country kabuki is that audience decorum is more in keeping with the old traditions of Edo-period city kabuki. They talk, drink, eat, and have a good time while casually observing the play. There is a very close connection between the audience and the performers, which is fast disappearing from the professional kabuki. If one has a chance to attend a folk-puppet play or a country kabuki, one will notice the difference immediately. There, the same spirit that permeated the European theatre through the Elizabethan age can still be felt. Modern-style solemnity and fierce concentration on the plot are out of place in such situations. This does not mean that the drama is ignored. Indeed, Japanese farmers have been known to leap on the stage to join in moments of great tension. The appeal of such folk theatricals is not the polish of their performance nor their music, but rather the rare identity established between the stage and the audience. It is a quality in the theatre arts almost unknown in present-day Western drama (see Plate 85).

The music of country noh is likewise of little interest except to the noh specialist. When the restricted style of noh singing is imitated in folk style the subtleties are lost. However, there are many clues as to the original style of noh in some of the folk productions. Mibu-kyogen (Plate 37) in Kyoto has been mentioned as a folk form that retains a staging method and pantomime tradition dating from the fourteenth century. While musically these various folk forms may not have much to offer,[5] they needs be mentioned as rare examples of the living reference materials available to the student of Japanese theatre.

This cursory glance at Japanese theatricals does not pretend to do adequate justice to the breadth and variety of such forms. However, this book is concerned with music, and the major musical elements common to such events have already been noted. That is, folk ceremonial music centers around drums and flutes with some singing. Folk dance adds shamisen though there are many old dances done to simple hand clapping. The folk dramas borrow from their professional models, simplifying the music according to the abilities of local performers.

Studying Japanese folk music is like stepping into a lush jungle. The beauty and diversity of forms and the number of un-named varieties are a veritable El Dorado to the folk-music treasure hunter. The past few pages have pointed out a few signs by which one can find for himself the trails that lead to the rich caches of folk song, dance,

[5] Mibu-kyogen uses one large fish-mouthed gong and two okedo drums, which are played in the same rhythm by one man. Occasionally a flute is added, playing the same tune regardless of which play is performed. There are a few special effects, but in general, the interest of the plays is pantomimic, not musical.

and theatre. This book began with a folk event and it is suitable that it should end in the same vein. The art music of Japan has contributed many beautiful and significant moments to the world of sound, but it is the steady stream of folk music that provides those basic, refreshing materials through which such art music grows. Whatever the future may bring, the past has shown a long and virile heritage of folk music in Japan.

EPILOGUE

In the past ten chapters we have viewed the multifarious musical products of Japan. We have seen them grow out of a Chinese, word-oriented tradition into a multiplicity of forms. The ceremonials of antiquity were preserved by the court musicians and dancers, while the message of Sakyamuni was memorialized through the music of the Buddhist church. The storytelling tradition flourished under the aegis of the Heike-biwa bards and was carried on by later biwa schools and by the exceptional joruri singers. At the same time, a host of folk theatricals combined to create one of the world's unique dramatic forms, the noh. This, in turn, joined with the joruri tradition to produce the kabuki. The instrumental orientation of gagaku was carried on in koto music, which joined with the shamisen and shakuhachi to form the basis of the music of the Edo period. The shamisen, in turn, was intimately connected with the kabuki. Thus, we find in the finest products of Japanese music today the residue of centuries of musical mixtures and refinements.

One might call folk music the catalyst which periodically accelerated the fusion of styles. At present, these folk arts are still a matter of local pride, but history has shown that such arts, though important catalysts for other forms, are themselves very susceptible to influence and change. In modern folk music, the unknown factor is mass communications. It is impossible to calculate the extent of help or damage of which this medium is capable. The communication centers may take over the functions of storytelling and entertainment, while advertisement may usurp religion. Nevertheless, the peasant's need for self-expression and his close connection with the basic forces of nature will prove, perhaps, to be antibiotics for this virulent infection which seems to be decimating the folk arts of the world. It is still too early for theories. It is better for us to learn to appreciate the wonderful Japanese folk tradition as it is, encourage it whenever possible, and hope that history will treat it kindly.

Time and again the Japanese compositional propensity for stereotyped melodic patterns has been noted. This is in keeping with a similar tendency found in all the arts in Japan. We have also seen the strong guild structure, the rote teaching methods, and the concomitant vague notation systems which have plagued Japanese music from its earliest times. Finally, we should notice once more the basic chamber-music concept of Japanese music. Though gagaku and kabuki music can be considered as orchestral, the fundamental compositional orientation of Japanese music is toward a subtle refinement of a limited tonal and instrumental spectrum.

The future of Japanese music depends, I think, upon the reaffirmation of this last concept. To the extent that Japanese music attempts to imitate the Western nineteenth-century sound ideal, it will lose its own most vital elements. In such a situation it is doomed to eventual failure. By the same token, to the degree that hogaku reverts to its overworked tonal systems, it will be unable to find truly new means of expression. In both Eastern and Western music, scales are expendable, compositional principles are not. If Japanese composers will rediscover the rich field of timbres and techniques available in traditional instruments and combine them with contemporary melodic principles and, perhaps, Japanese nondevelopmental forms, they might create one of the most original musics of the twentieth century. Japanese music will never match Wagner or early Stravinsky in terms of volume, but there is no reason why it cannot equal Mozart and late Bartok on the level of brilliance within a microcosmos. This is the problem and the hope I adjure to hogaku today.

APPENDIX ONE A TIME CHART OF JAPANESE MUSIC HISTORY

The study of Japanese music history is at such a stage of development that any dating is still tentative and open to considerable variation. This chart, shown on the following pages, is meant to aid the reader in seeing the over-all growth of Japanese music and the interrelations between its major forms. It should not be used in any more doctrinaire a fashion. Thus, for example, one can see that in the Heian period a separate shakuhachi tradition appeared out of gagaku. The beginning of the shakuhachi line is broken, as details concerning this early stage are as yet unknown. The line becomes solid in the Muromachi period with the appearance of the hitoyogiri, and in the eighteenth century a new shakuhachi tradition is seen. The influence of shakuhachi on jiuta is noted in the early ninteenth century when it was strong, though such an influence was felt earlier also. Such influences are noted by the direction of the arrows. In some cases the influence is mutual as between folk music and folk theatricals (shown in a broken line because of its historically indefinite nature).

Some forms became ancillaries to larger genres. This is shown by the merging of lines. For example, kyogen is seen growing out of folk theatricals, running parallel with noh, and eventually becoming part of the noh tradition. This line refers to the form of kyogen discussed in this book and does not attempt to trace further the many other theatricals which also use the word *kyogen* in their titles.

Thus, the inaccuracies of an outline have been preferred to the maze of a full graphic exposition of every form and influence. For example, the myriad forms of shamisen music have been reduced to the two general categories of utaimono and katarimono (see Chapter VIII). The influence of shamisen on kabuki is shown once, though new forms entered constantly from both major styles of shamisen music. A more detailed chart of shamisen music can be seen in the back of reference 49.

Visual aids are useful as long as their limitations are stated. This chart, used in conjunction with the text, may help the reader organize his general understanding of Japanese music history. It pretends to do no more than this.

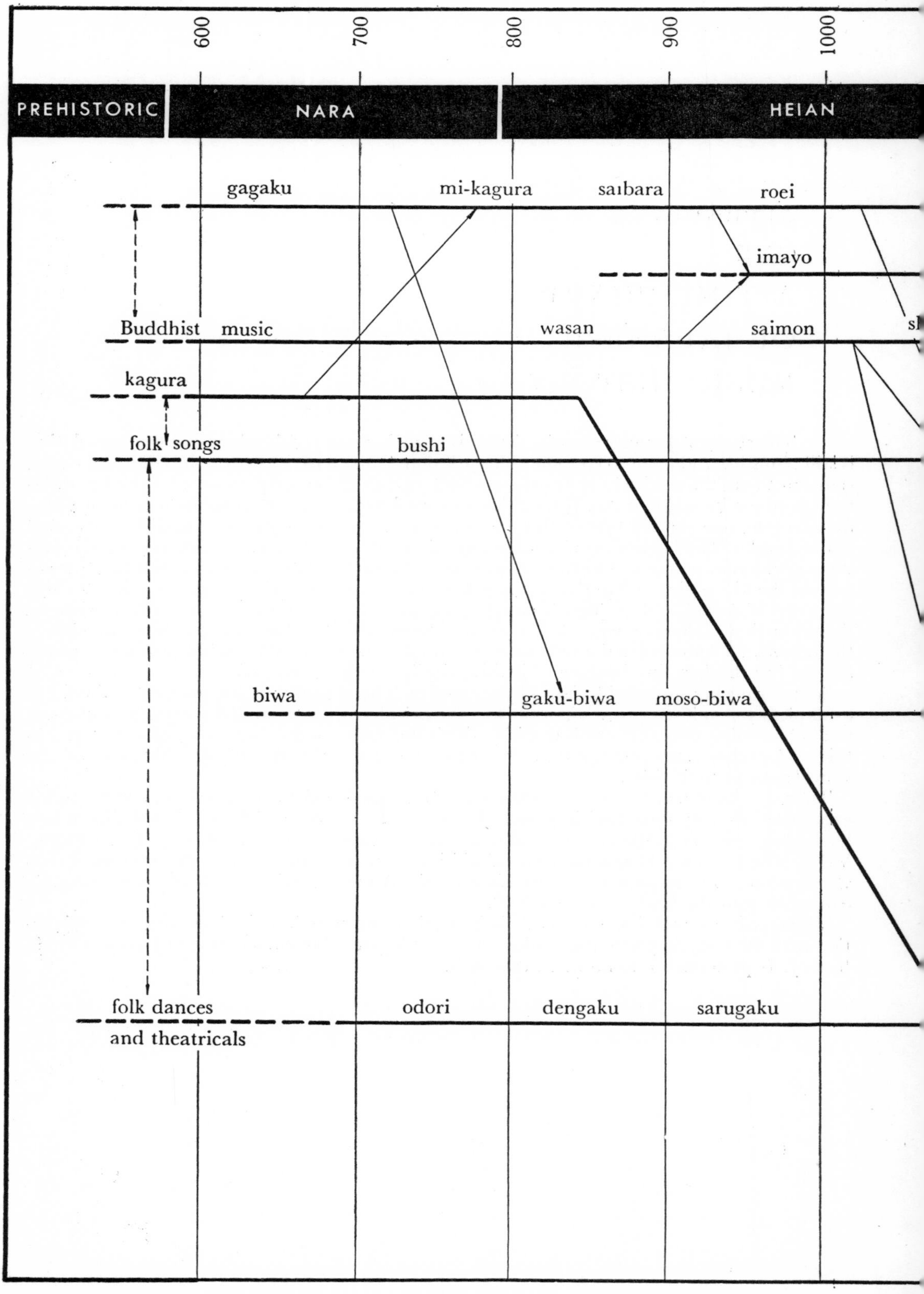

600 700 800 900 1000

PREHISTORIC | NARA | HEIAN

gagaku mi-kagura saibara roei

imayo

Buddhist music wasan saimon sh

kagura

folk songs bushi

biwa gaku-biwa moso-biwa

folk dances odori dengaku sarugaku
and theatricals

APPENDIX TWO

AN OUTLINE OF JAPANESE MUSIC NOTATION SYSTEMS

The problem of notation is somewhat specialized. Nevertheless, the fact that the topic is complicated does not lessen its importance to the general understanding of the entire music culture. Therefore, the following discussion has been appended in order that the reader of more technical bend will not be left destitute of any information concerning Japanese notation.

The history of the notation of early Christian music is a story of several centuries of evolution through a series of vague contour symbols to systems of relatively greater accuracy. The earlier systems grew out of a Greek tradition of contour notation into what is known as neumes. Early Japanese Buddhist music also began with a neumatic notation. However, in its evolution toward a more precise script, theology and Chinese systematics got in the way of practicality. The net result was the *go-on-hakase,* credited to Kakui (born 1236), a priest of the Shingon sect of Buddhism.

This system divides a range of fifteen notes into three "layers" of five notes each. Hence, the system is known also as the *go-on-sanju,* the five sounds and three layers. In actual practice, only eleven notes were used so that the bottom "layer" (*shoju*) actually consisted of only two notes, the middle (*niju*) of five notes, and the top (*sanju*) of four notes. The notation consisted of short lines which indicated specific pitches by means of the angle at which they were tipped (see Figure 22). The first layer is notated by the symbols 1–5, the second layer begins at 6 and goes through 10, and the symbols 11–15 are used for the top layer. The symbols in white are the notes not used, and, of course, the Arabic numerals do not appear in the original system. The dot on the end of the line establishes which way the line is pointing. Thus, for example, if we apply this system to a standard *ryo* scale, the lines could be transcribed into Western notation as shown in Figure 22.

It should be noted that some of the symbols point in the same direction (look at 4 and 12), but since the music (shomyo) is very diatonic, there is seldom any doubt as to which pitch is meant. However, the system is really efficient only when there are a very few notes to each word. As the vocal line became longer, the system became more

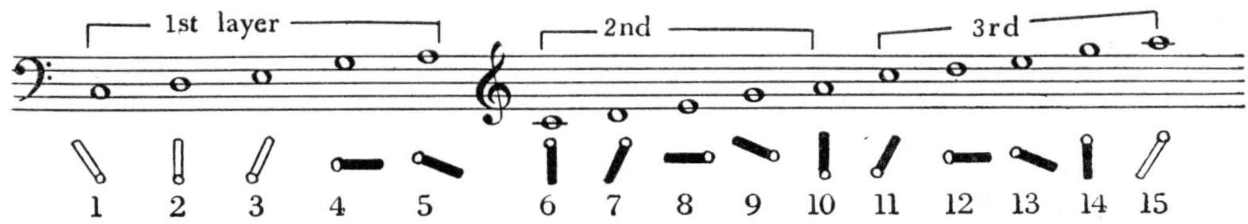

FIGURE 22. Go-on-hakase symbols

clumsy. Since the direction of the symbols has no relation to the contour of the melody, the notation is very confusing to the Western eye (see Figure 23). An additional complication is that special vocal melismas, dynamics, and tempo indications are written about the symbol in a direction dependent on that of the notation.[1]

This *go-onfu* (*fu* means notation) underwent many modifications. The simplest change was a reversing of directions so that the notation always led away from the words (Figures 23 and 24–B). However, few of the modifications ever approached a real visual representation of the contour of the melody. Unlike the growth of Western notation, the evolution of Buddhist chant moved away from the detailed system (go-onfu) toward even vaguer styles. One of the most famous styles is the *karifu* of the eighteenth-century priest, Kanko (Figure 24–A). This system is a shorthand version of go-onfu with the same style of melismatic annotations plus various notational refinements of rhythm and contour. The vagueness of the lines, however, could hardly be called a step toward greater accuracy. The other prevalent style of Buddhist notation is called *meyasu*, literally "easy on the eyes." This style is open to the greatest variation and tends to avoid cluttering the page with annotations. A twentieth-century version of meyasu is shown in Figure 24–C. All three scripts in Figure 24 represent the same musical passage as shown in the transcription above. From such examples it is obvious that Buddhist chant notation cannot be easily read without the aid of a teacher or a good deal of previous knowledge.

The above notations were intended primarily for the writing of shomyo chants. The notation of the music of wasan, koshiki, and other such shorter, more rhythmical forms is derived from a simple style of gagaku vocal music neumatic notation. The Tendai sect's version of meyasu notation also tends to show the general contour of the vocal line. Historically, the most important development in these simpler notations is *gomafu*,[2] in which teardrop-shaped lines are placed to the left of the words (Figure 25). These marks are symbols for longer stereotyped patterns and rhythms. However, the style of such music as wasan is simpler and less melismatic. This type of notation was impractical for any involved melodic style. It was further simplified by the heikyoku narrators into a form known as *sumifu*. The lines were put to the right, and certain indications were added concerning the biwa part. The most important outgrowth of these earlier systems, however, is the notation of noh singing. Early noh notation used sesame-seed-shaped symbols plus special signs to indicate stereotyped melodies, rhythms, or special singing styles. The system was vague and could not be read in any detail. In the Edo period it was subjected to greater regimentation so that each mark was given a rather definite meaning. Unfortunately, the various schools of noh applied different meanings to the same symbols so that any study of noh notation, like that of Buddhist script, must be sectarian. This style of notation (gomafu or gomaten) is used today without basic change (Figure 26). Again one should note that such a system is practical only with a music that is greatly restricted in melodic and rhythmic style. The notation and the power of tradition have worked together to inhibit any further significant development in noh singing.

[1] Japanese can be written left to right, right to left, or straight down. It is common to use all three systems within one publication. The newcomer to Japan is often confused by the many signs that read phonetically "ko-ba-ta." He soon becomes more flexible and reverses field to read "ta-ba-ko," or tobacco.

[2] Ref. 1, page 698 shows six different examples of the evolution of this style.

FIGURE 23. The go-onfu

FIGURE 24. Karifu, modified go-onfu, and meyasufu notations (below) and transcription in Western notation (above).

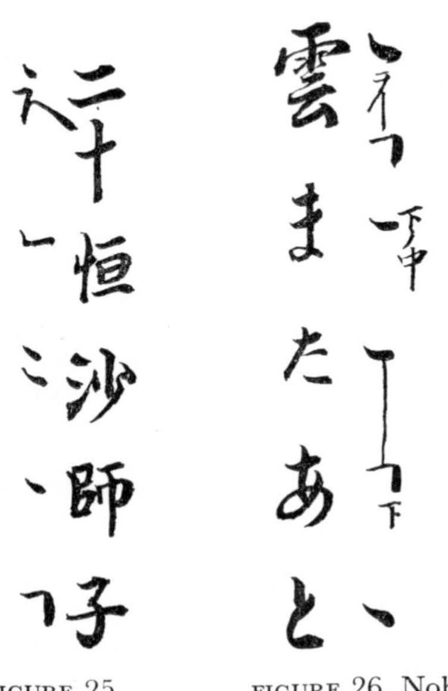

FIGURE 25. The koshiki gomaten notation

FIGURE 26. Noh vocal notation

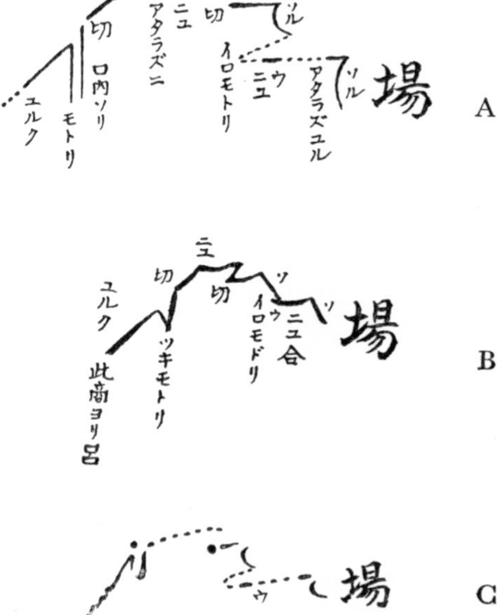

Instrumental Notation

The first important forms of instrumental music in Japan came from the Asian continent. Thus, the notation systems were also based on continental models, particularly Chinese. As in early European instrumental notation, a majority of the systems used were types of tablatures. They either indicated a string, a fingering position, or, in the case of woodwinds, a hole or fingering. Percussion notation became a more specialized field in early Japanese music than in Western music because of the greater variety of instruments used in ancient times. In the following discussion, an emphasis is laid on present-day systems, for it must be remembered that notation in Japan has always been primarily a supplement to rote teaching methods and as such is often very vague. Indeed, the tradition of secret pieces and clan-owned music made such a system necessary, however regrettable it may seem to the contemporary music researcher.

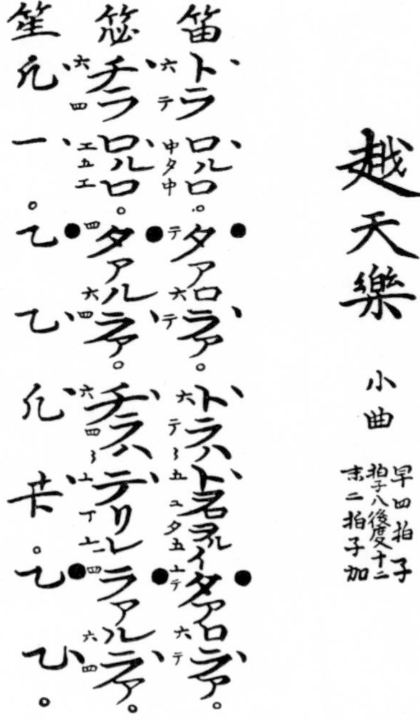

FIGURE 27. Gagaku notation

Gagaku Notation

The earliest notations for the wagon were modeled after Chinese cithern (*ch'in*) script. It consisted of the number of the string to be played while accompanying a song. These numbers were written to the right of the words, the rhythm being remembered by its connection with the vocal line (which was rote learned not notated). Later, as the wagon and the gaku-so were used within the gagaku ensemble, their notation became even simpler. Since these two instruments usually play stereotyped patterns, with occasional added notes, the notation need only list the name of the pattern and have interspersed numbers for any added notes and explanations for any special playing techniques that might be required. Rhythm was indicated by dots. The basic rhythmic unit was also indicated in a style much like the Western-style time signature at the start of a composition.

The gaku-biwa also inherited a Chinese system, but one based on a separate symbol for each of the four fret positions on the four strings (in some cases five).[3] In addition to representing the single positions (the actual pitch will depend on the tuning), these symbols also represent arpeggios of which the given symbol is the top note. Such arpeggios are the basic style of the gaku-biwa's music in the gagaku ensemble.

Figure 27 shows the notation of the hichiriki, the ryuteki, and the sho for the beginning of the piece "Etenraku."[4] The column to the right is the flute notation. It is based on two separate systems. First, there are the

[3] A chart of these symbols can be found on page 391 of ref. 25.

[4] A transcription of the hichiriki part can be seen in Figure 7. The entire piece is transcribed in ref. 23, I, 9–12.

FIGURE 28. Hichiriki and ryuteki notation symbols

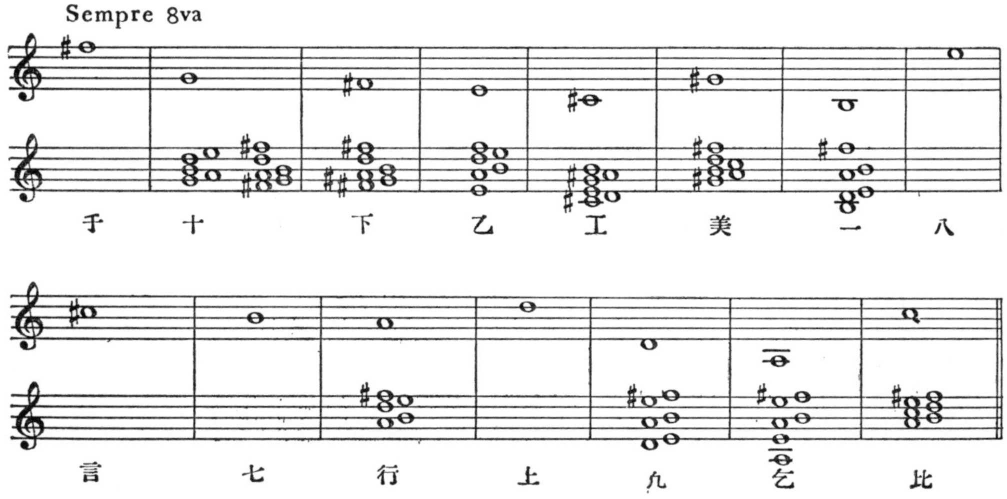

FIGURE 29. The chords and notes of the sho

larger symbols, which are a solfège system by which the player originally learned the music. The smaller figures to the left of this solfège represent fingerings on the instrument. One could notate violin music in an analogous system by writing a piece with only the words *do-re-mi*, later adding indications of the positions on the finger board that would produce those sounds. Unfortunately, the Japanese system is further complicated by the fact that most of the characteristic melismas are learned while memorizing the solfège so that they seldom are apparent to the eye. In addition, the words of the solfège do not stand for definite pitches and are only a few evolutionary steps above "la-de-da" singing as far as accuracy is concerned. Of course, the very restricted style of the music makes it possible to recognize "*ro-ru-ro*" as some standard phrase, but the point is that one must first know the music in order to read the notation with any accuracy.

Rhythm is indicated by dots along the right-hand side of the column plus white dots among the solfège for rests. The large dot represents beat four or eight, depending on the meter of the composition. This meter is indicated in the annotations below the title of the work. All three gagaku flutes use this style of notation.

The second column in Figure 27 is the music for the hichiriki. It is built on exactly the same principle as the notation of the flute except that the solfège is different as is the meaning of the fingering symbols. Figure 28 gives the pitches produced by the various fingerings on the ryuteki and the hichiriki. Since more than one note can be produced by a single fingering, further explanation is to no avail. One must either know the piece or find a teacher.

The left-hand column of Figure 27 is the notation for the sho. Each symbol represents the bottom note of one of the eleven chords of the sho or, in some cases, the note itself. These notes and chords can be seen in Figure 29. Rhythm is shown in the same method as mentioned above for the hichiriki.

As a rule, gagaku music is not written in score as shown in Figure 27. Rather, each man has a separate part book. In fact, individual musicians are sometimes unaware of what is going on in the other instruments. Such are some of the less salubrious results of rote teaching methods.

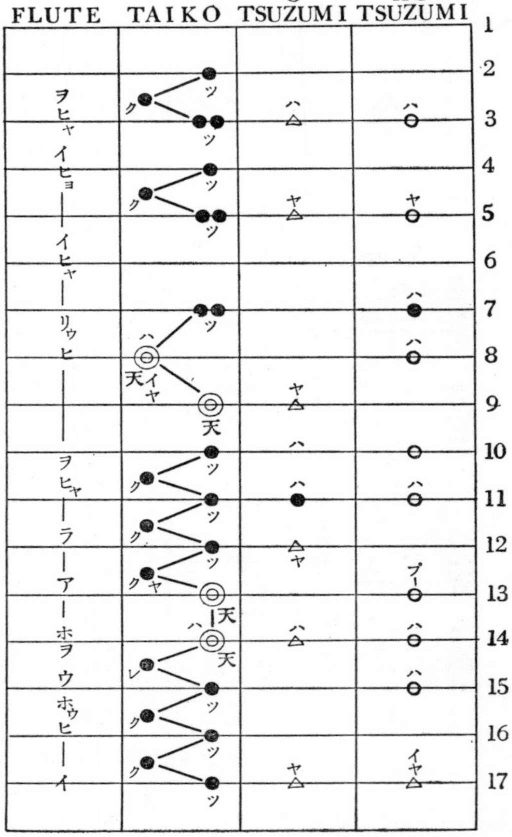

Finally we come to the notation of the percussion instruments in gagaku. The notations for all three instruments are normally combined in a single column. The beats are marked by Japanese numbers. The taiko left-hand beats (*zun*) are indicated by a dot to the right of the column. The symbol *chin* (金) is placed to the left or right of the numbers to indicate the proper strokes on the shoko. When the sticks are used together a *chin* is placed on both sides of the number. The kakko notation consists of two symbols. The first, *sei* (正), indicates a stroke with the right stick. The symbol *rai* (来) placed to the left of the numbers indicates a left-stick roll, while a *rai* on both sides of the numbers indicates a two-stick roll. *Rai* never appears by itself on the right. A detailed study of the rhythmic notation exists in English for those who wish to pursue the topic further.[5]

FIGURE 30. Noh hayashi section in traditional notation

Hayashi Notation

The three drums of the noh orchestra and the noh flute have developed notation systems based on the eight-beat phrase orientation of all noh music. The notation of all four instruments is written in vertical columns. Horizontal lines represent the beats. Sometimes dotted horizontal lines are added to represent the half beats. In other systems one occasionally finds the half beats represented by the lines and the beats by the spaces, but the normal procedure is to place the accent on the line. As a rule, each instrument has its own part book. Figure 30[6] is an artificial score compiled from these separate part books for the sake of comparison. Scores as such are rare in Japanese music (see ref. 31).

The flute part is shown in the left-hand column. It consists of phonetic symbols which represent a nonspecific solfège system designed to imitate the general contour of the melody rather than to indicate specific pitches. Since noh-flute music is characterized by a constant subtle variation of pitch, this notation suits it admirably. For the sake of sight reading or research, however, it is quite inadequate. The transcription of Figure 31 shows both the general pitch intended and the words of the solfège. The exact solfège used and the resultant melody

[5] See Harich-Schneider, etc. "The Rhythmical Patterns in Gagaku and Bugaku." *Ethno-Musicologica*, Vol. III, Leiden: E. J. Brill, 1954. 109 pp.

[6] Figure 30 is the first two lines of the basic melody (*ji*) of the noh dance piece "Chu no Mai." In order to illustrate the various symbols, two changes were made in the original parts. The last beat of the ko-tsuzumi part was not there in the original and the dot on beat 11 in the o-tsuzumi part was originally a triangle.

FIGURE 31. Transcription of Figure 30 in Western notation

Kesubi	Osameru Bachi	Osaeru Bachi	Cross Stroke	Large	Medium	Small	Types of Strokes
•	• •	•	㊈	◎	⦿	○	Stroke Symbols
ツ	ツ	ツ		テ, 天	ツ, テ, 天	ツ, テ, 天	Right Hand Solfege
レ, ク		ツ, レ, ク	天	天	ク, レ, 天	ク, レ, 天	Left Hand Solfege

FIGURE 32. Taiko notation symbols

vary from school to school as well as in different pieces. Also as the piece progresses, many unwritten melismas are added to the basic line. Since flute music consists of many standard melodies or pieces, only the titles are listed in the music scores to specific plays.

The right-hand column contains the ko-tsuzumi notation. The meanings of the symbols vary between schools but the ones in Figure 30 are standard. The circle represents the resonant sound *pon*, the dot is the lighter *chi*, the triangle is the hard *ta*, and the symbol プ is the soft *pu*. Occasionally one may see the phonetic letter ツ, which represents the very weak, loose sound *tsu*. The drum calls (kakegoe) are written in Japanese phonetics between the other symbols. Though they are written *ya* (ヤ) and *ha* (ハ) they usually are pronounced today as "*yo*" and "*ho*."

The o-tsuzumi notation appears in the second column from the right. The triangle represents the strongest beat, *chiyon*, a circle is the deader tone, *don*, and the dot is the light tone, *tsun* or *chin*. The drum calls are also marked between the symbols.

The taiko part is shown in the third column from the right. The system is divided into three types of symbols: 1) those which show the rhythm and the strength of the beat, 2) mnemonic syllables to further clarify the beats and aid memory, and 3) drum calls. Figure 32 shows the first two types of symbols. The fundamental stroke of the taiko *ten*, is shown by the symbol 天. This comes in three strengths, which are indicated by the size of the circle used in the notation. In addition, the special stroke *kashira*, in which the left-hand stick is placed on the right shoulder before striking (see Plate 43), has a special sign. Sometimes this special sign is not used, and it is written as shown on beats seven through nine in Figure 30. When the sticks are played very softly, they are indicated only by dots. If they are to be played *osaeru*, the sticks are left on the skin after each beat. If they are *kesubi*, the sticks are lifted. On beats three, five, and seven in Figure 30 there are examples of *osameru* in which both sticks are placed on the skin for a special dead effect. The various solfège syllables and signs are listed in Figure 32. Their pronunciation can be seen in Figure 31. The drum calls are found placed between the beats of the drum. Their pronunciation, like those of the other two drums, varies according to the situation. The tempo and character of the piece control this. The pronunciation of the same sound also varies depending on the drum part in which the sound appears. There is considerable variation between schools as well.

Figure 30 shows clearly the characteristic orientation of noh rhythm away from the first beat. In all separate part books the notation begins with the second beat. The effect, musically speaking, is to keep the flow of rhythm always "off balance." Patterns never seem to lose their dynamism but continue to push forward. It is somewhat like the effect Bach achieves by ending melodic phrases on the first beat of a measure instead of the last. When the hayashi parts are played separate-

FIGURE 33. A transcription of chirikara-byoshi (above) and traditional notation (below)

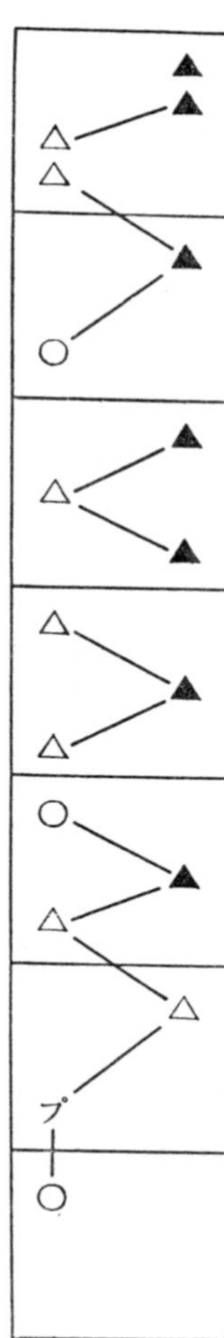

ly their natural phrase accents seem to fall elsewhere. When they are played together this simultaneous combination of varying rhythmic phrases produces one of the most distinctive qualities of noh music.

When this same hayashi is added to kabuki music the independence of the o-tsuzumi and ko-tsuzumi is more restricted. While they sometimes play straight noh-type rhythmic patterns, more often than not they play *chirikara-byoshi.* This is a more direct imitation of the rhythm of the shamisen melody. The taiko and flute, however, tend to continue with their noh-oriented patterns. As was explained in Chapter VIII, the tension between these two separate kinds of rhythm plus the shamisen melody create a system of tension and release similar to that produced in Western music by harmony, melody, and rhythm, the taiko and flute acting like the harmonic element of Western music.

The notation of kabuki drumming is similar to that of the noh. However, since the patterns are often much faster and syncopated, the o-tsuzumi and ko-tsuzumi parts are written together as shown in Figure 33. The o-tsuzumi is on the right side, and the ko-tsuzumi is on the left. The black triangles are for the o-tsuzumi *tsu,* and the white triangles represent *chiyon.* The transcription of Figure 33 includes the unnotated mnemonics. In both the case of noh and kabuki drumming, a professional book will usually carry only the names of the various patterns to be used in a specific piece. The exact placement and special variations are left to the memory of the player.

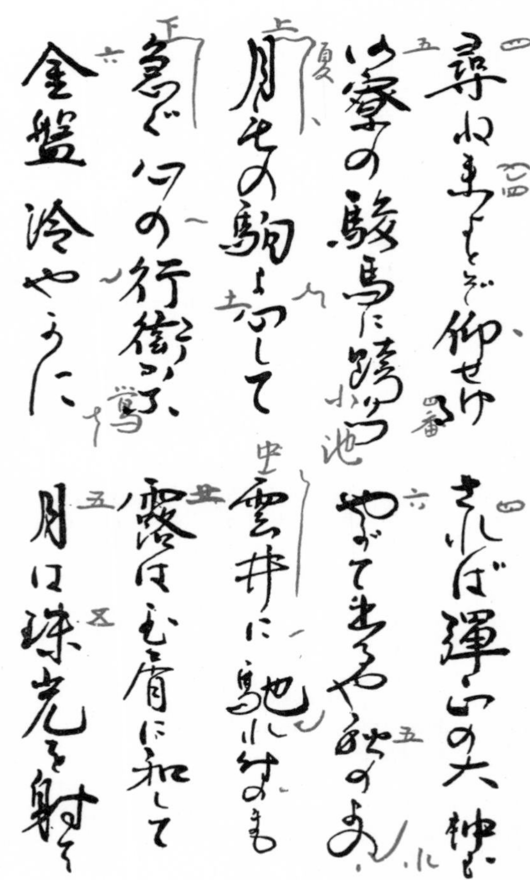

FIGURE 34. Biwa notation

Biwa Notation

The early Heike-biwa style of notation was relatively simple. It used the above-mentioned short lines (sumifu) placed to the right of the text as a general indication of the vocal line. Since the biwa normally played only between the sung phrases, there was no need to develop a notation that could be superimposed upon the existing vocal script. Instead, words and symbols were used between the phrases to indicate which stereotype pattern should be used. This type of notation has remained the basis of the Satsuma and Chikuzen music that followed. As used by these schools, each phrase of the poem is separated by a space. At the head of each column of text there is written the name of the biwa or vocal pattern to be used or the number of the note to be used as a reciting tone. Along the side of the text are found other symbols and wiggly lines which remind the musician of patterns to be used at that time. At the end of the phrase any special biwa interludes are marked by name. All these symbols can be seen in Figure 34.

During the early twentieth century there was an attempt to create a more accurate notation. This consisted of horizontal lines representing the strings of the biwa. Different length isosceles triangles and other figures were used to represent the various playing techniques. Another system of the twentieth century was similar to an ancient European notation. The biwa version consisted of seven lines representing the seven basic pitches of the scale. The text was written on the line corresponding to the correct pitch, and wiggly lines indicated the melismatic movement from one pitch to the next. The names of the biwa accompaniment patterns to be used were written at the beginning of each phrase. In all the biwa notations mentioned above, the signs for the vocal melismas and the biwa patterns are usually written in red while the text is in black. With the general deterioration of the biwa tradition since 1940, there has been little further development in biwa notation. Today, each teacher tends to use his own system based on one of the three main styles mentioned. The specific symbols used and their meanings vary to a discouraging degree. The biwa notation situation further aggravates the isolation of the various schools of biwa music.

Shakuhachi Notation

Figure 35 is the notation of the first phrase of the shakuhachi piece transcribed in Figure 16. This system is clearer than most of the notation styles studied so far. Basically, it consists of names for the different holes. Thus, it is like the Western fixed *do-re-mi* system in that the symbols stand for specific pitches and not merely melodic tendencies. The names for these holes in the three major schools of shakuhachi are listed in Figure 36. There are, of course, many pitches possible beyond the ones listed, which can also be played by the *meri-kari* system (see page 159). These have separate symbols.

Rhythm is indicated in two ways. First, the entire column has an imaginary zig-zag line running down the middle. The points of this line, like those in the taiko notation (see Figure 30), represent the main beats. Thus, the spaces between pitch symbols represent the general length of the pitches. Since shakuhachi music is very free in beat, no pressing need is felt for greater accuracy. The second rhythmic notation system consists of vertical lines placed to the right of the pitch symbols. One line indicates a basic beat, two a beat one half of that, and three a quarter of the basic beat. Thus, if we use a quarter note for the single line, two lines become an eighth and three lines a sixteenth note.

In addition to these signs, there are instructions as to special effects, breathing, and standard melismas. Of course, true to Japanese tradition, there are still many graces, etc., that are unwritten and must be learned from a teacher. Fortunately, for those who might want to put shakuhachi music into Western notation, there is now an instruction book on this process (ref. 44). However, such a notation will indicate only the basic melody and not the many subtle changes which are so characteristic of shakuhachi music.

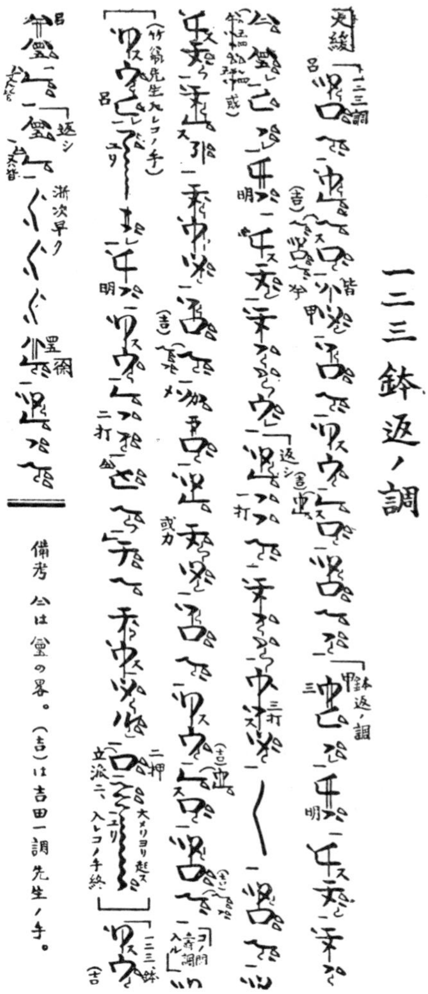

FIGURE 35. Shakuhachi notation of the Kinko school

Hole + Pitch	1st D	2nd F	3 G	4 A	5 C	6 D
MEIAN	フ	ロ	ウ	エ	ヤ	イ
KINKO	ロ	ツ	レ	チ	リ	ヒ
TOZAN	ロ	ツ	レ	チ	ハ	ヒ

FIGURE 36. Shakuhachi notation symbols

1	2	3	4	5	6	7	8	9	10	11	12	13
壹	貳	參	四	五	六	七	八	九	十	斗	爲	巾

FIGURE 37. Koto notation symbols

FIGURE 38. Yamada-school koto notation and transcription

Koto Notation

Until the nineteenth century, almost all popular Japanese music was not accurately notated. Koto books of the early Edo period give only the poems of the songs with a few private symbols that served as reminders of the music. The growth of purely instrumental pieces made the invention of a notation essential. Since the instrument was of Chinese origin, it was logical to turn to China for a notation system as well. This system consisted of a number for each string and dots of various sizes indicating rhythm.[7] The names of special playing techniques were written in or indicated by special signs. Today, this system is no longer used, though its basic idea has been retained.

There are two main systems of koto notation in use today, one for the Ikuta school and one for the Yamada school. They both use a common number system to indicate the strings. These signs are shown in Figure 37. As used by the Yamada school, the arrangement of these symbols more nearly resembles Western notation (upon which it is based). Figure 38 shows the first phrase of the piece "Chidori." Written horizontally, it resembles Western notation in its use of vertical lines to represent bar lines. The tuning and number of beats in a measure (usually two) are shown at the beginning of the piece and do not appear in Figure 38. Rhythm is indicated by the single, double, and triple bars as in the eighth, sixteenth, and thirty-second notes of Western notation. Rests are shown with short horizontal lines or circles. Special techniques are indicated by such signs as appear in the sixth measure of Figure 38. The symbols above the notation are a form of solfège by which the composition is learned. When there is a text, it is written below the notation. Though the vocal line differs somewhat from the koto melody, there is no separate notation for it. One must learn the vocal line as part of the entire piece. This system is second only to shamisen notation in its degree of accuracy. It is an interesting compromise of Eastern and Western principles of music notation.

The Ikuta-school notation for the same phrase from "Chidori" is shown in Figure 39. It is basically the same as the Yamada notation except that it is written Japanese-style in vertical columns. Half beats are indicated by shorter horizontal lines, the solfège is to the left of the notation, and special fingerings and techniques are noted to the right. Modern Ikuta pieces come in a special edition with traditional notation in one part of the book and a Western-notation transcription in the other part.

[7] An example of this notation with transcription can be seen in Piggott, ref. 9.

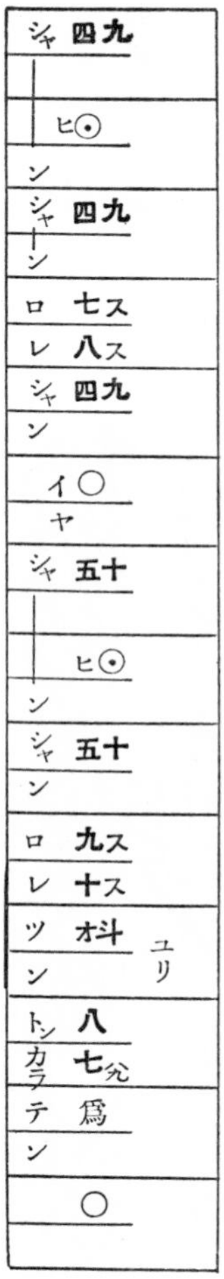

FIGURE 39. Ikuta-school koto notation symbols

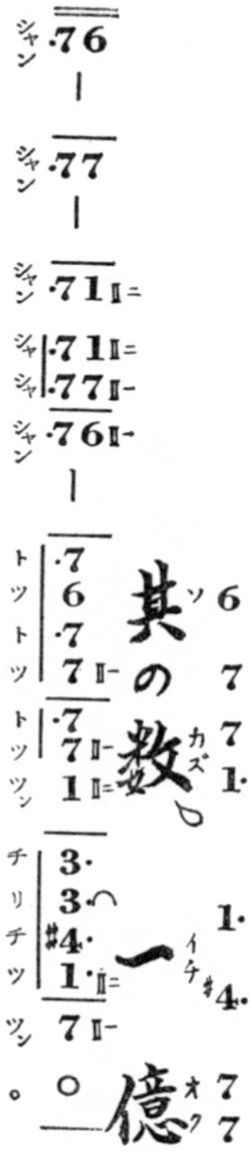

FIGURE 40. Shamisen notation

Shamisen Notation

There are a vast number of styles of shamisen music. During the Edo period, none of them were particularly concerned with the problem of notation. The net result was that the music of many of the old songs has been lost forever. In the last sixty years, however, there have been many attempts to create a satisfactory notation system. Of the several systems now in existence, two are most prevalent.

Figure 40 is the notation of the phrase *kangen* from the piece "Tsuru Kame" as used by members of the Kenseikai branch of the Kineya school of nagauta. This notation is rhythmically like the koto notation in Figure 38 except that it is written in vertical columns like Figure 39. The Arabic numbers represent diatonic pitches, the number ·7 being the lowest note. The exact pitch of this note will depend on the tuning of the instrument. If this note were B, then the number 7 would be the B an octave higher and the number 7· would be the B an octave above that. The fingerings are shown by Roman numerals (I, II, III), which stand for the strings, and Japanese numbers (一, 二, 三), which tell which finger to use. Special playing methods are marked to the side, for example, the left-hand pizzicato in the seventh bar. The small writing to the left of the music is *kuchi-jamisen*, the solfège by which one learns shamisen music. The words for the music are written to the right of the shamisen line, and the music of this vocal line appears to the right of the words. Since the vocal line is usually in syncopation with the shamisen part, this very loose vocal notation is convenient for the notator if not the researcher.

Figure 41 shows the same music as it is written in the so-called *bunkafu* shamisen notation. This is read like Western music from left to right. The Arabic numbers in this case represent finger positions on the finger board. The strings are indicated by the three horizontal lines. The disadvantage

FIGURE 41. A transcription of shamisen music in bunkafu notation

of this system is that the actual pitch of these symbols and their intervalic relations change if a different tuning is used. For example, the 4 in the first measure is the note A in hon-choshi but B in ni-agari. Since the strings are shown by the three lines, only the fingers need be noted in special fingerings. These are shown with Roman numerals. Rhythm is shown as before with short lines. Since circles represent open strings, this symbol is not used for a rest. Instead, one will see large black dots as in measure one. The bunkafu system is used in the notation of nagauta, kouta, Kiyomoto, and several other forms. Due to the central control of most of shamisen music publishing, it has become the most widespread system in use today.

There is also a third system that should be mentioned which combines elements of the two discussed above. In this style, the vertical orientation and Arabic number system of the first notation are combined with the three lines of the second. With a knowledge of these two main systems, however, the various offshoots from them can be read with a modicum of practice.

Finally, mention should be made of the notation of Gidayu-bushi (Figure 42). Its classic system is based on the same principles as biwa notation (compare with Figure 34). Some pieces recently have appeared in the above-mentioned bunkafu, though the system of secret signs and symbols for standard accompaniments, etc. is always used by professionals. Many people collect Gidayu textbooks for the beauty of their pages much in the way Westerners hang vellum pages from old church chant books upon their walls. Gidayu notation is even more vague than biwa notation, though the music itself is more highly developed. If one wishes to analyze Japanese music, it is best to start with the other shamisen forms, as their notation, particularly nagauta and kouta, are the most accurate systems developed in Japan.

FIGURE 42. Gidayu-bushi notation

Summary

During the past few pages we have discussed a vast number of disparate notation systems from the confusing and complicated shomyo style to the more precise shamisen systems. It is hard to make any general statement about so many different systems. However, one can note that instrumental notation has been more accurate in general than vocal. The ever-strong rote-teaching tradition in Japan has hindered the development of notation perhaps more than any other factor. The existence of secret pieces and interschool jealousy in all forms of Japanese music have proved a hindrance in many areas, including notation. With the entrance of Western culture, many of the secret pieces disappeared, though the interschool battles continued. However, Japanese musicians became aware of the need for notation if they were to compete with the easy access to Western music afforded by the Western music staff. In the area of notation, at least, the effect of Western music on hogaku has been salubrious.

APPENDIX THREE

WHERE TO HEAR JAPANESE MUSIC IN TOKYO

One of the purposes of this book is to whet the reader's appetite for the sight and sound of Japanese music. It would be a cruel jest to succeed in this endeavor only to leave the reader uninformed as to where such music can be found. Therefore, I have appended this short list of standard Tokyo concert halls at which one is likely to find Japanese music. I hope that the visitor to Japan and even the old Japan hands may find this of use in their hunt for musical souvenirs.

If one looks in the newspapers or in the weekly guidebooks of coming events, it would seem that traditional music had disappeared except for what is found in kabuki and noh. In truth, information on hogaku concerts is not available even in the normal Japanese press. For those who read Japanese, there are two sources of information. One is the magazine *Hogaku no Tomo*,[1] which prints a list of concerts for the next month and also lists radio broadcasts of traditional music. The other list is found in the magazine *Nihon Ongaku*.[2] Noh dramas and kabuki are listed in various English-language publications and so need not be mentioned here.

The most convenient cluster of concert halls centers around Tokyo Station. One is in the basement of the New Marunouchi Building directly across from the west exit of Tokyo Station. The information desk on the first floor will know the schedule for the week. Almost all concerts there are free, as they are usually student recitals. Koto, shakuhachi, and shamisen concerts are the most frequent.

Another very popular hall is on the eighth floor of the Nihon Sogo Ginko Building on the south corner of Gofukubashi, a short distance to the left from the east exit of Tokyo Station. Many of the best professional concerts are held in this hall. Such concerts are usually around noon on Saturdays. If one does not have an invitation, these professional concerts cost about eighty cents. Student recitals can also be heard here.

Many department stores in Tokyo have theatres. In such theatres one has an excellent opportunity to see amateur Japanese dance concerts. Koto, biwa, shakuhachi, and shamisen music can also be heard in such places. One of the most popular halls is in the Mitsukoshi Department Store just over Nihonbashi on the Ginza. The store publishes a list (in Japanese) of the month's program, which is available at the entrance of the theatre. Most such stores have an English-speaking receptionist at the information desk, who could eventually provide information on concerts. It is only fair to warn the newcomer that no question put in English or Japanese is ever answered simply. Perserverance is the price of success. Shirokiya, Matsuzakaya, and Isetan department stores are also used often.

The hall of the Dai-ichi Seimei Building two blocks north of the Nikkatsu Hotel is used for both Western-style and traditional music concerts. Such concerts are usually

[1] S. Kubo, editor. Tokyo: Hogaku-no-Tomosha, 1955. 34 cents monthly. Do not confuse this with the *Ongaku no Tomo* magazine.

[2] R. Fujita, editor. Tokyo: Nihon-Ongaku-sha. 1944–. 11 cents monthly.

professional, and admission is charged. Koto music and nagauta are the most common.

The Shimbashi Embujo in Ginza, two blocks from the Kabuki-za along the street in front of the Ginza Tokyu Hotel, is a common spot for dance recitals, as is the Asahi Seimei Hall in Shinjuku. The National Theatre of Japan (Kokuritsu Gekijo), 13 Hayabusa-cho, Chiyoda-ku, in back of the Imperial palace grounds, is also used for music and dance events, as well as for kabuki and bunraku plays. Dance recitals advertize in the monthly magazine, *Hogaku to Buyo.*

For the more adventuresome music lover, I recommend the Hommokute theatre near Hirokoji Station, the stop just before Ueno on the Ginza subway. This small second-floor theatre is one of the few remaining old-style halls. About one hundred people would completely fill its straw-mat audience area, while four people would fill its stage. Here one may hear many of the old Edo-period entertainments like Shinnai-bushi, old-style joruri, and various storytellers. One may even rent an Edo-style smoking pipe during the performance. This very charming theatre is difficult to find. Its address is 14 Kitadaimon-cho and it is located on the left-hand side of a small street just south of the famous Susumoto vaudeville house in Ueno. The latter theatre is also of interest for those who would like to observe *rakugo*, the famous monologue genre of Japan. However, one needs to know Japanese extremely well before one can appreciate the full humor of rakugo artists.

There are at least two opportunities to hear the Imperial gagaku orchestra every year. A public concert is given in the fall in Hibiya Hall and there is usually a private spring concert at the Imperial music building. Invitations to this concert are available through the Kokusai Bunka Shinko-kai (Society for International Cultural Relations). Occasionally, there are special performances at the Meiji Shrine but these cannot be predicted. There is an amateur group of gagaku musicians, who meet at the Onoterusaki Shrine every month. The exact day of their meetings can be learned from the shrine, which is near the Nippori stop on the Keihin line.

Religious music can best be heard in Kyoto where there are hundreds of temples, each with its own schedule of ceremonies. Tokyo is less populated with temples, but religious music can still be heard. The Asakusa Kannon Temple near the Asakusa stop on the subway is one of the largest temples in Tokyo and has two or more regular services every month at which some chanting is done. There are also various special services. The Zojoji Temple in Shiba Park is also a good place to ferret out Buddhist ceremonies. Shinto ceremonies with music are rarer but the Meiji Shrine has a few such events every year. Nichiren and Tenrikyo services are quite interesting but also quite early in the morning. Contact with such music is best made through a Japanese-speaking friend.

The short-time tourist will have to trust to luck for any opportunities of hearing court or religious music. However, in the concert field, he can predict his chances fairly easily. The big concert seasons for hogaku are fall and spring. If one goes to any of the department-store theatres or the other halls mentioned above on a weekend in September through early December, it is almost certain that there will be a hogaku concert scheduled. The same is true for the months of March, April, May, and early June. August and September are the times of the folk bon-odori festivals, and most local districts of Tokyo erect a stage and put on nightly dance parties during that time. The fall o-matsuri can be seen throughout the city during late September and early October. In early November there is an annual concert of folk theatricals from all over Japan presented in the Nihon Seinen-kan. For those interested in folk music, it is one of the best opportunities of the year to see a variety of Japanese folk arts. For those who are traveling about, the Japan Travel Bureau sometimes knows of local festivals of note.

The past two pages are by no means a complete list of music possibilities in Tokyo. However, it should provide a reader who is fortunate enough to come to Japan with a start on any music hunting expedition. If the hunt is successful, a knowledge of other less frequented theatres will be provided by the musicians met at the first concerts. Unless hogaku musicians develop a sudden sense for publicity, this method is the only practical means toward quick, direct contact with the beauties and artistic merits of Japanese traditional music.

APPENDIX FOUR
RECOMMENDED RECORDINGS

Discographies are dangerous. They become outdated as soon as they are written. However, one cannot write a book on such an unfamiliar field as Japanese music and not provide some modicum of information concerning how to hear this music without coming to Japan. Reviews of Japanese music records are found in the journal, *Ethnomusicology,* Vol. 11, No. 1 (1967) and Vol. 12, No. 3 (1968). Updating can be accomplished by reference to the *Schwann Catalogue* for Euro-American releases or the periodic lists in Japanese from major firms such as Nippon Victor, Columbia, Crown, Toshiba, King, and Polydor. Records from these companies can be ordered from the Bunkado Record Store, 14–1, 5-chome, Ginza, Chuo-ku, Tokyo. The store is across the street from the Kabuki-za. The selected list given below is based on 1972 materials and is organized under the general topics of the chapters of the book.

Chapter I: General

The UNESCO series released by Musicaphon includes six records on Japan (BM-30 L 2011–2016). They range from Buddhist chants, gagaku, and noh to koto, shakuhachi, and shamisen music. Their notes are tri-lingual. Japanese instruments are introduced on two Polydor records, *Nihon No Ongaku* (MN-9041–9042). The *Hogaku Taikei* printed by Chikuma Shobo is a thirteen-volume series (around $200) on Japanese music with extensive notes and pictures in Japanese. A Victor album from Japan is called *Traditional Music of Japan* (JL 52–54) and contains notes in English and Japanese by Shigeo Kishibe. Avoid Lyrichord or Nonesuch records unless you want second-rate performances and recordings and confused notes.

Chapter II: Religious Music

Polydor has provided two albums, *Shingon Shomyo* (MN 9021–9024) and *Tendai Shomyo* (MN 9011–9014). Each gives extensive history and theory as well as original and Western notations of each piece. Folkways produced the sounds of everyday chanting in *The Way of Eiheiji* (FR 8980). Shinto festival and pantomime music are given in Victor's *Edo No Kagura To Matsuri Bayashi* (SJ 3004). Separate records of each school are common in Crown and King records.

Chapter III: Gagaku

The two albums, *Gagaku Taikei,* by Victor, are divided into instrumental music (SJ 3002) and vocal music (SJ 3003) of the court. Court kagura is released by Polydor (MN 9031–9036). The King record, *Gagaku* (KC 1028), is a good sampler.

Chapter IV: Nohgaku

The most complete albums are those of Nippon Victor, *Noh* (SJ 1005, 1006). They contain preliminary history and music theory along with complete plays matched by texts, photographs, and explanatory commentaries concerning each part of the piece. *Hagoromo* and *Kantan* are available on the American Caedmon recording (TC 2019).

Chapter V: Biwa Music

Heike biwa is found on Phillips

Heikyoku (PH 7511). Satsuma biwa plays *Dannoura* on Victor (SJL 2099). A Chikuzen piece concerning a Meiji event is *Saigo Takamori* on Columbia (DLS 4138).

Chapter VI: Shakuhachi

Two records with some Zen-oriented English are *Shakuhachi No Shinzui* by Victor (SJL 2061, 2062). Another record, *Wadatsumi-do*, by Polydor, relates to komuso traditions (MN 4012).

Chapter VII: Koto Music

A set of Victor records called *Sokyoku To Jiuta No Rekishi* (SLR 510–513) is rather complete. The works of Miyagi are heard on Victor's *Miyagi Michio Sokyoku Zenshu* (JV 1013–1015). Older forms are heard in *Koten Meikyoku No Hikaku Kenkyu* by Toshiba (TH 7047–7050).

Chapter VIII: Shamisen Music

Almost every major piece from each genre is available on a Japanese record. The old Columbia *Azuma Kabuki* record (WL 5110) does give some good if over-recorded nagauta sounds. Try *Tsuru Kame* for nagauta on Crown (LW 5199) or *Dojoji* on Toshiba (TH 9008). For kouta, one can use *Kouta Shiki* on Victor (LR 533). Old shamisen forms are heard in *Bingokei No Joruri* on Victor (SJ 3011, 3012). For Naniwa, try *Mori No Ishimatsu* on Teichiku (NL 2015). In Gidayu, any scene from *Chushingura* may be obtained from the King series (KC 1006, 1009, 1010, 1012, 1019). A Chikamatsu play, *Ten No Amijima*, is on Victor (SJL 2067). The famous *Terakoya* scene is recorded on Victor (SJL 118, 119). Classical dance music is illustrated sectionally in three important albums of *Nihon Buyo Ongaku* by Victor (SJ 3013–3015).

Chapter IX: Kabuki Music

Complete kabuki plays on two Victor recordings are *Sukeroku* (SJ 1001) and *Kanjincho* (JL 105). For single scenes, buy Suzugamori by King (KC 1029). Off-stage music is explained in detail in two Victor albums, *Kabuki Geza Ongaku Shusei* (SJL 2010–2012) and *Kabuki Geza Uta Shusei* (SJL 2091–2095).

Chapter X: Folk Music

Folkways has a good album of Japanese regional music with English notes (FE 4534). More complete Japanese collections are found in such series as King's *Nihon Minyo Daizenshu* (KR 121–130).

A SELECTIVE ANNOTATED BIBLIOGRAPHY

The following list of recommended readings is so organized that those desiring to pursue further the topic of a specific chapter may quickly learn which sources are most germane. While most of the books are rather specialized, I have tried to include books of use to the general reader whenever they are available. The books listed under "General" are those I would consider to be part of a basic reference library on Japanese music. Reference to any of these books within the text of this book are indicated by the use of their bibliographic prefix number. These numbers are also used to cross reference the Bibliography itself. Thus, 1, 616 refers to page 616 of Iba's *Nihon Ongaku Gairon* and 6, II, 206 refers to page 206 of volume two of the *Ongaku Jiten*. This list is by no means comprehensive. Those who wish a broader selection should refer to the "Bibliography of Asiatic Musics, Tenth Installment," compiled by Richard Waterman and others which appeared in the March, 1950 issue of *Notes* magazine. It is hoped that there will soon be a supplement listing in that magazine of sources in Japanese as well.

Chapter I: General Reference

1. Iba Takashi (伊庭孝), *Nihon Ongaku Gairon* (日本音楽概論). Tokyo: Koseikaku Shoten, 1928. 999 pp.

   "An Outline of Japanese Music." An extensive discussion of scale structures, instruments, and forms. The best single reference book on Japanese music.

2. *Japanese Music and Drama in the Meiji Era*. Komiya Toyohashi, ed. Trans. by E. Seidensticker and D. Keene. Tokyo: Obun-sha, 1956. 535 pp.

   A historical chronicle. The music section reveals the political intrigue and jealousy that plagued the hogaku world at that time.

3. Kikkawa Eishi (吉川英士), *Hogaku Kansho* (邦楽鑑賞). Tokyo: Hobun-kan, 1952. 442 pp.

   "The Appreciation of Japanese Music." Scripts to a series of broadcasts concerning various forms of Japanese music. A good beginning book on Japanese music.

4. *Koji Ruien* (古事類苑). Goto Ryoichi (後藤亮一), ed. Tokyo: Ruien Kankokai, 1931. Vols. 43 and 44.

   "Selected Ancient Texts." These two volumes (marked as Part I and II) are devoted to ancient writings on music and dance.

5. "Music in Japan," *Western Influences in Modern Japan*. Inazo Nitobe and others. Chicago: University of Chicago Press, 1931. pp. 469–523.

   A summary of both traditional and Western-style music in Japan.

6. *Ongaku Jiten* (音楽事典). Shimonaka Yasaburo (下中弥三郎), ed. Tokyo: Heibon-sha, 1955–57. 12 Vols.

   "The Music Dictionary." The most useful and most recent Japanese music reference book.

7. *Ongaku to Shakai* (音楽と社会). Nakajima Kenzo (中島健蔵), ed. Tokyo: Sogen-sha, 1953. 333 pp.

"Music and Society." Volume 4 of the series called *Sogen Ongaku Koza*. From pages 235 through 264 there is a concise outline of Japanese music written by Kishibe Shigeo. It is the only article which approaches Japanese music along ethnomusicological lines.

8. Peri, Nöel, *Essai sur les Gammes Japonaise*. Bibliothèque Musicale de Musée Guimet. Series 2, No. 1. Paris: Geuthner, 1934. 70 pp.

A convenient discussion of Japanese scale systems and their construction.

9. Piggott, Francis, *The Music and Musical Instruments of Japan*. London: B. T. Batsford, 1893. 230 pp.

The pioneer work by a Westerner on Japanese music. Useful for koto music and the general listing of oriental instruments. Shows an understandable lack of perspective.

10. Sansom, G. B., *Japan: A Short Cultural History*. New York: Appleton-Century-Crofts, 1931. 554 pp.

The best general background book in English. Music is set in its historical perspective.

11. *Sekai Ongaku Zenshu* (世界音楽全集). Subtitled *Gesammeltewerke der Welt Musik*. Kanda Hosui (神田豊穂) and others. Tokyo: Shunju-sha, 1930–. 118 vols.

"A Collection of World Music." Volumes 17, 18, 22, 25, 27, 43, and 48 contain transcriptions of various Japanese musics.

12. Sunaga, Katsumi, *Japanese Music*. Tokyo: Maruzen Co., 1936. 65 pp.

One of the Tourist Library Series. A concise layman's book on Japanese music.

13. Takano Tatsuyuki (高野辰之), *Nihon Kayoshi* (日本歌謡史). Tokyo: Shunju-sha, 1926. 1090 pp.

"The History of Japanese Songs." Primarily a study in texts.

14. ——, *Nihon Kayo Shusei* (日本歌謡集成). Tokyo: Shunju-sha, 1929. 11 vols.

"A Collection of Japanese Songs." Annotated texts from all forms of music.

15. Tanabe Hisao, *Japanese Music*. Tokyo: Kokusai Bunka Shinko-kai, 1936. 33 pp.

A short lecture on Japanese music with some pictures.

16. ——, (田辺尚雄), *Nihon no Ongaku* (日本の音楽). Tokyo: Bunka Kenkyu-kai, 1954. 337 pp.

"Japanese Music." The latest version of Dr. Tanabe's many other books. A good general survey of the subject.

CHAPTER II: RELIGIOUS MUSIC

17. *Bukkyo Ongaku no Kenkyu* (仏教音楽の研究). Vols. 12 and 13 of the *Toyo Ongaku Kenkyu*. Tokyo: Toyo Ongaku Gakkai, 1954. 320 pp.

"Research on Buddhist Music." A special edition of the *Journal for Research in Asiatic Music*. The lead articles are on Tendai and Shingon shomyo. There is a short English summary.

18. Iwahara Teishin (岩原諦信), *Shomyo no Kenkyu* (声明の研究). Kyoto: Fujii Sahee, 1932. 656 pp. plus 100 pp. of music.

"A Study of Shomyo." A detailed study of the Nansan school of shomyo.

19. Tanabe Hisao (see 16), *Shukyo Ongaku* (宗教音楽). Tokyo: Toho Shoin, 1934. 128 pp.

"Religious Music." Covers early Shinto music, mentions Confucian music, and sidesteps the important points of Buddhist music.

20. *Yuki Matsuri* (雪まつり). Compiled by the Education Committee of Nagano Prefecture, Nagano: Nagano-ken Insatsujo, 1955. 132 pp.

"The Snow Festival." Still photos and the script from a movie made of this festival by the Iwanami Shoten. Also commentaries.

See also 1, 616 and 641 plus specific articles in 6.

CHAPTER III: GAGAKU

21. Harich-Schneider, Eta, "The Present Condition of Japanese Court Music," *Musical Quarterly*, Vol. 39 (January, 1953). pp. 49–74.

The most useful English summary of the essentials of gagaku.

22. Kishibe, S. and Leo Traynor. "On the Four Unknown Pipes of the Sho," *Toyo Ongaku Kenkyu*, No. 9 (March, 1951). pp. 26–53.
One of the few detailed studies of a Japanese instrument in English.

23. Shiba Sukehiro (芝祐泰), *Gagaku* (雅楽). Tokyo: Ryugin-sha, 1955–56. 2 vols.
Scores of gagaku music in Western notation with short commentaries and photos of instruments.

24. ——, "The Tones of Ancient Oriental Music," *KBS Bulletin*, No. 13 (July 25, 1955). pp. 6–8.
A discussion of the music theory of gagaku.

25. Tanabe Hisao (see 16), *Nihon Ongaku Kowa* (日本音楽講話). Tokyo: Iwanami Shoten, 1919. 764 pp.
"Lectures on Japanese Music." Concerns primarily gagaku music. See also 6, II, 206 and related articles. 3, 355–72 is a layman's explanation.

CHAPTER IV: NOH MUSIC

26. Ko Yoshimitsu (幸祥光), *Ko-ryu Ko-tsuzumi Shofu* (幸流小鼓正譜). Tokyo: Nohgaku Shorin, 1955. 163 pp.
The fundamental music and style of the Ko school of drumming.

27. Komparu Soichi (金春惣一), *Komparu-ryu Taiko Zensho* (金春流太鼓全書). Tokyo: Hinoki Shoten, 1953. 322 pp.
Textbook for Komparu-school taiko.

28. Miyake Koichi (三宅衍一), *Fushi no Seikai* (節の精解). Tokyo: Hinoki Shoten, 1955. 105 pp. plus notation.
A detailed explanation of noh singing. A textbook for students.

29. ——, *Jibyoshi Seikai* (地拍子精解). Tokyo: Hinoki Shoten, 1954. 223 pp.
A textbook on noh rhythm.

30. ——, *Shidai Kara Kiri Made no Utaikata* (次第からキリまでの謡ひ方). Tokyo: Hinoki Shoten, 1952. 169 pp.
Discussion of the musical problems in singing each section of the noh drama.

31. Morita Misao (森田操), *Yokyoku-mai Hyoshi Taisei* (謡曲舞拍子大成). Osaka: Yoshida Yokyoku Shoten, 1914. 71 pp.
One of the few books in which hayashi is written in score.

32. *Nohgaku Zensho* (能楽全書). Yabe Ryosaku (矢部良策), ed. Tokyo: Sogen-sha, 1933. 6 vols.
A set of studies on all phases of noh including some materials on its music.

33. Peri, Nöel, *Le No*. Tokyo: Maison Franco-Japonaise, 1944. 495 pp.
Translations of plays and an introductory essay.

34. Tazaki Nobujiro (田崎延次郎), *Kadano-ryu O-tsuzumi Kaitei* (葛野流大鼓階梯). Tokyo: Hinoki Taiko-do, 1925. 80 pp.
Notation and instruction in the fundamentals of the Kadano school of o-tsuzumi drumming. See also related articles in 6.

35. Waley, Arthur, *The No Plays of Japan*. New York: Grove Press, 1957. 319 pp. Original edition, 1920.
A reprint of Mr. Waley's fine translations of various plays with an informative introductory essay.

CHAPTER V: BIWA

36. Aramaki Mamoru (荒牧守), *Tsuzoku Biwa Shidan* (通俗琵琶史談). Tokyo: Keiundo Shoten, 1923. 236 pp.
A short history of biwa with plates showing different shapes.

37. Kanetsune Kiyosuke (兼常清佐), *Nihon no Ongaku* (日本の音楽). Kyoto (?): Hattori Shoten, 1913. 509 pp. plus 40 pp. of music.
A study of Heike-biwa and jiuta.

38. Kishibe Shigeo (岸辺成雄), "The Origin of the P'ip'a," *The Transactions of the Asiatic Society of Japan*, Second Series, Vol. 19 (December, 1940). pp. 261–304 and plates.

A detailed study of the types of three lutes that entered Japan.

39. Nakayama Taro (中山太郎), *Nihon Mojin-shi* (日本盲人史). Tokyo: Seikokan, 1934. 452 pp.

A history of Japanese blind men. Includes blind music professions. See also articles in 6 and 1, 417–445.

CHAPTER VI: SHAKUHACHI

40. Kamitsuki Enzan (上月円山), *Shakuhachi Seisaku-ho Taizen* (尺八製作法大全). Tokyo (?): Takeda Toshado, 1933. 2 vols.

The only book on Japanese instrument construction. Deals only with the shakuhachi.

41. Kozan Kyoshi (虚山居士), *Meian Suisho-ho Kikai* (明暗吹籥法基階). Tokyo: Oya Shobo, 1930. 232 pp.

History of the Meian school of shakuhachi.

42. Kurihara Hiroshi (栗原広), *Shakuhachi-shiko* (尺八史考). Tokyo: Kawase Junsuke, 1920. 263 pp.

A general history of shakuhachi music.

43. Nakao Rinzo (中尾琳三), *Tozan-ryu-shi* (都山流史). Tokyo and Osaka: Soke, 1932. 724 pp.

History of the Tozan school.

44. Tanaka Inzan (田中允山), *Gosenfu Kara Shakuhachifu no Torikata* (五線譜から尺八譜のとり方). Tokyo: Ongaku no Tomo-sha, 1956. 228 pp.

Explains how to transcribe shakuhachi notation into Western script.

45. Yoshida Seifu (吉田晴風), *Shakuhachi no Gakuri to Jissai* (尺八の楽理と実際). Tokyo: Koran-sha, 1949. 237 pp.

A scientific study of the theoretical and actual pitches of the shakuhachi. See also 6, 39 and 16, 209–243.

CHAPTER VII: KOTO

46. Kishibe, Shigeo, "Classical Japanese Koto Music," *KBS Bulletin*, No. 21 (November and December, 1956). pp. 3–4.

A good English summary of koto music.

47. Nakajima Toshiyuki (中島利之), *Sokyoku no Chishiki* (箏曲の知識). Tokyo: Maekawa Gomei-gaisha, 1936. 369 pp.

Discussion of basic koto music.

48. Takano Ryu (高野劉), *Koto Danmono-keishiki no Kenkyu* (箏段物形式の研究). Vol. I of *Nihon Ongaku Riron*. Tokyo: Toen Shobo, 1935. 85 pp. plus music.

A strange attempt to fit koto music into sonata-allegro form. See also related articles in 6 and 1,356–416 and 39. Also 9 and 37.

CHAPTER VIII: SHAMISEN

49. Asakawa Uichiro (浅川卯一郎), *Nagauta no Kiso Kenkyu* (長唄の基礎研究). Tokyo: Hogaku-sha, 1955. 288 pp.

A survey of most of the elements of nagauta.

50. *Gidayu Dokushu Shinsho* (義太夫拙習新書). No author listed. Osaka: Osaka Bunraku-sha, 1920. 3 vols.

Notated Gidayu music with explanations.

51. Kineya Eizo (杵屋栄蔵), *Nagauta no Utaikata* (長唄のうたひ方). Tokyo: Sogen-sha, 1932. 2 vols.

Studies in the nagauta repertoire.

52. Machida Kasho (町田嘉章), *Nagauta no Utaikata to Hikikata* (長唄のうたい方と弾き方). Tokyo: Hoki Shoten, 1934. 330 pp.

Informative book on general nagauta technique and repertoire.

53. Nakagawa Aihyo (中川愛氷), *Sangen Gaku-shi* (三絃楽史). Tokyo: Dainippon Geijitsu Kyokai, 1951. 1016 pp.

The basic reference book on all shamisen music.

54. Wakatsuki Yasuji (若月保治), *Ningyo-Joruri-shi Kenkyu* (人形浄瑠璃史研究). Tokyo: Sakurai Shoten, 1943. 1162 pp.

The history of puppet joruri. See also 6, IV, 329–34 and articles on each music form.

CHAPTER IX: KABUKI

55. Atsumi Seitaro (渥美清太郎), *Hogaku Buyo*

Jiten (邦楽舞踊辞典). Tokyo: Fuzambo, 1956. 459 pp.

A dictionary of the major dance pieces from the kabuki and the general Japanese dance repertoire.

56. ——, *Kabuki Nyumon* (歌舞伎入門). Tokyo: Tokai Shobo, 1948. 419 pp.

See also 6 and 53.

57. Ernst, Earle, *The Kabuki Theatre*. New York: Oxford University Press, 1956. 296 pp.

Technique, history, and aesthetics of kabuki. Bibliography of other non-Japanese sources appears in back.

58. Halford, Aubrey S. and Giovanna M., *The Kabuki Handbook*. Tokyo: Tuttle, 1956. 487 pp.

Summaries of famous plays and introduction to kabuki theatre and techniques.

59. Iacovleff, A., and S. Elisseeff, *Le Theatre Japonaise* (*Kabuki*). Paris: Jules Meynial, 1933. 94 pp.

Introduction to kabuki with lovely plates.

60. Kawatake Shigetoshi (河竹繁俊), *Kabuki-shi no Kenkyu* (歌舞伎史の研究). Tokyo: Tokyo-do, 1943. 680 pp.

A standard Japanese historical reference.

CHAPTER X: FOLK MUSICAL ARTS

61. Embree, John F., *Japanese Peasant Songs. Memoirs of the American Folklore Society*, Vol. 38. Philadelphia: The American Folklore Society, 1943. 96 pp.

An excellent study of songs from one area.

62. Fujita Tokutaro (藤田徳太郎), *Nihon Minyo-ron* (日本民謡論). Tokyo: Banrikaku, 1940. 408 pp.

A general study of Japanese folk music.

63. *Geino Jiten* (芸能辞典). Kokugeki Kojokai publication. Tokyo: Tokyo-do, 1953. 795 pp.

A dictionary of theatre arts in Japan.

64. Honda Yasuji (本田安次), *Tokyo-to no Kyodo Geino* (東京都の郷土芸能). Tokyo: Ikkodo Shoten, 1954. 308 pp.

A discussion and list of folk theatricals 1928–around the Tokyo district.

65. *Minzoku Geijitsu* (民俗芸術). Odera Yukichi (小寺融吉), ed. Tokyo: Minzoku Geijitsu no Kai, 32. 60 issues.

The defunct "Folk Arts" magazine. Available in complete sets. Many excellent field studies.

66. *Minzoku Geino* (民俗芸能). Honda Yasuji (see 64) and others. *Dento Geijitsu Koza*, No. 4. Tokyo: Kawade Shobo, 1954. 289 pp.

Miscellaneous essays on Japanese folk theatricals.

67. Nakayama Yoshio (中山義夫), *Nihon no Minyo* (日本の民踊). Tokyo: Kaku Shobo, 1955. 265 pp.

Music and instructions for Japanese folk dances.

68. *Nihon Minyo Taikan* (日本民謡大観). NHK music staff. Tokyo: Nihon Hoso Shuppan Kyokai, 1953–55. 3 vols.

The best collection of Japanese folk music. Present volumes cover Kanto, Tohoku, and Chubu districts.

69. Shimofusa Kanichi (下総皖一), *Nihon Minyo to Onkai no Kenkyu* (日本民謡と音階の研究). *Ongaku Bunko*, No. 75. Tokyo: Ongaku no Tomo-sha, 1954. 105 pp.

A study of Japanese folk music scales. See also articles in 6.

INDEX AND GLOSSARY

This glossary-index is designed to be of use to both the general and the reference reader. All major music terms have been defined briefly and musicians identified. Many terms have several meanings and extensive ramifications, but they are defined here only as used in this book. Japanese characters have been included whenever possible. Important alternate versions are shown in brackets. Names of cities, historical persons, periods, and literary manuscripts have not been rendered in Japanese nor further identified since they are more readily available, though long marks appear on all Japanese words. The policy of capitalization and hyphenization was devised by Mr. Ogimi Kaoru, to whom I here express my thanks for help with many vexing editorial problems. My thanks also to Professor Ashikaga Ensho for authenticating the Japanese in this index.

Numbers in parentheses refer to plates, the letter "d" refers to a drawing, and "fig." indicates a figure. The letter "f." means that there is a further reference to the subject on the following page and "ff." means that there are references for several pages.